2nd Edition

Buying
Property

FOR

DUMMIES®

D1248580

2nd Edition

Buying Property

FOR

DUMMIES®

by Karin Derkley

WILEY

Wiley Publishing Australia Pty Ltd

Buying Property For Dummies®, 2nd Edition

published by
Wiley Publishing Australia Pty Ltd
42 McDougall Street
Milton, Qld 4064
www.dummies.com

Copyright © 2011 Wiley Publishing Australia Pty Ltd

The moral rights of the author have been asserted.

National Library of Australia
Cataloguing-in-Publication data:

Author:	Derkley, Karin
Title:	Buying Property For Dummies / Karin Derkley
Edition:	2nd Australian ed.
ISBN:	978 0 7303 7556 2 (pbk.)
Series:	For Dummies
Notes:	Includes index
Subjects:	House buying — Australia
	Real estate business — Australia

Dewey Number: 643.120994

About the Author

Karin Derkley began as a journalist in 1992 writing up the property listings for local paper *The Melbourne Times*. She went on to write for various sections of *The Age*, *The Sunday Age* and several other magazines. For five years she worked as a senior writer and then as deputy editor at *Personal Investor* magazine. She is now a regular contributor to the 'Domain' section of *The Age*, and writes on property investment for *AFR Smart Investor* magazine. Karin writes extensively about the ups and downs of the property market; about the art of unearthing the perfect home; about negotiating through the mortgage maze; about the ordeal — and occasional delights — of renovating; and about how to present your house to sell in a difficult market. Living through the experience of purchasing and renovating her own home, and being regularly solicited for advice by friends and family on the purchase and sale of their properties, she is all too familiar with the pitfalls and pleasures of home ownership and investing.

Dedication

To my friend Lisa who has been a constant personal and professional support.

Author's Acknowledgements

Thanks first to acquisition editors Lesley Beaumont and Anthony Stone who drummed up my enthusiasm for the project in the first place. Also, to Charlotte Duff who carried out the perhaps more difficult task of sustaining that enthusiasm right to the very end. My biggest thanks must go to my editor Robi van Nooten who tirelessly and cheerfully worked with me to turn my prose into a style worthy of a *For Dummies* book.

I must also acknowledge the assistance of Mal James of James Buyer Advocates, who was always happy to help with his insights into the real estate industry. Shane Oliver, chief economist of AMP Capital Investors, assisted greatly with his timely responses to requests for data. And thanks to Alison Verhoeven from REIA, for supplying helpful data.

The input and support of many friends has been invaluable, both in volunteering their own experiences and in providing encouragement throughout the process. Special thanks to Jan and Julien, through whose first-home-buying eyes I have been able to relive the excitement and anxiety of buying one's first property; to Shannon who shared her experience of becoming the owner of a house-and-land package; and to Jenny M who so generously volunteered her insights into the selling process. I also acknowledge the many people I have interviewed in my years as a property writer, who have given me their personal perspectives on buying, selling or investing in property.

Thanks also to my family who have watched the process of putting together a book unfold in my corner office. To my husband Iain who has been unfailing in his support and belief; and to my children whose regular cries of 'Haven't you finished that book yet?' goaded me on to its completion.

Publisher's Acknowledgements

We're proud of this book; please send us your comments through our online registration form located at http://dummies.custhelp.com.

Some of the people who helped bring this book to market include the following:

Acquisitions, Editorial and Media Development

Project and Copy Editors:
Robi van Nooten, On-Track Editorial Services; Charlotte Duff

Acquisitions Editors: Rebecca Crisp

Editorial Manager: Hannah Bennett

Production

Graphics: Wiley Art Studio

Cartoons: Glenn Lumsden

Proofreader: Liz Goodman

Indexer: Don Jordan, Antipodes Indexing

Contents at a Glance

Introduction *1*

Part I: The Great Australian Dream *7*

Chapter 1: Assessing the Dream: Buying Property 9

Chapter 2: Squeezing Your Foot onto the Property Ladder................23

Chapter 3: The Position or the Property..43

Chapter 4: Dealing with Property Professionals 55

Part II: Finding Your Dream Home *67*

Chapter 5: The Search Is On 69

Chapter 6: Buying a Piece of History 87

Chapter 7: Renovator's Dream (or Nightmare) 103

Chapter 8: Nice and New...125

Chapter 9: Building from Scratch...139

Part III: Borrowing For, Buying and Protecting Your Home *155*

Chapter 10: Climbing Aboard the Mortgage Merry-Go-Round 157

Chapter 11: Going, Going, Gone: Buying at Auction 183

Chapter 12: Making an Offer: Buying Through a Private Treaty Sale..195

Chapter 13: Sold to the Highest Bidder! Now What? 207

Part IV: The Part of Tens *223*

Chapter 14: Ten Things to Remember as a First Home Buyer..........225

Chapter 15: Ten Areas (Almost!) to Check at Open Homes 233

Index *243*

Table of Contents

· ·

Introduction *1*

About This Book...1
How to Use This Book 2
Foolish Assumptions..3
How This Book Is Organised..3
    Part I: The Great Australian Dream 3
    Part II: Finding Your Dream Home 4
    Part III: Borrowing For, Buying and Protecting
        Your Home...5
    Part IV: The Part of Tens...5
Icons Used in This Book..5
Where to Go from Here...6

Part I: The Great Australian Dream *7*

Chapter 1: Assessing the Dream: Buying Property......... 9

Looking at Whether You're Ready to Buy a Home 10
Renting versus Buying 11
    Liking the advantages of renting...................................12
    Disliking the disadvantages of renting 13
Understanding How Your Home Is an Investment...............14
Owning Your Home Is Tax-Friendly...............................16
The Government's Leg-Up—the First Home
    Owner Grant 17
Getting Ready to Scrimp and Save.................................18
Agonising Over the Time to Buy 19
Searching for Your Ideal Home.....................................20
Smartening Up Your Home..21

Chapter 2: Squeezing Your Foot onto the
Property Ladder...................................... 23

The Costs of Buying a Home...24
    Drumming up the deposit 26
    Begging to borrow..27
    Government slugs and sweeteners...............................28
    Paying off the lawyers 30
    Counting every last bit and bob 30

Calculating Your Monthly Outgoings 32
    Home maintenance costs 33
    Rates, fees and insurance 34
    Regular living costs 35
    Plans for the future 35
Looking at Funding Strategies 35
    First Home Savers Accounts 36
    Staying with the parents 37
    Doing it solo 38
    Getting together with friends 38
    Asking the parents to help out 39
    Investing in shares and managed funds 41

Chapter 3: The Position or the Property 43

Dreaming Up Your Perfect Home 44
Must Haves, Like to Haves and Mustn't Haves 44
Trading Off Location against the Perfect Home 49
    Spotting up-and-coming suburbs 50
    Moving to the fringes 51
    Escaping to the country 52
    Going high rise 53

Chapter 4: Dealing with Property Professionals 55

Working with Real Estate Agents 55
    Understanding a real estate agent's motivation 56
    Getting to the truth on property value 57
    Getting a real estate agent to help you
        find a property 59
Putting In an Offer 60
Dealing with Buyers' Agents 60
    Finding a competent buyers' agent—avoiding
        the pitfalls 61
    Counting the costs of using a buyers' agent 63
    Negotiating a purchase on your behalf 64
Understanding What (Selling or Buyers') Agents
    Can and Can't Do 64

Part II: Finding Your Dream Home 67

Chapter 5: The Search Is On 69

Setting Up Your Search Strategy 70
    Keeping track of all the information 70
    Doing the research 71

Narrowing Down the Search 76
  Paring down the properties 76
  Understanding real-estate speak 77
  Doing the drive-by 78
  Checking out trains, trams and buses 79
  Strolling to the corner shops 79
Assessing the Properties on the Short List 79
Attending an Open for Inspection 81
  Working out a schedule of visits 81
  What to look for during an inspection 82
Taking a Critical Look at a Property 84
Getting a Pre-Purchase Building Inspection Done 85

Chapter 6: Buying a Piece of History 87
The Pros and Cons of Buying a Period Home 88
  Impressive pros 88
  Not-so-impressive cons 89
  Living with the idiosyncrasies of a
    period home 89
Dealing with Heritage Restrictions 90
  Renovating your period home 92
  Restoring original features 93
Architectural Periods and Styles 94
  Colonial style: 1788–1830s 95
  Georgian period: 1810s–1840s 95
  Victorian styles 96
  Federation or Edwardian style: 1901–16 98
  Queenslander: 1880s–1940 99
  Californian bungalow: 1916–1940s 99
  Early modern: 1915–1940s 100
  Modernist: 1945–70 101

Chapter 7: Renovator's Dream (or Nightmare).......... 103
Tackling a Renovator's Delight 104
  Making the place livable 104
  Progressing from livable to lovable 105
Planning the Job 107
  Obtaining the necessary permits 107
  Getting the work done 110
Doing It Yourself 110
  Deciding whether you're up to the job 110
  Becoming an owner–builder 113
  Taking out home warranty insurance 115
  Calling in qualified tradespeople 116
  Acting as project manager 117

Hiring Designers and Project Managers...............................117
    Resolving complex renovation situations..................118
    Handing over the project management.....................119
Hiring a Builder...119
    Getting a quote..120
    Signing the contract...120
Living Through the Building Process 121
    Moving out until the dust settles...............................122
    Staying put during renovations.................................122
Funding Your Renovation 123

Chapter 8: Nice and New **125**

Buying Into a Housing Estate..126
    Checking out an estate..127
    Studying the developer 128
The House First or the Land? 129
    Getting the land first, then the house......................129
    Taking the package...130
Looking Behind the Facade of the Display Home..............131
    Knowing about inclusions...132
    Deciding on some optional extras 132
    Upgrading to a better model 133
    Getting finance through the developer.....................133
Your Dream Home: From Plans to Completion 134
Project Building 135
Buying 'Off the Plan'...135
    Imagining your home from a glossy brochure..........136
    Finding out everything you can 137

Chapter 9: Building from Scratch **139**

Starting with a Block of Land..140
    Assessing a block of land...141
    Working with a less-than-great block of land...........142
Designing Your Dream Home 142
    Finding someone to turn your vision
        into reality 143
    Harnessing an architect's vision 143
    Deciding on a building designer.................................145
    Getting a draftsperson to draw your design...........145
    Choosing an architect or building designer..............146
Moving from Concept to Contract 148
    Drawing up the concept plans 148
    Developing the design 148
    Finalising the plans 148
    Signing contracts and project managing..................149

Building a Home of Your Own.................................149
The responsibilities of the owner–builder 150
Looking at your options 152
Taking a course for owner–builders.........................153
Getting council approval...............................153
Getting on with tradespeople...................................154

Part III: Borrowing For, Buying and Protecting Your Home.................................... 155

Chapter 10: Climbing Aboard the Mortgage Merry-Go-Round 157

Understanding How a Mortgage Works...............................158
Qualifying for a Loan...159
Lending criteria 159
Providing documents to your lender 161
Choosing the Home Loan That Suits You and
Your Hip Pocket 162
To fix or not to fix 162
Splitting the difference 164
Introductory illusions 165
No-frills variable 165
Standard variable vanilla..............................166
Line of credit loans 167
Going professional.....................................167
Shopping Around for Your Lender...............................168
Stand-alone mortgage 168
The mortgage as the core of your finances..............169
Who's who of mortgage lenders 171
Choosing the right mortgage broker for you 172
Deciding to change your mortgage lender 174
When You're Not the Standard Mould...............................175
Accessing no-doc and low-doc loans.......................176
Looking around when your credit is impaired.........177
Understanding Your Credit File and What to Do
about a Bad One 179
Bypassing the Banks Altogether.............................180

Chapter 11: Going, Going, Gone: Buying at Auction. 183

Assessing the Pros and Cons of Auctions............................184
Estimated Selling Prices and Other Half Truths.................185
Understanding Auction Day...................................186
Introducing the property...................................187
The bidding war 187

Vendor bids 187
Bidding rules and regulations..............................188
On the market..189
Passed in..190
Tactics to beat the auctioneers at their
    own game...190
You make the winning bid — now what?.................192
Making an Offer after a Property Is Passed In...................192
Making a Pre-Auction Offer 193
Signing (After Reading) the Contract...............................194

**Chapter 12: Making an Offer: Buying Through
a Private Treaty Sale** **195**

Checking Out a Private Treaty Sale 195
Negotiating a price.......................................196
Beating down the price 198
Making an offer..199
Putting conditions on your offer................................202
Understanding what happens after the
    vendor agrees to your offer 203
Avoiding being 'gazumped' 204
Looking at Other Selling Methods.............................205
Set sales 205
Expressions of interest 206

Chapter 13: Sold to the Highest Bidder! Now What? **207**

Signing on the Dotted Line......................................208
Knowing what to look for in a contract of sale........208
Making special conditions on the contract 209
Exchanging contracts and handing over
    the deposit...210
Argh! We made a mistake: Enter, the
    cooling-off period 211
Waiving your cooling-off period 213
Securing Your Final Loan Approval.....................................213
Getting a Valuation Done..214
Settling on Your Property.......................................215
Insuring Your Biggest Asset 217
Insuring the building.....................................217
Calculating the costs of rebuilding your home........218
Insuring your possessions 220
Calculating the value of your possessions 221

Part IV: The Part of Tens 223

Chapter 14: Ten Things to Remember as a First Home Buyer................................... 225

Buy When You're Ready to Buy..225
Think Outside the Square..226
Look at Your First Purchase as a Springboard..................227
Borrow No More Than You Can Afford...............................227
Another Property Is Always around the Corner 228
Don't Pay Too Much for a Property.....................................228
Keep Your Emotions in Check When Looking
    at a Home...229
Be Sceptical of Selling Agents...229
Renovating Can Wait 230
The Mortgage Does Go Down — Eventually......................230

Chapter 15: Ten Areas (Almost!) to Check at Open Homes....................................... 233

Kitchen...233
Bathroom 235
Lounge..236
Dining Room 237
Bedrooms...237
Laundry..238
Garage 239
Backyard or Balcony...240
Street Appeal..241

Index... 243

Introduction

. . . .

*B*uying a home is one of the biggest things you're going to
do in your life (along with getting a job, getting married or
having a baby — but they're the subjects of other *For Dummies*
books). Buying for the first time can be especially daunting:
How do you know if you're getting a good deal? Why is one area
better than another to buy into? Is this property any good?
If you're like most first home buyers, you're going to have to
borrow an enormous amount of money, which can be a nerve-
wracking experience in itself. You have to deal with real estate
agents and understand how property sales work. You also have
to get all the legal stuff sorted.

Buying property is likely to be a far less stressful process when
you go into the experience with some knowledge of how it all
works. If you understand why some suburbs are more likely to
grow faster in value than others, for instance, or the advantages
(and extra costs) of having a mortgage offset account, you're
going to be better able to make informed decisions and less
likely to make expensive mistakes. You're also in a better
position to ensure that any professionals you deal with do their
job properly.

In *Buying Property For Dummies*, 2nd Edition, I give you
that baseline of knowledge about real estate and property
buying, and the financial and legal stuff that goes along with
it. I also muster together lots of tools and practical ideas on
how you can improve your chances of doing well out of your
dealings in property.

About This Book

Much of the information in this book comes from knowledge
I've gained over many years working as a property writer. Much
of it also comes from insights from the many people who've
talked to me over the years about their own property buying
experiences — friends buying or selling their homes, as well
as property investors who have accumulated large portfolios
of properties.

Some of the information is more factual, such as the rules that apply to property transactions or the kinds of permits you need to renovate a home. Other information is in the form of tips and insights, such as how to organise all the paperwork you collect during your search for a home, and the tell-tale clues that suggest a suburb is about to take off in price.

While I try to present as much up-to-date and accurate information about each stage of the home-buying process as possible, the intention of this book is as much to be your ally in a challenging and exciting journey as to be a factual guide. Buying a home is as much an emotional experience as it is a transaction, and understanding what you're likely to come up against during the process helps give you the confidence to deal with the highs and the lows.

Be warned: The laws and regulations governing property dealings, and subjects such as first home-owner grants, contracts and stamp duty, change all too rapidly. Even over the months of writing this book I notice that some rules have changed, while others are in review. As part of your research, you may need to contact the relevant government authorities to check on current rulings.

How to Use This Book

Buying property involves a number of stages, each requiring a different area of knowledge and with its own dynamic and its own complications.

While the book is set out in a logical order — you probably should work through the costs involved in buying a home and establish what you can afford, for instance (this information is contained in Chapter 2) before you start thinking seriously about what and where you want to buy (look for help on this in Chapter 3) — you may prefer to start by dreaming about what you want your perfect home to be like, and where. After you work out what you can actually afford to buy, you can start thinking about what you can live without in the trade-off between the perfect location and the perfect home.

Note: In this book, I use $450,000 as a typical price for a first home. This figure is higher than the national average for a first home (at the time of writing, the national average was around $300,000), but this figure is closer to the typical cost of a first home for many buyers in the major cities around the country.

For those buying in more affordable areas of the country, you can have the satisfaction of scaling down my calculations and projections by a third or so.

Foolish Assumptions

In this book, I make some general assumptions about who you are:

- ✔ You may never have bought your own home before, and are now seriously hankering after your own four walls. That may be because you've been renting for some time and feel like you're throwing your money away on rent. Or you may be living at home with your parents and you feel that owning your own home is an important next step on to the property ladder. Or perhaps your friends have started buying their own home and you feel it's time you did too.

- ✔ You may know people, such as your parents or friends, who have bought their own home and are suggesting you ought to take the step to home ownership and you're not sure whether it's the right thing to do now.

- ✔ You may have previously bought your own home and are looking to upgrade and would like to be more knowledgeable and confident about going into the process the second (or third) time.

- ✔ You're looking for information about the process of buying a property that's presented in a way that doesn't assume you have an economics, law or accounting degree.

If any of these statements apply to you, you're in the right place.

How This Book Is Organised

This book is organised into four parts so you can go directly to the topic you need to know about first. Here's a brief overview of each part.

Part 1: The Great Australian Dream

Many people in Australia consider buying a property to be something of a rite of passage. But although home ownership can be an important foundation for both building your family life and your financial security, it's a big step to take — both financially and psychologically.

The first two chapters in this part give you a clear idea of the costs and responsibilities involved in buying and owning a property to give you a better understanding about whether you're now ready for this step. You find out about ways to save the money you're going to need for a deposit and other upfront costs and how you can join forces with others to make the dream come true. Chapter 3 covers how to go about finding a property that meets both your needs and your budget, and that holds (and hopefully grows) its value over the years. And because you're almost certainly going to be dealing with real estate agents in your home hunting, Chapter 4 gives you some insights into how to deal with property professionals in the long process of searching for your home.

Part II: Finding Your Dream Home

Having worked out a good idea of the type of property that suits your needs and wants, now is the time to actually look at what properties are out there and narrow down the field to the ones that most closely match your wish list. This process is a job that can well take months, so getting a system to help you manage the deluge of information you collect in the process is going to make the job a lot more efficient and stress free. Chapter 5 covers finding potential properties and keeping track of all the information you gather on each.

What kind of home do you look for? An established home in an established suburb, a brand-new home in a new housing estate, or perhaps an apartment? This part takes you through the issues associated with each option. You find out what's involved in buying and restoring a period home (Chapter 6), and the challenges involved in renovating a property with more imperfections to start with (Chapter 7). Building a brand-new home — whether a house-and-land package, or an architect-designed home on your own piece of land — involves dealing with people such as developers, builders and architects as well as negotiating the many rules and regulations put in place by local councils to ensure that any new construction is safe and solid. Chapters 8 and 9 cover building a new home.

Part III: Borrowing For, Buying and Protecting Your Home

Even the most modest home costs a small fortune these days, so one of your first tasks is to go cap in hand to a lender to ask to borrow an enormous amount of money that you're to spend the rest of your life (or so it can feel) paying off. Many people these days build their entire financial affairs around their mortgage, using it as an endless ATM from which they finance not just renovations on their home, but cars, entertainment systems and holidays. Chapter 10 helps you find the right kind of mortgage — balancing flexibility with low cost.

Chapters 11 and 12 look at how you actually go about the purchase of your new home. Whether you buy your new home at auction (Chapter 11), through a private treaty sale or through some other method (covered in Chapter 12), these chapters set out the information you need to confidently put in your best offer. Chapter 13 covers what happens when you sign on the dotted line, getting the legal part of the transaction right, and then ensuring that you properly insure what may well be your biggest ever asset.

Part IV: The Part of Tens

In many ways, the chapters in this part are the most important chapters of the book for first home buyers. Chapter 14 sums up the crucial points you need to remember when buying your new home. For example, pay only what you can afford to borrow, be careful of selling agents and keep your emotions in check. Follow this advice and your first property experience can be a happy and profitable one. Chapter 15 covers what you should look out for when inspecting properties.

Icons Used in This Book

In this book, I use icons as a quick way to go directly to the information you need. Look for the icons in the margin that point out specific types of information. Here's what the icons I use in this book mean.

This icon points you to a website that gives you more information on a subject or has a handy tool that you can use.

This fine piece of art flags information of note to store in your memory bank.

The Technical Stuff icon points out material that generally can be classified as dry as a bone. Although I think that the information is interesting, it isn't vital to your understanding of the issue. Skip it if you so desire.

The Tip icon points out practical, concise information and insights that can help you make the right decisions when buying property.

When you see this icon, you can take advantage of my experiences and those of people I've spoken to over the years. I've learnt from every one of these stories.

This icon cautions you about potential problems or threats to your financial health.

Where to Go from Here

For Dummies books are designed so that you can dip in anywhere that looks interesting and get the information you need. This is a reference book, so don't feel like you have to read an entire chapter (or even an entire section for that matter). You're not going to miss anything by skipping around. So, find what interests you and jump on in!

Part I
The Great Australian Dream

Glenn Lumsden

'Now there are three of us, I think it's time we sell the tree house and move up to a bouncy castle.'

In this part ...

*A*re you ready to buy a home? Is renting better than buying? Is now the right time to buy? In this part, you find the answers to these questions and more. I help you assess whether home buying is really for you, and cover the how, when, where and why, including costs, location and using professional real estate agents and buyers' agents.

Chapter 1

Assessing the Dream: Buying Property

- -

In This Chapter

▶ Deciding whether you're ready to buy

▶ Weighing the pros and cons of renting versus buying

▶ Looking at your home as an investment

▶ Getting a helping hand from the government with the First Home Owner Grant

▶ Thinking laterally to put the deposit together

▶ Understanding the property market cycle

▶ Starting the search for your dream home

- -

*B*uying property is ingrained in the Australian psyche. If you haven't already bought your own home, you probably spend a fair bit of time wondering if you should or fending off questions from others as to 'when' or 'why not'. Even with the boom in property prices tapering off somewhat, buying a home still costs a fortune, so it would be understandable for you to wonder: Am I better off renting than buying? If I buy, when do I get into the market and how? Can I even afford to live where I want? If I get a mortgage, will I be able to eat out/see a movie/ buy a new piece of designer clothing ever again?

This chapter helps you decide whether entering the property market is right for you and gives you some know-how to make the process less stressful if you do decide to buy. I compare the advantages and disadvantages of renting, and look at how your home really is an investment. I also cover some of the ways the government gives first home buyers a helping hand and provide some tips on how to build that all-important deposit.

Looking at Whether You're Ready to Buy a Home

Before you leap into the all-consuming tasks of saving for, researching and spending every weekend inspecting potential properties, thinking about whether you're truly ready to take on the commitment of home ownership is a worthwhile exercise.

In Australia, many people buy a home because they're expected to. As soon as you're a certain age and you've got a steady job, you've settled down with someone or you've got kids, the common assumption is that your next step is to own your own bit of bricks and mortar. You may also take on board the idea that the earlier you get your foot on the property ladder, the better off you're going to be financially later on. That idea may well be true, but buying a property is such a big commitment that you need to do it when you're truly ready — financially as well as psychologically.

Buying a home is very costly. You need a large upfront sum and then you need to be able to keep repaying the mortgage payments month after month, as well as covering all the costs of owning your own home — costs such as rates and insurance, and bills for maintenance and repairs, such as emergency plumbing and regular house painting that your landlord, or your parents, have previously paid for. (See Chapter 2 for a blow-by-blow account of the costs of buying and holding onto a property.)

Covering those costs can exclude the possibility of doing other things in your life — things like studying, going overseas, setting up a business or travelling around Australia. You may have to cut back your spending on entertainment, dining out, clothes, music and other luxuries. Strict budgeting involves sacrifices — something you need to be ready for.

If you buy before you're ready, offloading a property isn't easy, and deciding to rent it out and become a landlord isn't something to go into lightly either.

Ready to make the dream a reality?

If you're like most Australians — about 70 per cent — the time comes when you get a yearning to put down stumps on a place you can call your own. You may also start to experience a desire to benefit from that great financial leg-up that home ownership confers in Australia.

If you answer yes to the following, you're seriously ready to consider taking the plunge:

✔ Do you find yourself poring over the property pages in your local newspaper and visualising whether a particular place could be your dream home?

✔ Do you slow down when going past properties that are for sale, or pop in to those that are open for inspection 'just out of curiosity'?

✔ Do you look at auction results to see how much properties are selling for in a suburb you'd like to live in?

✔ Do you study the floor plans of homes for sale, mentally knocking out a wall here or adding an extra bedroom there?

✔ Do you dream about colour schemes, built-in shelving or planting a garden that you can watch grow over the years?

✔ Do you spend hours doing budgets to see how long you need to save up a deposit on your own home?

✔ Do you take your own lunch in to work and put the money saved into a special account called 'home deposit'?

Renting versus Buying

Why not just continue to rent? After all, in lots of countries many people live in rental housing all their lives. In Denmark and Germany, for instance, less than half the population own their own homes. The rest rent for most of their lives — including well-off people with good jobs — and no-one thinks anything of it.

The main reason renting isn't as common in Australia as it is in many European countries is security of tenure. Being a tenant simply isn't as secure here as in countries such as Germany and Denmark. Tenants in those countries enjoy many protections that make renting for the whole of their lives feasible. Governments are a major landlord, renting out good quality housing to middle-class people as well as to people on low incomes — and often for life. Even in private rental housing, the law strongly protects tenants' interests — they have long leases and strict controls apply to how much landlords can raise rent.

A neat little calculator on the website www.yourmortgage. com.au gives you a wealth comparison between renting and buying a home after seven years. The calculator makes some assumptions — such as that, if you rent, you invest the money that would otherwise have gone to repaying your mortgage, and that, if you buy, your home increases in value by 8 per cent a year.

Liking the advantages of renting

Renting a property has lots of advantages over buying one:

- ✔ **Affordability:** You can often afford to rent a bigger, more comfortable property in a nicer suburb than you could afford to buy yourself. (I lived for some years in quite up-market suburbs that I knew I couldn't even dream of buying into myself.)

- ✔ **Convenience:** The other really big advantage is that a rental property isn't your responsibility. If something breaks down or the property needs a paintjob, the problem belongs to the landlord, not to you.

- ✔ **Flexibility:** When you rent, you have flexibility to do what you want. If you want to up and leave after your lease runs out, nothing is tying you down.

- ✔ **Financial benefits:** Some people also argue that you may be better off financially by renting rather than buying. That argument presumes you invest the extra money you would have spent on buying and holding onto a property into something such as shares, or even an investment property. The money you spend covering the expenses on any investment, including interest payments, property management costs, repairs and maintenance, is tax deductible, whereas everything on your own home you pay for out of after-tax money.

The catch when you invest the money you would otherwise spend on your own property is that you pay tax on the earnings and profit you make from an investment. You pay income tax on rental income or dividend income from shares. At the time of writing, you also pay capital gains tax on half your profits when you come to sell your shares or an investment property.

✔ When you retire, you can sell your home, buy a smaller one or one in a cheaper area and live off the change.

✔ You can take out a *reverse mortgage* against your home's value. This option gives you a lump sum or a regular income that you (or your children) only have to pay back (with interest) when you sell your home.

Owning Your Home Is Tax-Friendly

A good reason the family home can be your platform for building your long-term wealth is that in Australia the government regards the family home very favourably when it comes to the tax system and to the social security system.

When you sell your home, the tax office doesn't charge capital gains tax against the profits you make on the sale. You can use that money to upgrade to a bigger or better family home, sell that to buy another, and so on until you retire and sell to buy a smaller, cheaper home. You finally get to live on the change, without ever having to pay a cent of tax on the profits.

Similarly, our retirement system assumes that you own your own home when you retire and recognises this by not counting the family home as an asset when assessing your eligibility for a government pension. This approach by government may not sound very important now if you're still young but, when you retire, getting even a small amount of pension means you can get concessions on things like your pharmaceutical bills, your council rates and other bills.

By not owning a home when you retire, you actually get penalised twice. Not only do you have to pay rent but, also, the government counts the money invested anywhere else, such as in shares or investment property, as an asset so that you may miss out on the benefits home owners may be receiving. (Non–home owners are allowed a higher amount of assets before they start losing their pension, but the extra allowed is a little over $130,000 — not quite the value of the average family home.)

Disliking the disadvantages of renting

Renting can come with unpleasant side effects, and owning your own home has many advantages:

✔ **Landlord involvement:** In Australia, tenants are largely at the mercy of the goodness or otherwise of their landlords. Laws do exist to protect tenants being unfairly evicted and against outrageous rent rises or other harassment. But you can rarely get more than a 12-month lease, and landlords can ask tenants to leave the property as long as they give notice. (The number of days a landlord is required to give you as notice varies depending on the reason and by state or territory.) Some landlords can take weeks to respond to an urgent call for repairs to a heater or hot-water system. Others like to take advantage of a law that allows them to inspect their property every three months, a provision that can feel rather invasive if you consider the property as home.

✔ **Money down the drain:** You don't see any benefit from the money you pay on rent month after month, year after year. Your landlord is the one who benefits if the property grows in value, and all while you help him pay off his investment. Consider that over ten years or so you may be paying several hundred thousand dollars into someone else's pocket rather than paying off a property of your own that could be growing in value.

✔ **Restrictions:** You're restricted by what you can and can't do to a rental property. If you hate the wall colour, you may not be allowed to change it. Also, you may not be able to knock down walls, put up shelving or make other changes that can make the home more liveable.

One landlord didn't allow us to put any picture hangers on the wall, so for a year our walls were bare of the paintings and pictures we love.

✔ **Uncertainty:** Renting in Australia can be a rather precarious experience for another reason. A property you grow to love and care for as your own home can suddenly be sold from underneath you, leaving you out on the street looking for another roof over your head.

Owning your own home has advantages

When you weigh up the pros and cons of renting, you need also to consider the advantages of owning your own home:

- No-one can kick you out — as long as you make your monthly mortgage repayments.

- You can paint the walls any colour, hang pictures wherever you like, and knock down walls as you wish (subject to council approval, of course).

- If as a result of your home 'improvements' the property goes up in value, you're the one who benefits when it sells — not your landlord.

- Your mortgage repayments are like forced savings into a growth asset that you can sell at a profit or rent out one day.

- When your property goes up in value, you can borrow against it to renovate or to invest in something

else — like another investment property or shares.

- Inflation has a positive effect when you're a home owner, increasing the value of your home and decreasing proportionately your interest payments to your income. Rent, on the other hand, tends to rise with inflation.

- When you retire you have a home to live in rent-free.

- If when you retire you need extra money, you can sell your home if necessary and buy something smaller and cheaper — and keep the change.

- You don't pay capital gains tax on the profit from selling your home.

- When you retire, the value of your home isn't counted towards your assets when you're being assessed for your eligibility to receive the pension.

Understanding How Your Home Is an Investment

Buying a property isn't like buying a car or spending money on a big overseas trip. The value of a car starts falling the moment you drive it out of the car saleyard, and the money you spend on an overseas trip is gone forever (although travel has plenty of other invaluable benefits). But the money you spend on a well-chosen property is likely to increase in value over the years.

Being at the mercy of the landlord's investment

We had a wonderful landlord for our lovely rental home for some years. He inspected the house just once in the four years we lived there, only too delighted that we took care of the house and the garden as though it were our own. We had started saving, aiming to buy our own home six months down the track. About a month into our savings program, our

landlord called to tell us apolog cally that he had to sell the prop We had 90 days to find and move a new home, which upset our sav program dramatically. In the we found a home to buy, but remember vividly the sense of lessness at being forced out rental property we thought of home.

Property is a *growth asset* — the longer you hold on to i more it grows in value. The money you spend on buying property now may double in value if you come to sell it years. (This prediction is based on the property price g by an average of 7.5 per cent per year — a fairly conser assumption. According to a report prepared for the Au Securities Exchange by Russell Investment Group, resid property prices nationally went up on average by arou 9.8 per cent per year in the 20 years to 2009.) Your pro grow in value even more if you buy in a high-growth ar you add value by improving the property — putting in redecorating, renovating (see Chapter 7) or extending

Having the flexibility to improve your home makes it important investment. In fact, in Australia, a good arg exists for regarding your home as a core investment, which you can build your wealth over the long term. the following options for making money from the val home:

- You can borrow against the value in your home other investments — another investment prop portfolio of shares.

- You can sell your home to buy a bigger home suburb that may increase even more quickly

The Government's Leg-Up — the First Home Owner Grant

State and federal governments recognise the plight of first home buyers and so offer a small (some would say 'token') handout of a few thousand dollars towards the purchase of your first home. The First Home Owner Grant (FHOG) was set up in 2000 specifically to compensate first home owners for the effect of GST (goods and services tax) and offers first home buyers a cash amount of $7,000 that must be spent on the purchase of your home.

The FHOG is paid by each state and territory government — each has particular rules and idiosyncrasies that change from time to time. Some states, for instance, offer a further first home buyer's bonus or rebate to help first home buyers with the cost of *stamp duty* (a state tax on the purchase price of a property). In most states and territories, concessional stamp duty rates are available on property purchases up to a certain price. Some states offer the concessions to first home buyers with families, or those with concession cards. (I go into more detail on stamp duty concessions in Chapter 2.)

In Victoria and South Australia, the focus is more on promoting the purchase of new homes (see Chapters 8 and 9 for more on buying or building a new home). These two states offer the following, on top of the $7,000 FHOG:

- ✔ South Australia offers an additional $8,000 First Home Bonus Grant if you buy or build a new home.

- ✔ Victoria offers an additional $13,000 for its First Home Buyer Bonus if you buy or build a new home. Plus, if you buy or build a new home in a regional area in Victoria, you not only can get the additional $13,000 First Home Buyer Bonus but also a further $6,500, because it's in a regional municipality.

In Western Australia, first home buyers can apply for a Home Buyers Assistance Account, which offers up to $2,000 for the incidental expenses of buying an established or partially built home valued at up to $400,000 through a licensed real estate agent.

Go to fhogOnline at www.firsthome.gov.au and click on your state or territory for up-to-date information on the First Home Owner Grant and your eligibility.

If you're counting on the First Home Owner Grant to help you to pay for the property at settlement, you need to apply through an 'approved lender' (ordinarily your lender). Otherwise, you receive FHOG after settlement. (I go into more detail on the settlement process in Chapter 13.)

Getting Ready to Scrimp and Save

If you've already started to look around the suburbs for a home to call your own, you no doubt have come up against the harsh reality that properties are expensive. Properties are frighteningly expensive. Even with a supposed slowdown in property price growth in late 2010, property prices are still outrageously high for the first home buyer.

High property prices make coming up with the money to buy your first home a feat that can take up to a few years. You need to go into that feat with a battle plan (as well as lots of determination). (Chapter 2 gives you lots of ideas as to how you can achieve that seemingly impossible goal.) You probably need to cut back on expenses — forgoing your spring wardrobe this year or even going back home to stay with the parents for a while. You may have to find an extra source of income. If you're going it alone, joining forces with others to be able to afford something more to your liking may be a possibility. You may also have to scale down your expectations a little.

The most likely scenario is that you have to think a bit laterally. For many first home buyers, buying a home involves scaling down your choice a little — at least for a while. You may need to consider something a bit smaller than you'd prefer, or something that your mother may quietly regard as something of a dump — albeit one with renovation potential. (Turn to Chapter 7 for lots of ideas on how to go about renovating a home in a way that adds value instead of just costing you money.) Alternatively, you can consider an area previously off your radar. First home buyers have had to go outside the square (or outside the obviously desirable part of town) since people started building their own houses. If you choose well, you may find you benefit from being a pioneer in one of these up-and-coming areas. (See Chapter 3 for advice on the trade-offs between property and position, as well as hints on how to identify an area about to boom.)

Assessing your commitment

Some years ago, my parents suggested that my husband and I would be better off putting the money we were planning to spend on an overseas trip towards a deposit on a home instead. But we simply weren't ready to make that commitment then. Given how much we had to tighten our belts in the first few years after we bought our first home, I'm glad we had that last splurge on an overseas trip. It sustained us for the years we had to cut back on our spending just to cover the mortgage payments.

Agonising Over the Time to Buy

First home buyers can spend a lot of time mulling over when is a good time to buy. But while you probably should avoid buying when the news is full of stories of how the property boom has become unsustainable, an obviously perfect time to buy a home doesn't knock on your door either.

When property prices are rising, you can feel like everything is priced out of your reach. But if you wait another few months, hoping the bubble might pop, you may end up having to pay another 25 per cent due to prices rising still higher. When property prices are flat, you face the chance that prices are even lower in six months' time. Even when prices are falling, you have no absolutely certain way of telling whether they're at the bottom.

The fact is that if you're buying a home to live in and you're planning to hold onto your property for the long term — at least five years — when you buy doesn't really matter. (If you're buying for investment purposes, you should go in with at least a five-year outlook as well.)

Historically, property prices tend to go up — over the long term. But over the short term they can go sideways and even decline for periods. During the slowdown that followed the global financial crisis, property prices fell in some areas by as much as 20 per cent. But unlike individual shares, for instance — the value of which can reduce to nothing — over the longer term, property generally tends to hold its value rather than fall.

Waiting for the property bell to go 'ding-a-ling'

When my husband and I decided to buy our home in 1999, we thought we were buying at outrageously high prices that were sure to drop in a year or two, but the market has continued to rise over the years, even if there have been a couple of periods of slower growth along the way. The problem is that you don't get a bell ringing at the bottom or at the top of the property market and, if you wait for the perfect time to buy, you may end up waiting forever.

Of course, enormous variations exist in the rate at which the value of property increases, depending on where it is and what it is. Properties in areas of high demand, close to the centres of major cities and other high employment areas tend to increase in value faster than properties in a fringe suburb or a country town a long way from desirable amenities. Scarcity value also affects the rate at which a property's value increases. Prices go up when more people want to buy properties than properties are available. A shortage of land in a sought-after area — say, near the centre of a city or on waterfront locations — makes that land increasingly valuable over the years. Conversely, some apartments may be less likely to grow in value as fast as houses, partly because it's easier to build more of them, but also because they have a lower land to value ratio. (See Chapter 3 for an explanation of land to value ratio.)

Ordinarily, the value of property is rarely completely wiped out, unlike (occasionally) the value of a company's share price. Even if you do happen to buy at the top of the property market and prices go flat for the next few years, if you can afford to hang on for a few more years, you're likely to catch the next boom that may push prices up to a more comfortable level.

Searching for Your Ideal Home

As soon as you make the decision to buy, get ready to have the job of home hunting take over your whole life for a while. Looking for a home — the perfect home — can become rather obsessive. You can spend your days scouring property pages, your nights pondering whether a particular place fits your bill, and your weekends traipsing down one hallway after another.

Having a system that culls down the available properties according to your set of criteria can save a lot of time and hassle. (Chapter 5 is full of hints about how to organise your search strategy.) Scaling down your hopes and expectations to fit the reality of what you can afford to buy may be one of the first challenges. But after you learn to look for potential, instead of expecting to find the perfect home, the home-seeking process may actually become more exciting.

Smartening Up Your Home

One of the nicest things about owning your own home is that you can make it your own. If you don't like the colour of the walls, you can paint them however you like — with lime green feature walls or elegant aubergine. You can knock down walls and create your entertaining paradise (subject to council approval). (See Chapter 7 for the rules and regulations and lots of tips on renovating a property.) Or you can build a peaceful garden retreat that no-one can disturb without your permission.

Some of these changes can add value to your home when you come to sell it, although not always by quite as much as you may like to think. One of the most challenging tasks you have, though, is to find the right people to help you realise your makeover dreams — the designers, builders and various other essential tradespeople who are crucial to making sure this kind of project doesn't end up as nightmare. (Chapter 9 has plenty of guidance for dealing with the design and construction process involved in building or renovating a home.)

Chapter 2

Squeezing Your Foot onto the Property Ladder

* *

In This Chapter

▶ Counting the costs of buying a home

▶ Working out what you can afford each month

▶ Pulling together the money you need

* *

*B*uying a home is a huge financial commitment — the biggest you're probably going to make in your life. So, home ownership isn't something you should rush into or be pressured into doing before you're ready, financially or psychologically. Unless you're lucky enough to have come into a windfall or a big inheritance, you're almost certainly going to need to borrow a hefty sum from the bank — which usually means you have to come up with quite a bit of money upfront as a deposit. You also need to have the means to keep up the mortgage repayments for years to come, as well as pay all the other costs associated with owning a property of your own.

Before you launch yourself into home ownership, do the maths and work out what you can afford to repay on the mortgage each month. Banks can be only too happy to lend you as much money as they think you can afford, ignoring the fact that you occasionally like to go out to the movies or take a holiday now and then.

While covering your financial commitments may well mean making sacrifices in some other parts of your life, making payments on your home shouldn't stretch you so thin that you have nothing left to cover other essentials — such as health insurance, good food and exercise and the occasional night out with family and friends. You may, however, have to rein in your taste for fancy shoes and the latest techno gizmos and learn to cook and eat at home instead of eating out most nights.

Don't lose sight of the fact that, over time, that huge amount of money you owe on your mortgage is going to shrink. Inflation and rising property prices are the friend of the home owner. If you're renting, your rent tends to rise over the years with inflation. But as a home owner, as long as your loan amount and interest rate remain the same, your repayments eventually decrease as a proportion of your income.

In this chapter, I set out all the costs involved in becoming a home owner — from putting down the initial deposit right through to paying the legal fees and the removalist. I explain the kind of regular expenses a home owner may expect to pay, and then discuss your options for raising the necessary finances.

Note: Interest rates and other costs involved in buying a home — for example, building inspection fees, mortgage fees and so on — may change, even while you're reading this book. So too may government legislation regarding home purchasing and mortgages change in the various states and territories. Always stay aware of current costs, especially during the purchase process.

The Costs of Buying a Home

The median Australian house price changes over time. The median price means the middle price of all the sales that have occurred in a particular period. At the time of writing, the median Australian house price was $533,243, while the median price for a unit was $384,000. However, first home buyers tend to buy at a lower price point. According to a 2010 report by www.ratecity.com.au, the average (not the median) price for a house bought by a first home buyer was just under $300,000. I use $450,000 for calculations in this book, because that's closer to what first home buyers are paying in capital cities around Australia.

Based on a $450,000 purchase price and taking a 10 per cent deposit as average, you may need to come up with $45,000 just to be able to get a bank to lend you the rest of the money to cover the whole purchase price of your house. You may be able to get a home loan with a deposit of just 3 per cent, but the bigger the deposit you can save the more likely a lender is to give you the money you need to borrow.

The deposit isn't the end of the costs you have to cover out of your own pocket when you buy a property. Each Australian state and territory imposes levies on the actual purchase and on the land transfer, and most impose a stamp duty on the mortgage itself as well (although only on mortgages over a certain amount). You also have the costs of establishing the mortgage and the legal fees associated with the transaction. The following is a full list of your cost factors, which I explain further in this chapter:

- ✔ Building inspection fee
- ✔ Deposit
- ✔ Legal fees
- ✔ Mortgage establishment fee (also known as an application fee)
- ✔ Mortgage insurance (if you borrow more than 80 per cent of the value of the property)
- ✔ Mortgage registration fee
- ✔ Registration of transfer of land
- ✔ Stamp duty on purchase
- ✔ Stamp duty on mortgage
- ✔ Title search fee
- ✔ Valuation fee

Table 2-1 is an estimate of the costs involved in the purchase of a property for $450,000. The amount of stamp duty levied varies between states and territories, as I explain in the section 'Government slugs and sweeteners' later in this chapter.

Table 2-1   Expenses for a $450,000 Property Purchase

Expense	Cost
Building inspection fee	$350
Deposit of 10 per cent	$45,000
Land transfer registration fee	$131 (Tas) to $2,896 (SA)
Legal fees	$1,000
Mortgage establishment fee	$600

(continued)

Table 2-1 *(continued)*

Expense	Cost
Mortgage insurance	$6,700
Mortgage registration fee	$90 (Tas) to $135 (WA)
Mortgage stamp duty	$0
Petrol costs	$200
Stamp duty	$0 (NSW, NT, Qld and WA) to $18,970 (Vic)
Title search	$15
Valuation fee	$250
TOTAL	$54,336 min to $76,116 max

When you hear stories of people who bought an inner-city terrace 20 years ago for $60,000 or so that is now worth ten times as much, worth remembering is the fact that, back then, $60,000 was a lot of money. Down the track, the twin effects of rising wages and rising property prices have steadily eroded that amount, making the original outlay seem outrageously small. The same is likely to happen with the home you buy now — eventually. The short-term sacrifices you make now are going to be worth it in the long run.

Drumming up the deposit

Be careful not to go in over your head with your borrowings — you need to make sure you can cover those repayments for the next few years.

If you can manage to raise a deposit of at least 20 per cent of the value of the property, you benefit from not having to pay the substantial extra cost of mortgage insurance. *Mortgage insurance* doesn't protect you; it is insurance you pay to protect the interests of the lender against the risk that you default on the loan. Mortgage insurance can add almost $7,000 to the costs associated with buying a $450,000 home. With a 20 per cent deposit, you also benefit from lower monthly repayments and have a larger equity stake in your home that you can draw on if necessary down the track. For most people, though, coming up with a 10 per cent deposit is enough of a challenge, leaving them with little choice but to cop the cost of the mortgage insurance. (See Chapter 10 for more information on mortgage insurance.)

Bear in mind that if you buy at auction, you're expected to pay a deposit (usually around 10 per cent of the purchase price) on the spot. If you make an offer for a property through a private treaty sale, you're ordinarily expected to pay a holding deposit that can range from $1,000 to 10 per cent of the purchase price. (This holding deposit doesn't guarantee your purchase — for more information see Chapter 12.) You need to come up with the 10 per cent deposit (or whatever other sum you negotiate with the vendor) at the time you exchange contracts for a property purchased through a private treaty sale. If you don't have money for the deposit on hand, you may be able to raise the amount through a short-term loan or a gift from family, or through a deposit guarantee (see the sidebar 'Deposit guarantees' at the end of this chapter). Depending on how much finance you're able to raise through your lender, you may be able to pay some or all of the loaned money back when it comes to finalising the transaction on settlement day.

Begging to borrow

You might think that lenders would be satisfied with the more than $1 million you're to pay them back over the next 30 years on the $405,000 you originally borrow to buy your $450,000 property. (That scenario assumes an interest rate of 7.5 per cent over 30 years. As interest rates go up, the total amount you pay back is more, while lower interest rates result in a smaller interest bill.)

But, guess what? You also have to pay upfront and along the way for the privilege of borrowing that money. Expect to pay your lender the following:

- ✔ **Mortgage establishment fee:** Most lenders charge an upfront *mortgage establishment fee* of around $600. This fee covers the lender's costs of processing a loan and mortgage; it can also be referred to as an *application fee*.

- ✔ **Service fees:** Along the way, depending on your loan, you may also pay ongoing administration or account-keeping fees to cover the lender's cost of maintaining the loan account. These fees may be levied on a monthly, quarterly or annual basis and can add another few thousand to your costs over the life of your loan.

✔ **Valuation fee:** This fee covers the lender's cost of valuing your property to ensure that it is really worth the price you're planning to pay for it. This fee is generally around $250, although some lenders may include the *valuation fee* with the mortgage establishment fee.

All these costs can sometimes be negotiable, depending on the size of your loan, whether you have other facilities with the lender, and how hard lenders are currently competing with each other for business. (Turn to Chapter 10 for more tips on how to reduce the costs of your loan.)

Government slugs and sweeteners

Government charges such as stamp duty are the next biggest sums you have to cough up when you buy a property. If you haven't factored these costs in at the beginning, they can really blow out your budget. There's nothing more disheartening than having scrimped and saved for a deposit for the home of your dreams, only to find out that you're going to be slugged with another several thousand dollars on top of it, depending on which state you live in.

Every state has its own stamp duty levels, established for various historical quirks. In many states and in the Northern Territory, first home buyers receive concessions on the stamp duty they pay, usually up to a maximum purchase price. At the time of writing, for a property bought for $450,000 you'll pay no stamp duty in New South Wales, Northern Territory, Queensland and Western Australia. In the ACT you'll pay $17,750, in South Australia you'll pay $18,830, in Tasmania it's $15,550, and Victoria demands the biggest slug of all at $18,970. (Remember, these figures can change so keep an eye on your government's legislation.)

As well as these stamp duty concessions, there are other incentives to assist first home buyers to buy their first home. At the time of writing the federal government is offering a $7,000 First Home Owner Grant. States and territories may also offer their own grants and incentives on top of this amount. First home buyers in Victoria, South Australia and Queensland can receive First Home Buyer Bonuses for buying a new home, while in Victoria and Queensland you can get an extra incentive again for buying a new home in a regional area.

Here is a summary of the stamp duty concessions and other first home incentives offered:

- **Australian Capital Territory:** First home buyers who earn up to $116,650 may be entitled to a partial stamp duty concession on homes of up to $375,000.

- **New South Wales:** No stamp duty on homes priced up to $500,000 and concessions on duty on homes valued between $500,000 and $600,000. (NSW also has First Home Plus One, which allows first home buyers who buy at least 50 per cent of a property, with a non-first home buyer buying the rest, to still qualify for some concessions.)

- **Northern Territory:** A concession of up to $26,730 off the duty payable on the first $540,000 of the property's value and phasing out on houses costing less than $750,000 and land costing less than $385,000.

- **Queensland:** A stamp duty concession of up to $8,750 for properties valued at up to $500,000 and phasing out on purchases above $550,000.

- **South Australia:** The stamp duty concession for first home buyers has been replaced by the First Home Bonus Grant of up to $8,000 for new properties of less than $450,000.

- **Tasmania:** A stamp duty concession of a maximum of $4,000 for homes priced up to $350,000, or of $2,400 for vacant land up to $175,000.

- **Victoria:** For first home buyer's with at least one dependent child, a full exemption of stamp duty on homes up to $150,000 and a concession rate of duty on homes of up to $200,000. Victoria also offers a First Home Bonus of $13,000 for new homes values at up to $600,000 (up to June 2011), plus an additional $6,500 if you buy a new or established home in a regional municipality in Victoria.

- **Western Australia:** No stamp duty on homes up to $500,000 or vacant land up to $300,000, and a partial exemption on homes up to $600,000 or vacant land up to $400,000.

Stamp duty concessions, rebates and grants for first home buyers change regularly depending on government priorities, so you're best to check with each state's and territory's revenue office for up-to-date information.

Stamp duty on the mortgage

No states or territories currently levy a stamp duty on mortgages at the $450,000 price level.

Paying off the lawyers

Buying a property is a major legal transaction, and lawyers cost money. You pay for the lawyer's time in handling the transfer of your property from the seller to you, and you also pay for what's known as disbursements — the cost of other services undertaken during the transfer process. Disbursements cover such things as title search fees, the land transfer registration fee levied by the state government to cover the transfer of the title of your new property, checks on any outstanding matters with council and utilities, right down to the cost of your lawyer's phone calls, stamps and faxes. (You can find more detailed information about the legal processes involved in buying a property in Chapter 13.)

This whole process is known as *conveyancing*, and it culminates in *settlement*, which is the final handover of the property in exchange for your money. The cost of conveyancing varies enormously. A number of non-legal practitioners have stepped into this field in recent years, offering fixed-fee conveyancing services. A local specialist conveyancer may well have as good a knowledge as a solicitor of the kinds of issues you're likely to face with your specific property. Some people, however, believe that a property purchase is too large and too important a transaction to leave to anyone other than a qualified solicitor.

Counting every last bit and bob

If you want to properly budget your property purchase, you should factor in other costs, such as the cost of searching for your dream home. Additional costs may include

- ✔ **Body corporate or owners' corporation fees:** If you buy a unit or an apartment that is part of a property that has more than one owner, you need to make allowances for the additional costs involved with maintaining and insuring the property. These costs may include annual body corporate or owners' corporation fees that cover general administration, maintenance, insurance and other ongoing costs, as well as contributions to a maintenance fund.

✔ **Home building insurance:** Most lenders require you to take out home building insurance for your own property in case of fire or other structural damage. (After all, until you've paid it off, your property actually belongs to the lender, so the lender has an interest in protecting 'its' asset.) You might be able to get away with the bare minimum but, given the money you've just invested in your home, making sure you're covered at least for the replacement value of your home is in your best interests.

If you buy an apartment, the building insurance that is included in your body corporate or owners' corporation fees only covers the exterior and common areas of your apartment building, not the internal walls or any fixtures or fittings of your individual apartment. As such, you still need separate home insurance to cover you for any damage to your flat or apartment caused by an internal fire or flooding.

✔ **Building inspection:** As soon as you find a property you're keen on, you should arrange to have a *building inspection* done before you finalise your purchase. A building inspection can range from an overview that tells you about significant building defects or problems, such as rising damp, movement in the walls (cracking), safety hazards or a faulty roof, to more detailed and expensive inspections that include an estimate of the cost of fixing major problems, a list of minor problems and a recommendation of the repairs and maintenance work needed. If the property is located in an area where termites are known to be a problem, you should also consider getting a *pest inspection* done.

✔ **Contents insurance:** You should also consider contents insurance to cover you for loss of your valuables and other possessions by fire, flood or theft. (You can find more information on insurance in Chapter 13.)

✔ **Removal costs:** You have to move home, a task that, depending on how much furniture you need to relocate and how picky you are on the process, could range from $100 for the hire of a truck and one strong man to several thousand dollars for the kid-glove treatment. Add to this amount the costs of making basic repairs and buying new furniture and you have a more accurate picture of how much you're going to be up for in order to move into your new home.

> ✔ **Travel expenses:** You're likely to go through quite a bit of fuel if you're looking for a property or attending auctions almost every weekend for three months or so. Then your lunch and refreshments, which, unless you pack your own, could add $50 or so to your search costs every weekend.

Calculating Your Monthly Outgoings

After putting together a realistic picture of what your initial outgoings are going to be when you purchase the property, you need to look at how much you can afford on a monthly basis. In this section, I cover the sort of costs a home owner has to pay on a regular monthly basis, and also discuss costs you may incur in the future that you haven't yet considered.

Many home-lending websites have calculators that give you an insight into exactly how much you're going to be up for when you purchase a home, depending on its purchase price, how much you want to borrow and which part of Australia you live in. But be cautious of the amounts they suggest you can borrow. Some assume that you can spend half your household income on mortgage repayments.

Money for curtains

When I was 13, we moved to a new housing estate. All around us new houses were being built. Many of them were bigger and fancier than our own, but one thing struck me. So many of these grand new houses had sheets screening the windows instead of curtains. I wondered, 'If they could afford to buy such a big new house, why can't they afford nice new window coverings?' Just years later, I realised that it was possible for mortgage repayments to take up almost your entire disposable income — leaving you with little money for curtains, plants or furniture, let alone entertainment or holidays.

Traditionally, lenders preferred borrowers' mortgage repayments not to exceed a quarter of their pre-tax income. In the past ten years or so, lenders have become a lot more generous — or greedy, depending on how you look at it! The idea now is that repayments should take up no more than 30 per cent of your income. If repayments go beyond this percentage, home buyers are said to suffer from *mortgage stress* (that is, the cost of repayments makes it difficult for them to cover the cost of other essentials). Even so, recent research from the Australian Bureau of Statistics indicates that on average Australians are paying 34 per cent of their income, more than $1,900, in mortgage repayments (which means many are paying a lot more).

Your ongoing costs don't end with the mortgage repayments. The costs of owning and maintaining a property can come as quite a shock to those who have been renting or living at home with family. In Table 2-2, I set out the costs a home owner repaying a $405,000 loan at an interest rate of 7 per cent may expect to pay each month.

Table 2-2	Checklist of Monthly Home-Owning Costs
Expense	*Cost*
Mortgage repayments on $405,000 principal and interest loan (at 7% interest over 30 years)	$2,694
Maintenance, house-painting, gutters, etc.	$250
Insurance	$150
Rates/Body Corporate fees	$150
TOTAL	$3,244

Home maintenance costs

When you're renting, if the plumbing suddenly dies on Christmas Eve, the problem is the landlord's. The landlord is also the one responsible for ensuring the outside of the property gets a paint job every five years, for paying rates, insurance and so on. When the property is yours, all those costs fall on you, and if you're putting every last cent into just covering the mortgage repayments, those extra costs may well be the last straw.

Setting up a separate savings account with $2,000 or $3,000 to cover ongoing maintenance and repair costs is a good idea — and keep it topped up as you go along. If you have the money readily available, if something disastrous happens — like the hot-water system packing in just before the rellies come to stay — you don't have to scramble around for funds, or eat into your holiday savings. The money in your savings account could also cover the cost of attending to one big maintenance job each year — say replacing gutters, repairing the roof, painting the exterior of the property — that may well save you thousands on the flow-on problems that can result if you ignore such maintenance jobs, such as water damage from broken tiles on your roof.

Rates, fees and insurance

Other ongoing costs you need to budget for include council rates and insurance. If you buy a unit or an apartment, you'll also need to factor in body corporate or owners' corporation fees.

Council rates can add another thousand dollars or more to your annual outgoings, depending on the city or region in which you live and the value of your home. Most councils now allow you to pay rates on a quarterly or even monthly basis, and you need to account for that in your budget.

If you own an apartment, flat or strata-title unit, you also need to allow for regular body corporate or owners' corporation fees, which go towards the general administration and upkeep of the common areas. These are usually annual fees, but you can also pay them quarterly.

As the owner of an apartment or unit, you may also be asked to contribute to a special levy to cover one-off large-scale repairs or refurbishments to your building. Before purchasing your property, find out if any such payments are required in the near future.

While you may be required to take out home insurance as part of your mortgage establishment, you also need to take account of this as an ongoing cost. You should also add contents insurance to your coverage, and many insurers give a discount for bundling home and contents insurance. You may also get further discounts if you also insure your car with the same provider. You can make these payments on a monthly basis, but don't neglect to review your coverage each year to ensure you are properly covered — especially as you start collecting more expensive belongings around your home.

Regular living costs

To get a sense of how much you can really afford to pay on a mortgage, you should set out all your regular expenses, including your food bill, your telephone, internet and electricity costs, clothing, health insurance and car running costs. Don't forget entertainment, holidays and gifts — while recognising that you might need to cut back on these expenses in the first couple of years of your mortgage. After you clearly establish your spending each month, you have a better idea of how much you can really afford to repay each month.

Plans for the future

Don't forget to plan for the future. What happens if you want to go back to study or travel for an extended period? What if you decide to have children and lose part of your household income for some time? What if, as is always likely, interest rates rise by a percentage point or so? A rise from 7 per cent to 8 per cent doesn't seem that big, but if you've borrowed $405,000, it can add almost $300 or so a month to your repayments. Building a buffer of 10 per cent or so into your monthly budget is a good idea and allows for those kinds of contingencies.

A bit scary isn't it? You can understand why people often don't have enough money left to buy curtains in their first year or so of home ownership.

Looking at Funding Strategies

How are you going to pull together that $55,000 to $75,000 you need upfront to buy a $450,000 home? If you're saving up from scratch, you need to put away around $2,500 a month for two years to save that amount of money. Doing that isn't a bad discipline, given you're going to be paying that much on your mortgage after you've bought your property. But it may be a challenge if you're paying rent or have other financial commitments, such as a car loan.

So what are your options? You can try to increase your income by asking for a pay rise or taking on a second job. You can reduce your expenses by forgoing unnecessary spending on entertainment and luxuries. Or, as long as both you and your parents are happy about this option, you could choose to stay at home rather than move into a rented property while you save up your deposit. Alternatively, you may decide to lower your sights and look for a less expensive property. In this section, I discuss various ways of funding your property-buying venture.

Where's the best place to save for your deposit? The high-interest-bearing online savings accounts that have proliferated in recent years are hard to beat. These accounts offer interest rates as high as, and sometimes higher than, term deposits, and let you access the money within a day or two of requesting a drawdown rather than having to wait for a maturity date to be reached, as would be the case with a term deposit. You can also easily set up this type of savings account to automatically deduct a fixed amount from your primary bank account whenever you're paid.

First Home Savers Accounts

First Home Savers Accounts were set up by the federal government in 2008 to help first home buyers save for their first home. The big benefit of the accounts is that, at the time of writing, the government contributes an extra 17 per cent to the first $5,500 you save in the account in any year. The other benefit is that any interest you earn on your savings is taxed at just 15 per cent instead of at your marginal tax rate, as would happen if you saved the same amount in a regular savings account or other investment.

To be eligible for these benefits you need to be aged between 18 and 65, be a genuine first home buyer (not an investor) and contribute at least $1,000 per year for four financial years before withdrawing the balance. Anyone can contribute to the account on your behalf, but the maximum account balance is currently $80,000. (This maximum account balance and the contribution threshold are indexed to the CPI, and are adjusted periodically in increments of $5,000 and $500 respectively.)

Most of the major banks offer First Home Savers Accounts, including the ANZ, the Commonwealth Bank and ME Bank, as well as several credit unions and building societies. Interest rates offered on these accounts vary from around 3 per cent to 6 per cent.

Using a First Home Savers Account can mean you end up with more funds for your deposit. For example, if you save $400 per month for five years in a First Home Savers Account, you end up with nearly $32,000, around $5,000 more than the $26,700 you end up with if you put the money into a regular account instead.

More information about First Home Savers Accounts is available at www.homesaver.treasury.gov.au and www.firsthomesaver.com.au.

Staying with the parents

Children are staying at home much longer than ever before, often well into their twenties, and sometimes longer. Part of the reason is the huge expense involved when children move out on their own — saving up a deposit on a property while you're paying market rent is very difficult. And if you and your parents get on well enough, staying in your parents' home is probably the best way you can quickly save to buy your own property.

The important thing is to ensure the arrangement works for all parties concerned. If you're going to live at home, a couple of rules can make life easier for everyone. Remember to

- ✔ **Carry your weight around the home.** Help with the cooking and cleaning and the numerous everyday chores of daily living. Just think of it as good practice for when you're living on your own in your own home.

- ✔ **Pay rent.** Another guideline is that if you have a job and you're living at home beyond the age of 21, you really should pay your parents some kind of rent or board. What you pay may be well below market rates, but the gesture is important: It shows respect for the fact that you're living at home beyond a reasonable age, covers the considerable costs of feeding and housing you, and is a good practical discipline.

Some parents arrange to have their child's board, or part of it, put into an account as a form of forced savings for the deposit on that child's future property purchase. If your parents are considering doing this for you, you may want to be able to use these funds as proof of savings when you come to apply for a home loan down the track. If so, ask your parents to put the account into your name rather than theirs, and perhaps into a First Home Savers Account (see preceding section). See Chapter 10 for details of the kind of things lenders look for when they receive an application for a loan.

Doing it solo

Part of the reason house prices have risen so much in the past decade or so is because many homes are now bought by two-income households. If you're a single person, you may find covering the costs of buying on your own very difficult. So what can you do?

The most obvious solution is to buy at a lower price point. You may have to think long term, aiming to buy a unit or an apartment first, and use it as a springboard to buy something bigger down the track. Even with the price rises of the past few years, finding a unit for $300,000 or so in the major capital cities, or a small two-bedroom cottage elsewhere is possible.

If you buy well, when you choose to sell up, you can expect good demand from buyers in the same position as you were in when you first bought. Alternatively, you could use this property as the beginning of an investment property portfolio and rent it out. Either way, your position allows you to borrow against the equity you've built up (through your repayments and the increase in the property's market value) and use it as a deposit for your next bigger and better property.

Getting together with friends

An increasing number of single people are getting together with friends, siblings or other relatives rather than a life partner to buy a property. There's nothing to stop you doing this, and it can be a great way of increasing your buying power, as long as you're aware of a few of the pitfalls of doing so.

In terms of finance, lenders treat friends or relatives purchasing together like any other borrower. All the buyers' names are on the title deed and on the mortgage and all parties are liable for the loan repayments.

When assessing how much you can borrow, most lenders take your combined incomes into account. However, they usually calculate your living expenses individually, as distinct from a couple that has shared expenses. This approach can have an impact on how much you can borrow. For example, a single adult's living expenses might be calculated at $2,000 per month, and two individual adults at $4,000 per month. The living expenses of a couple, on the other hand, might be calculated at $3,000 per month.

Legally, a purchase made by friends is treated differently from a purchase made by a couple. When a couple purchases a home, they're defined as 'joint tenants' and are said to have an equal interest in the whole of the property. Friends or relatives buying a property together are defined as 'tenants in common', and have shares in the property depending on how much they have contributed to the purchase. For instance, if three people are purchasing the property, one person might contribute half the purchase cost, and the other two might contribute a quarter of the cost each.

The consequences of such joint purchases are seen when the property is sold, or when one party moves on or dies. In a joint tenancy, if one partner dies, the ownership of the house automatically goes to the other partner. But in a 'tenants in common' arrangement each party can pass on their share of the property to someone else through their will; they can also sell their share of the property to someone else.

If you're going to enter into a joint-purchase arrangement with friends, you need to make sure your legal agreement is drawn up very carefully. Some things your lawyer should consider are

- ✔ What happens if one party wants to sell the property?
- ✔ What happens if one party wants to sell just their own share of the property?
- ✔ What happens if one party is unable to meet the loan repayments?
- ✔ How is the property to be valued if one party wants to hold on to the property and the others want to sell?

Asking the parents to help out

A mark of how difficult it is to buy a house these days is that parents are so keen to help out ... or perhaps this option is one of the few ways they can finally get the kids off their hands!

Lump sums to help with the deposit

Many parents or grandparents offer their children or grandchildren a lump sum gift towards a deposit. That can be a huge help, particularly if the amount increases your deposit beyond the magic 20 per cent that eliminates your need to pay for expensive mortgage insurance. Such a gift doesn't help with your savings history, though, if you're applying for a regular loan. For that, you usually need to be able to show that you can save up at least 10 per cent of the deposit yourself.

However, lenders have come around to the idea that even though you may not have a savings record now, or even have the income to service a loan, your family may be in a position to help you out, especially if they have built up equity in their own homes over the years.

Lenders like St.George Bank and the Commonwealth Bank now offer products that allow a member of your family to take out a mortgage on their own property and give you the money towards the purchase of your property. You and your family decide whether the money is a deferred loan or a gift.

Second mortgages

Another option is that a family member takes out a second mortgage on the property you're buying to help you meet the repayments. Under this option, the family member gives you the money to put towards the property purchase. They're then responsible for the amount of their individual loan. You can arrange it so that at a point down the track, you buy out this family member, giving them an amount that reflects any increase in the value of their portion of the loan.

Properties owned by your parents

Many parents buy a property for their children to live in until they can afford to buy it from their parents. The children may pay their parents rent, perhaps at lower than the market rate. This approach can be a way in which parents can ensure their children are safely housed in the future, without rent 'going down the drain'. However, you must remember that when the property does finally change hands, you're going to need to pay your parents a fair market price (one that is comparable with other similar sales in the area).

If your parents are planning to buy a property to sell to you some time in the future, you should be aware that, depending on how much the value of the property has risen, your parents could be up for a hefty capital gains tax bill when they eventually sell on to you.

Investing in shares and managed funds

One other option for raising money to buy a home — although you need to be aware that this one is risky if you have a short time frame to work with — is to invest your money in a potentially high-growth asset, such as shares, either directly or through a managed fund, rather than just putting the money in the bank.

Most fund managers that invest in Australian or overseas shares recommend that you hold the managed fund for at least five years and preferably seven years: This advice is sound because, unlike a term deposit or an online savings account, the returns on the sharemarket aren't guaranteed. The sharemarket can go up 30 per cent one year and drop 20 per cent the next. Such a roller-coaster isn't so much of a problem if you have enough time to ride out the ups and downs, but predicting whether the sharemarket is likely to go up this year or down is almost impossible. If you need to use the money for a deposit in a year the sharemarket drops, you may not benefit at all.

Managed funds or shares are best used if you have at least a five-year time frame to save up for your home deposit. If you don't have a great deal of investment experience or money to start off with, a good low-cost option is to use an index fund that invests in the whole sharemarket rather than pay a professional fund manager to pick a few potential winners. Most funds allow you to start off with one or two thousand dollars and then let you add a couple of hundred dollars a month in a regular savings plan.

Investing in the sharemarket is something you should only contemplate if you have clear picture of the risks involved and know that you have the personality and the time frame to tolerate those risks. I strongly recommend you get professional advice from a financial adviser if you're thinking of entering the sharemarket.

Deposit guarantees

A deposit guarantee (sometimes called a deposit bond) is an alternative way to raise the cash deposit required when you first purchase a property. Deposit guarantees are generally used when you have cash tied up in other investments such as shares or a term deposit, or where you're waiting on the money to come through on the sale of an existing property. Deposit guarantees are often a lot quicker to get and cheaper to use than a personal or a bridging loan. After you apply for a deposit guarantee, you can hold onto it for up to six months while you're looking for your ideal property; after that, you need to renew it.

Deposit guarantees can be purchased from most lenders and some specialist providers like Deposit Power and Deposit Bond Australia, and cost from 1 to 10 per cent of the deposit amount, depending on the amount and its term. A deposit guarantee for a $45,000 deposit on a $450,000 home, for instance, may cost about $540. When you finalise the property purchase (such finalisation is known as *settlement*), the full purchase price includes the deposit amount.

In order to qualify for a deposit guarantee, you must be able to prove that you have enough funds to settle on, or finalise the purchase of, the property. Meeting a lender's criteria is a similar process to that for a standard loan application, including assessing that you have adequate income to meet the financial commitments. For standard rules of assessment to apply, you also need to be an Australian resident or a corporate entity.

Deposit guarantees don't come without risk. If you fail to finalise the property purchase, you still owe the deposit issuer the money you borrowed as well as any costs or expenses they have incurred. Deposit bonds (as they were then known) become notorious during the recent off-the-plan investment apartment scams that proliferated in Melbourne and Sydney. In those cases, people obtained multiple deposit bonds with the intention of making quick money by selling their off-the-plan properties before having to settle. When they couldn't find a buyer and were unable to pay the balance of the deposit or the sale price, many faced financial ruin.

Chapter 3

The Position or the Property

In This Chapter

▶ Envisioning your ideal home

▶ Listing the important features you want in a home

▶ Trading off location against facilities

*Y*ou've made the big mental shift to thinking of yourself as a potential home owner. Now, you can spend your thinking time on how you're going to translate your dream into reality. At this time, two big questions require your attention — and the criteria for one can almost certainly affect the other:

✔ What kind of a home are you looking for?

✔ Where do you want to live?

Property gurus often cite location as the most important factor in choosing a home. And it's true; a well-located home is more likely to hold its value in a flat market, and grow its value faster in a strong market, than one in a poorly located area. However, unless you've got plenty of money to play with, you may need to make some compromises on either the location or the kind of home you would like to buy.

If location is absolutely most important to you — either because you want to live close to your workplace or for more emotional reasons, such as living near grandparents, or perhaps because you believe a particular location is a sensible investment decision — you first may want to research the kind of properties you're able to afford in that area. Based on that information, you may need to scale down your expectations and settle for something smaller and less fancy than you had your heart set on, or you can investigate purchasing an unrenovated bargain with potential to improve.

On the other hand, if the style and comfort of the home is more essential to your happiness as a home owner than location, you may need to make other trade-offs. While you may not be able to afford to buy in a particular suburb, an adjacent suburb may have homes that fit your criteria, and at a price you can afford.

The more flexible you are with what you want from your home and its location, the more quickly you're likely to have success with your home hunting. Having a clear awareness of the importance of each feature about the home or location is very important. Some features may not be negotiable for you, while others may just be nice to have, if possible. This chapter shows you how to work out what those criteria are so you can go out into the marathon task of home hunting with a clearer picture of what you're looking for.

Dreaming Up Your Perfect Home

You may have your idea of the perfect home. It may be a clean-lined and architecturally designed apartment with smart modern appliances, or a cosy cottage full of old-world character, with a sunroom where you can curl up with a good book. Finding something that matches those dreams can be a difficult balancing act between imagination and practicality. You need to be able to imagine what kind of features are going to make you happy, but also be prepared to make the inevitable compromises when you're restricted by either your budget or the property choices that are available in the area you'd like to live.

Must Haves, Like to Haves and Mustn't Haves

Your first step before looking for your ideal home is to sit down and make a list of the kinds of features that are important to you in a home. Eventually, you may have to make compromises on some of these criteria but, right at the beginning of the exercise, you may as well be completely open with your hopes and dreams. You never know — you may just come across a home with a sunroom facing a view that you always dreamed of enjoying.

If you're planning to buy with someone else, being clear on the essential criteria for you both is particularly important. You may have other features you like, but which you're prepared to use as a trade-off for others the co-purchaser may prefer. For example, while you may insist on a study as a must-have inclusion, you may be able to negotiate your wish for central heating with the garden shed he craves. Remember, also, to make a note of features you absolutely can't live with. This list may include a home on a busy road or one with an outdoor toilet.

This list gives you some criteria and features you may like to consider when you complete your own list:

- **Apartment/house:** If you like the idea of apartment living, this choice may be an easy one. For others, it may be the trade-off they're prepared to make in order to be able to afford to live in the location of their choice. If you decide on an apartment, you may also like to think about whether you'd like to live on the ground floor, with the possibility of a courtyard garden, or whether you prefer the security of living on an upper level.

- **Bathroom:** Having two bathrooms or more is no longer seen as a luxury, but extra bathrooms are likely to jack the price up considerably. If you absolutely must have a second bathroom, you may need to move your search further out of the city, or look for a property with the potential to add another bathroom down the track.

  What about a bath? Some people wouldn't dream of living in a home where they can't have a long soak in a tub now and then. If you have or are planning to have children, a bath is pretty much a must-have.

- **Building material:** In many areas you don't have a choice between brick veneer, timber, stone or whatever is commonly used as a building material. But for some people, the material from which their home is built is paramount. Some building materials can look ugly — think 'brick' cladding from the 1960s and 1970s — but remember that in most cases you can paint or render, or improve the exterior in some way. Unless you have a very strong preference, you may be best to leave this feature open. One exception may be properties constructed using asbestos. Asbestos is a safety hazard and can be expensive to remove safely. A building inspection report should be able to uncover any existence of asbestos in a property.

✔ **Floor plan:** You can have any number of properties with three bedrooms, a kitchen, bathroom and living area — how they're put together makes all the difference. You may have heard about 'logical' floor plans. This concept refers to the way space flows through a house so that you move easily from one room to another; doors and windows seem to be where they ought to be and dead ends are eliminated. You may have a preference for the kitchen to flow into the dining area, the laundry to have a door out to a hanging area and, as is increasingly demanded in Australian homes, that the living area or kitchen/family room opens to an outdoor entertaining area.

✔ **Garden:** The world may be divided between those who dream of their own patch of land, with flowers, veggies and room for a dog to run about, and those for whom a garden is just one more hassle. If two or more of you are purchasing the property, make sure you're clear on how important this feature is to you all. If you like a garden, you may also like to think about what size and style you prefer. You may be lucky to find your perfect garden, or you can look out for one with the potential to be transformed.

✔ **Mod cons:** Dishwashers, European appliances, central heating and cooling systems, security alarms and smart new bathrooms add to the comfort and pleasure of your home. But are they the criteria by which you measure the desirability of a home?

 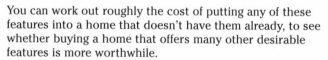

You can work out roughly the cost of putting any of these features into a home that doesn't have them already, to see whether buying a home that offers many other desirable features is more worthwhile.

✔ **Number of bedrooms:** A single person or couple can theoretically live with just one bedroom, but an extra bedroom or two can give you space for a study, a home gym/theatre, or somewhere for your cousin to stay. Depending on how long you plan to stay in the home, you might also like to plan ahead for children.

✔ **Off-street parking/garage:** Having the option of off-street parking, even if the space is just a private driveway, can add several thousand dollars to the price of homes in some inner-city areas. If on-street parking is easily available, this facility may be something you can live without. If you're looking in suburbs and country areas, the choice may be whether you want a lock-up garage or not, and how big.

✔ **Period home or something more modern:** Buying a home that has age and character can raise challenges not every one is keen to take on (see Chapter 6), but some people wouldn't dream of buying anything else. Evidence suggests that period homes grow in value faster than more modern homes. You may, however, prefer the cleaner lines and often more logical floor plans of a modern home, or even choose to buy something brand new (see Chapter 8).

✔ **Pools, spas and other luxuries:** Pools and spas, and even tennis courts, never seem to add quite as much to the price of a home as they cost to build in the first place, so don't discount a potential property as out of your price range just because it has any of these facilities. Remember, though, that you may have to compromise with the loss of garden space — for example, in the case of a pool or tennis court — plus the extra costs in maintaining the facility. In an apartment or unit development, amenities like pools and gyms add to your annual body corporate or owners' corporation fees (fees that cover the costs of common property facilities that are available to everyone in the development to make use of; for example, garden areas or a swimming pool), so make sure you really intend to use them or you may come to resent the extra costs.

✔ **Position to the sun:** Australian architects and home designers now incorporate the way the sun shines into homes and gardens. Here's how a home's aspect benefits from the sun and light:

- North-facing living areas filled with sunlight in winter (but without the full blaze of sun in summer) are ideal.

- East-facing homes get morning light.

- West-facing homes get hot, direct sun in summer unless screened in some way (look for awnings or summer foliage).

- South-facing homes or gardens are in shade most of the time in winter.

If you like to entertain outdoors, you may prefer a north- or west-facing garden. However, you may be willing to settle for an easterly or southerly aspect as a good trade-off for some other more important feature.

✔ **Renovator's dream:** Some people thrive on the challenge of completely remodelling a home. Others couldn't think of anything worse than living in chaos for months, and getting out the tools and paintbrushes every spare moment. A home that requires a bit of work may be more affordable than one that has been freshly made over, but if it requires major structural work to be liveable, make sure that you and whoever you're buying with are up to the task.

✔ **Storage areas:** Talk to any disgruntled home owner and one of the biggest sources of complaint is often a lack of storage space. You may want storage for clothing and books, kitchenware, camping or sporting gear and garden equipment. You can always buy wardrobes, shelves and even a shed, but you may want to check that any home you look at has the space to fit in these hideaways.

✔ **Views:** I grew up with a fabulous view looking out over Hobart's Mount Wellington, the Derwent River and the Tasman Bridge, and when I moved to Melbourne I was shocked to realise that very few people had any kind of view. A view, whether of water, mountains, a forest or park, or even the city lights, is a wonderful bonus. If you can afford a home with a view, such an asset ensures your property always keeps its value. But, again, a view is one of those factors you may need to use as a trade-off to get the kind of house or the location you have your heart set on.

Table 3-1 presents one way to collect your thoughts when making your checklist of must haves, like to haves and mustn't haves for your dream home.

Table 3-1   Checklist of Features You Look for in a Home

Feature	How Important Is It?		
	Must Have	Like to Have	Mustn't Have
1. House, townhouse or apartment			
2. Town or country			
3. Renovations required? (a) None (b) Cosmetic renovation (c) Serious renovations			

Feature	How Important Is It?		
	Must Have	Like to Have	Mustn't Have
4. Style of property (a) Modern home (b) New (c) Period			
5. View			
6. Position to the sun			
7. Building materials (a) Brick veneer (b) Double brick (c) Weatherboard (d) Other			
8. Number of bedrooms			
9. Logical floor plan			
10. Number of bathrooms			
11. Bath			
12. Study			
13. Central heating/cooling			
14. Off-street car parking			
15. Garage			
16. Storage			
17. Other (a) Pool (b) Spa (c) Tennis court			

Trading Off Location against the Perfect Home

As soon as you work out the features you're looking for in your ideal property, you're better able to know whether you're going to have to trade off the location you prefer against the style of home you like. This decision making is very personal. For instance, initially you may look for a large spacious house with a big backyard. But, soon, you realise that to get that space you have to move a long way from friends, your children's school and the inner-city life you're used to. Eventually, you decide to stay near your community, which more than compensates for the smaller house and yard you settle for.

In another scenario, you may make the opposite decision and move a couple of suburbs out and be happy for the extra living and outdoor space that the home provides for the children.

If you're determined to live in a particular location, you may want to look for properties that are a bit run down or have some other flaw — a location next to a big block of flats, perhaps — that makes them less desirable to others and, therefore, lower in price.

You can usually change something about the property itself by renovating or landscaping or even knocking it down and starting again. A flaw in the location is a lot harder to come to terms with. For instance, you can screen the noise from a busy road with a high wall and double glazing. But your location next to an electricity substation is more difficult to remedy. Always take into account the effect of these external factors on the future re-sale value of your home.

Spotting up-and-coming suburbs

You may have your heart set on a particular suburb. But, if that suburb is beyond your price range, why not look one or two suburbs farther afield? You're certainly not alone. First home buyers have always had to strike out to new frontiers, and as long as you look astutely, your chosen suburb can be a good investment decision. Many suburbs once considered 'off the radar' are now considered 'sought-after'. Consider suburbs like Brunswick in Melbourne's north or Newtown in Sydney's inner west. People who bought in these suburbs ten years ago or so are doing very well indeed. And the suburbs have flourished around them, becoming more attractive with interesting shops and cafes, and better facilities.

Drive around and see how many houses in a suburb are being renovated. Apart from increasing the aesthetic value of the area, renovations are a good indication of how optimistic owners are about the value of their homes increasing. Also, look at the kinds of shops and cafes that are opening up in a suburb.

Suburbs that are close to public transport, freeways (but not too close), universities or a good shopping area are likely to hold or increase their value. Contact the council and ask if any planning proposals are on the agenda.

Moving to the fringes

The fringes of Australia's cities are expanding every month as land becomes available to new housing estates. In these places, you can buy newly (or recently) built homes with all the mod cons for much less than the price of similar properties closer to the city. Some developers even offer terms that mean you don't have to come up with a full deposit (although watch out for catches in these kinds of arrangements, as Chapter 8 outlines). These estates can be ideal for young families, or those planning them, because they're often full of children and facilities catering to their needs. These areas also often offer the added attraction of proximity to the countryside, with its fresh air and opportunities for outdoor activities.

New housing estates can often lack access to public transport, shopping centres, medical facilities and facilities for teenagers — including secondary schools and sporting facilities. Before you buy into a housing estate, check that it has the kinds of facilities you and your family need, or that it has plans to build them in the future. Public transport is especially important. Without it, you and your family are completely reliant on the family car.

Buying into a new house-and-land package estate isn't always the best investment decision. The value of a property is related to the rarity value — that is, the rarity of the land it stands on, which is why inner-city properties and waterfront properties cost so much. You can't build more land in the inner city and water frontages are finite spaces. By their nature, outer suburban housing estates can be replicated, a factor that undermines the re-sale value of any one property.

In terms of eventual re-sale value, best buys in housing estates are those that have a unique characteristic — being adjacent to a golf course or national park, for instance. You can also financially do better on an estate that has easy freeway access or public transport into the city. An individual property that is next to a lake or park, or a short walk from shops, may be easier to sell down the years as well.

Escaping to the country

Newspaper articles regularly cover people who have left the city to move to a coastal or country town or onto a rural property. The stories talk of the fresh air, the animals and the beautiful country vistas, the friendliness of the local community — and the size of the new country abode bought with the sale price of the city home.

'Sea-changing' — and its rural counterpart 'tree-changing' — are growing trends in Australia, especially for people who have retired from the workforce or who have worked out a way of being able to work mostly from their rural home. If you're in that position, you may well be able to find a property that has all the space, land and features you dream of, at a fraction of the price of a similar property in the city.

Where should you look? You may be considering areas you already have a connection with, perhaps through family or friends who have already made the move. Tune in to their much-needed information on whether the area is likely to be one that is going to provide you with the facilities you're looking for on a day-to-day basis. Otherwise, do your research by driving around different regions, checking the For Sale ads in the local real estate agents and reading any independent market information you can find about an area.

You can get a sense of how an area has been growing in value (or not) and even get a sense of who lives there by accessing free information available online. Home Price Guide (www.homepriceguide.com.au), RP Data and www.realestate.com.au all offer access to basic median price, growth and demographic information on many country towns around the country. For a fee, all of these services also offer more in-depth research reports, which give you detailed information on recent sales in particular streets or even on a particular property.

Properties in most coastal and country areas had big rises in value in the early 2000s, but for years before that many areas barely moved in price, and many areas have done little since. Those regions that are more likely to hold or increase their value over the next few years are those within two hours' drive of a major city centre, with easy access via freeways and increasingly, public transport, and that are close to beaches or places of great natural beauty.

Be careful not to buy into an area just because it grew strongly in price over the past few years. Last year's great investment strategy isn't necessarily going to be repeated this year, or the next.

Going high rise

Apart from Sydney, high-rise apartment living is a relatively new lifestyle choice for Australians. Australians have traditionally liked their backyards, even if it's just a plot of concrete, and haven't liked to live too high off the ground. But, for better or for worse, urban planning now caters for living in multi-unit, high-rise developments, convincing many Australians that this option is a glamorous choice.

Certain advantages come with living in a high-rise apartment block. Apart from the potential for spectacular views, many newer developments are beautifully fitted out with all the mod cons. Some also offer amenities like pools, gyms and cafes, as well as the benefits of a concierge and security systems.

Indeed, given the prices of houses in some parts of the major capital cities, an apartment is the only option many people have for owning a home. Certainly, if you can't afford anything other than a tiny, run-down dump in the inner city or a bigger property way out of town, an inner-city apartment may seem like a gift from heaven.

Don't expect your apartment purchase to always be a great investment decision. As with outer suburban housing estates, the problem with high-rise apartments is that they're in good supply and it isn't that hard to build more. Which means that, by the time you come to sell yours, you may well be competing with other apartments that are newer and fancier. Apartments also have a low land to value ratio.

Land to value ratio is an indicator of the proportion of the total value of your property that can be attributed to its land value. Because land appreciates, while buildings depreciate, the higher the land to value ratio the better. The land to value ratio on a freestanding house in some highly desirable inner-city areas can be as high as 80 per cent (or, in other words, on a $1 million property, the land is valued at $800,000). With apartments, the land to value ratio is arrived at by dividing the value of the land on which the block is built by the number of apartments on that block. So if there are 50 apartments, the land to value ratio for one apartment is a 50th of the value of the land. That means you can't rely as much on the rise in the value of the land to boost the value of your apartment in the long run. Smaller blocks of, say, four to six apartments have a much higher land to value ratio, so can be expected to increase in value over time more than multi-unit developments.

To maximise the opportunity for your apartment to hold or increase its value, look for one with scarcity value.

To improve the scarcity value of your apartment

- ✔ Choose a good location — across from a beach or park, or near an interesting shopping area.

- ✔ Choose one with a view if possible, but make sure that the view can't be built out, or you may end up looking at another apartment building.

- ✔ Look for a good design and floor plan. Avoid low ceilings and poky rooms. The input of a known designer can help with the value.

Living out-of-season

You may experience a particular temptation to move into an area where you've enjoyed your summer holidays. Living in the off-season in a coastal getaway or rural paradise can be quite different when the tourists have gone home and many of the cafes and shops have closed their doors. Are local doctors, supermarkets, banks and other kinds of facilities that you're going to need when you're living there always available? If you have a family or are planning one, you might also like to check the local schools and other facilities, such as sporting facilities.

Chapter 4

Dealing with Property Professionals

. . . .

In This Chapter

▶ Dealing with real estate agents

▶ Making the initial offer

▶ Using a buyers' agent

▶ Getting a feel for what real estate agents and buyers' agents are allowed to do

. . . .

*A*lmost every property transaction in Australia involves a real estate professional. Occasionally, though, a property is sold privately, without any agent being involved. If you see a property you like in a newspaper or on a property website, nine times out of ten you need to contact the real estate agent handling it in order to get more information, organise an inspection and put in an offer.

In this chapter, I look at how real estate agents work, how to recognise a good agent and how to get one on side to help you in your search for your dream home. I also look at the growing trend for using buyers' agents to help find a property and negotiate a sale without you ever having to talk to a real estate agent yourself.

Working with Real Estate Agents

Rightly or wrongly, real estate agents don't have a great reputation in Australia. But that's not to say they're all bad. Agents are salespeople, and salespeople do what they can to get a sale. The good ones do so by earning your trust, giving you the information you need and following through on their promises; the poor ones can be either lazy, incompetent or, at worst, underhand in their efforts to make a sale.

Dealing with a real estate agent you can trust means checking that your agent is a member of the Real Estate Institute of Australia (REIA) in your state or territory. Members of the REIA are committed to providing a service with professional standards, and they follow a strict code of conduct. REIA members can also undertake a wide range of professional development opportunities, which enable them to continually update their skills and service. The quickest and easiest way to check out your agent is to visit the REIA website at www.reia. com.au. You can also phone them on 02 6282 4277.

From 2012, real estate agents will be licensed and regulated on a national basis, replacing the former state-based real estate agent licensing system.

Understanding a real estate agent's motivation

When you're dealing with real estate agents (known also as *selling agents*) as a property buyer, the first and most important piece of information to remember is that their primary obligation is to look after the best interests of their client. That means they're working for the seller (ordinarily known as the *vendor*) of the property — not for you, the purchaser. (Agents have a legal obligation to act for the vendor, so they're not acting wrongly at all.)

Many selling agents are on fairly low-base salaries and make most of their money from the commission they make on the sale of a property. The *commission* they earn is a percentage of the sale price of the property. Sometimes the commission is tiered, so the agent may get an extra bonus if they sell the property above a certain pre-agreed price. Understandably then, the primary motivation of a selling agent is to sell a property for as much as they can possibly get. When the property sells, the agent gets paid.

For a selling agent to sell a property at the highest possible price, she aims to encourage the interest of as many buyers as possible and promote competition among them. Everything an agent says and does is motivated by this aim. When you regard everything a selling agent tells you in this light, your expectations are more likely to match the outcomes achieved.

Not all properties are quick and easy for a real estate agent to sell. Sometimes, when a property is taking months to sell, an agent's primary motivation is just to get a property sold and off his books so he can make time for other properties. This scenario can provide a window of opportunity for the canny home buyer (see Chapter 12 for more on negotiating with the agent).

Getting to the truth on property value

One of the biggest criticisms of selling agents is that they're flexible with the truth.

- **Dealing with the purchaser:** When selling a home, the agent's in a position to quote buyers a lower price than you might think a property should sell for. Some states now have guidelines to curtail this practice — called *underquoting* — by forbidding agents to state a price below the vendor's asking price or their own current estimate of the likely selling price. But agents generally quote at the lower end of their own estimated range, a practice they defend by arguing that their role is to maximise the number of people who make an offer or attend an auction. A favourite saying of real estate agents is 'Quote 'em low, watch 'em go; quote 'em high, watch 'em die.'

- **Dealing with vendors:** When trying to get the listing of a property, a selling agent may over quote the price she thinks the property is going to sell for — at least at first. Then, if the property fails to draw offers at that price, she may backtrack, talking down the original quote.

Ordinarily, a selling agent talks up the value or features of a property — just as any salesperson does. He places more emphasis on this aspect of a sale if the property is lagging on the market. The agent can also exert pressure on you as a potential buyer in more subtle ways by suggesting that the vendor is anxious to sell and that if you put in a good offer you may be able to snap it up quickly. Another ploy is to talk up the interest of other buyers in a property in an attempt to get you to raise your offer price.

Be sceptical about an agent's selling approach, and do as much research as possible in order to see through the smokescreen to the most likely truth. Here are some questions to ask that may help show a selling agent you're alert to separating truth from trickery:

- ✔ Are there any problems with the property?
- ✔ Has the vendor already bought elsewhere?
- ✔ Have you received any other offers?
- ✔ How long has the house been on the market?
- ✔ Why is the vendor selling?

Don't count on getting straight answers to these questions, but the way the agent answers them may give you clues as to whether she's a trustworthy professional or one to be wary of.

You can't always rely on an agent to tell you the whole truth about a property. While the contract will inform you of any really important issue about a property (a problem with the title, for example), an agent is unlikely to draw your attention to the fact that a property has rising damp or that a freeway is going to be hugging your letterbox in the near future.

You can investigate issues relating to a property by organising a pre-purchase *building inspection report* and getting your solicitor to do some research on the title. A building inspection report checks the overall condition of the property inside and out. See Chapter 5 for all you need to know about this pre-purchase report.

Laws in most states and territories now prohibit some of the misleading practices that were widely used by selling agents until recently. One of the most notorious was 'dummy bidding' at auctions, where agents planted employees or friends among the auction crowd to pose as a buyer and bid the price up to a pre-determined level. Some agents were also known to take imaginary bids from non-existent bidders. Today, agents in the Australian Capital Territory and some states must register all bidders to prove that every bid is genuine. (You can find out more on dealing with the auction process in Chapter 11.)

Getting a real estate agent to help you find a property

If you think finding a new home is just a matter of ringing a local selling agent, telling her what you're looking for, and then sitting back to wait for the agent to send properties your way, think again. Some selling agents may work like this — for instance, in quiet suburbs and country areas. However, in inner-city areas, unless you've got a couple of million or so to spend, mostly you're on your own in your search.

As the average first home buyer, you need to do a bit of work to chase up properties for yourself. Agents are working for the sellers of a home, not the buyers, and most have enough on their hands chasing the next commission to concern themselves with every potential buyer who walks through the door.

The best way to get an estate agent to help you is to show that you're serious. Start by calling the agent and ask if any of the properties on their books might suit your requirements. When you're asked to leave your name and number, don't expect a call back right away with the first suitable listing. Be proactive and call again every week or so to show you're a genuine, or motivated, buyer.

If you find an agent prepared to help you find a home, make sure you do your homework. Be clear about what you're looking for and what you can afford. Busy agents don't pay much attention to someone who walks in saying: 'I'm not sure what I'm looking for, but I want to buy a house.' Before you contact any agent, review your list of must haves for your dream home (I show you how to put this list together in Chapter 3). Remember to be realistic and a little bit flexible with your wish list.

Some people hope that by developing a relationship with an agent they're likely to hear about and, perhaps, purchase a property before the property is officially listed. An agent, however, is unlikely to accept any offer before getting as many buyers interested as possible.

Give the selling agent a rough (but accurate) idea of the price range you're looking at, but don't tell him your upper limit. Very often the prices he quotes miraculously inflate to match your top price.

Putting In an Offer

If you're keen on a particular property and want to make an offer, you need to do so through the agent. Each state and territory has its own procedure for putting in an offer. In some jurisdictions, you need to make an offer in writing, sometimes by using a special form. Agents are only obliged to forward formal written offers to vendors. (Find more information about putting in an offer in Chapters 11 and 12.)

Be aware that the agent may use your offer as proof to all potential buyers that other people are interested.

Putting in an offer, even in writing, does not guarantee that you are the buyer of a home. It is not until both you and the vendor sign a contract of sale and you pay a deposit that the transaction is finalised.

Dealing with Buyers' Agents

A growing demand in recent years for agents who act for the buyer means another style of agents has entered the property market. *Buyers' agents*, also called buyers' advocates, are often ex-selling agents who use their inside knowledge of the industry to help buyers find a suitable property and negotiate on their behalf.

Sit back, put the kettle on and your feet up while you read about how you can let a buyers' agent do the leg work and take the hard work, and the stress, out of looking for your property.

Buyers' agents claim to help buyers by

- ✔ **Getting you access to properties not yet advertised** — 'the silent listings'.

- ✔ **Looking for faults and flaws in a particular property** — both in terms of structure and suitability to your needs.

- ✔ **Removing emotion from the purchasing decision and process** — you can hand over the emotional and stressful aspects of looking.

- ✔ **Saving you the time and stress of finding suitable properties** — you tell the agent what you're looking for, how much you can spend and where you'd like to buy, and he comes back to you with a selection of properties that may fit your bill.

- ✔ **Using their understanding of the property market, as well as their inside knowledge of the tricks and traps of the real estate trade to get you a better price on a property** — agents can advise you whether your preferences are realistic, given how much you have to spend.

Finding a competent buyers' agent — avoiding the pitfalls

Like selling agents, buyers' agents need a real estate agent's licence, and are regulated by the real estate agents Act and regulations in each state.

Theoretically, this legislation ought to protect you from disreputable conduct among buyers' agents. But an Act doesn't protect you from incompetence. Here's why:

- ✔ An incompetent buyers' agent isn't any better at finding you a good property at a good price than you are — and the agent charges you a lot of money for the service.

- ✔ Some incompetent buyers' agents may become victims of a selling agent's ploys and actually end up pushing up the price of a home by signalling their interest too strongly.

How do you find a competent buyers' agent? The easiest way is to get a referral from someone you trust and respect. To put your mind at ease about a buyers' agent's competence, especially if you have to resort to finding an agent through the *Yellow Pages*, here are some questions you can ask:

- ✔ **Can you make available details of some examples of successful purchases from the past six months?** Having access to the names and numbers of two or three clients so you can interview them, instead of relying purely on testimonials, acts as a confidence safety net.

- ✔ **Do you also act as a selling agent?** Buyers' agents can also be selling agents but not for the same property.

✔ **Do you ever recommend against buying a property?**

✔ **How do you charge?** Check how much the agent's formula works out in dollars on the particular price of the house you're considering.

✔ **How many properties have you bought for clients over the years?** To be worth your hard-earned money, buyers' agents need a very good understanding of the property market in general, and specifically what makes a good property.

✔ **How many times have you bought a property prior to auction?**

✔ **What experience do you have in real estate?** Preferably, the agent has years of experience in real estate, both as a selling agent and as a buyers' agent. The agent also needs to have mastered the art of negotiation. Note, though, that some good buyers' agents haven't worked as a selling agent.

Many buyers' agents claim to be property investment consultants. While many agents do have a lot of knowledge and experience to offer someone who is looking at property as an investment, your best bet is to approach this advice with a grain of salt. Some are really just in the business of promoting properties they're earning a commission from. Check what kinds of properties they're recommending to you. Be suspicious if they're newly built properties and if the properties seem to be a part of a multi-unit development.

To juggle or not to juggle

Some buyers' agents act as selling agents simultaneously. As long as they're not simultaneously buying and selling the same property, the law allows this juggling of roles. But is it ethical? Some buyers' agents say they refuse to act as selling agents, claiming it causes a conflict of interest and arguing that an agent should clearly be acting either for buyers or sellers.

Counting the costs of using a buyers' agent

If engaging the services of a buyers' agent sounds like the answer to your prayers, remember to investigate the costs.

Buyers' agents can charge for their services in three ways:

- ✔ **Flat fee:** Where you pay a fixed amount for the agent's services no matter what the eventual purchase price of the property.

- ✔ **Percentage fee of your budgeted purchase price:** If you're looking for a property around the $450,000 mark, for instance, the buyers' agent may charge you a 2 per cent fee of $450,000 whether he's able to buy a property on your behalf for $430,000 or $465,000. This percentage fee is agreed to at the beginning of the search process.

- ✔ **Percentage fee of actual purchase price:** The buyers' agent charges you 2 per cent of $465,000 (where that amount is the actual purchase price).

Sometimes agents charge an engagement fee of several hundred dollars upfront as a form of retainer for their services. When they find and successfully purchase a property on your behalf, you're charged a further 'success fee' that may be charged in any of the three ways just outlined.

If you engage the buyers' agent solely to make a purchase on your behalf — either through a private sale or through an auction — the agent is likely to charge you a lower fee than if sourcing the property as well. The costs to you may include an engagement fee, whether the agent's successful or not, as well as a success fee if the agent makes the purchase.

Whichever way a buyers' agent charges you, the agent is required by law to give you a clearly set out listing of all fees, including an estimate of the real dollar value. For example, on a property value of around $450,000, the agent can't just tell you that the charge to you is 2 per cent of the eventual purchase price of your home. The agent must set out the dollar value of $9,000, plus any other engagement fees, building and pest inspection fees and legal fees.

Negotiating a purchase on your behalf

Even if you feel confident to find a suitable home yourself, you can engage a buyers' agent to make the actual purchase on your behalf.

Buyers' agents claim that, because they understand the psychology of negotiation and can see through the ploys so often employed by selling agents, they can sometimes get a property for a better price than you could on your own. Or, a buyers' agent can help ensure you don't miss out on a property — for instance, if you don't have the expertise to put in an offer that an agent is going to take seriously.

Getting someone to bid on your behalf is especially helpful in the frenzied atmosphere of an auction. A buyers' agent can be very adept at working an auction crowd, and at intimidating the auction agent and other bidders to get a good price on auction day. Some buyers' agents have become notorious for their entertaining techniques on auction day — a performance that they justify as a response to the theatre and frenzy of the average auction.

Understanding What (Selling or Buyers') Agents Can and Can't Do

The government regulator, the Australian Competition & Consumer Commission (ACCC), is responsible for ensuring small businesses comply with the *Trade Practices Act 1974*. The ACCC, in consultation with the Real Estate Institute of Australia (REIA), makes available a guide specifically for the real estate industry. This guide, *Fair and Square: A Guide to the Trade Practices Act for the Real Estate Industry*, informs real estate agents about their rights and responsibilities under the Trade Practices Act.

Agents must not

- ✔ Make false or misleading statements about a property.

- ✔ Make predictions about property trends that they can't substantiate.

- ✔ Make property valuations that are unrealistic.

    ✔ Make a 'dummy bid'.

    ✔ Remain silent when they have a duty to disclose information of relevance to a buyer.

Agents should not

    ✔ Use high-pressure techniques or harassment to further sales.

    ✔ Use their inside knowledge to take advantage of consumers, especially the vulnerable.

You can visit the ACCC website for a copy of the guide at www.accc.gov.au.

If you come across a situation where you believe a property agent has infringed these rules, your first port of call should be your state or territory consumer agency. See Table 4-1 for contact details of your state or territory office.

Table 4-1	Contacting Your Local Consumer Agency	
State/Territory	*Contact Details*	
ACT	Office of Regulatory Services www.ors.act.gov.au	Tel: (02) 6207 0400
NSW	Office of Fair Trading www.fairtrading.nsw.gov.au	Tel: 13 32 20
NT	Dept of Justice — Consumer Affairs www.nt.gov.au/justice/ consaffairs	Tel: (08) 8999 1999 or 1800 019 319 (NT only)
Qld	Office of Fair Trading www.consumer.qld.gov.au	Tel: 07 3405 4059
SA	Office of Consumer and Business Affairs www.ocba.sa.gov.au	Tel: (08) 8204 9777
Tas	Consumer Affairs and Fair Trading www.consumer.tas.gov.au	Tel: 1300 654 499
Vic	Consumer Affairs Victoria www.consumer.vic.gov.au	Tel: 1300 558 181
WA	Dept of Commerce — Consumer Protection www.commerce.wa. gov.au/ConsumerProtection	Tel: 1300 30 40 54

Part II
Finding Your Dream Home

Glenn Lumsden

'It's nice, but we really had our hearts set on something with a giant underground secret cave and connecting bat-poles.'

In this part ...

*1*n this part, you find out about how to search for the home you really want. From using real estate agents and websites to help you with your search to knowing what to look for during an inspection, this part has it all. Investigate the pros and cons of period homes, renovating, choosing a house-and-land package, or building from scratch as an owner–builder.

Chapter 5

The Search Is On

• •

In This Chapter

▶ Planning your property search

▶ Homing in on the most likely places

▶ Gauging short-listed properties before inspection

▶ Inspecting properties that interest you

▶ Turning a non-emotional eye on the property

▶ Having a professional building inspection done

• •

*A*s soon as you work out what kind of property you're looking for, you can strap on your boots and start pounding the pavements in the search for your perfect home. Sometimes you can be lucky and find a new home without too much effort but, for most of us, home hunting is a big job that can take weeks or even months. For some people, finding the perfect home at the right price can become something of an obsession that occupies every waking minute (and sometimes invades their dreams as well). I know people who, every weekend, still pore over the property lift-outs — even though they've owned their own home for years.

Whether you're an obsessive type or a practical type who would rather get the job over and done with quickly and easily, in order to maximise your chances of finding the right property you need to know what you're looking for, know where to look and be organised in your search. In this chapter, I discuss the different ways in which you can search for your new home and how you can make the whole process easier.

Setting Up Your Search Strategy

Before you start looking for a property, work through the features in the checklist of must haves, like to haves and mustn't haves for your dream home in Chapter 3. Make at least rough notes of the kind of property you're looking for and some of the important features you hope to find in it. Some preliminary benchmarks are especially important if you're property hunting with others: Benchmarks help to guide your search strategy and narrow down the number of properties you need to look at. Almost certainly you're going to change and refine some of your criteria as your search continues, but at least you have something to start working with.

You should have received pre-approval for a home loan amount before you start your serious search for a new home. (See Chapter 10 for information about housing loans.) When you know how much you can borrow, you have a clearer picture of how much you can afford to spend on your new home — thus saving you the heartache of falling in love with a place only to find that that property is beyond your means.

Keeping track of all the information

As you go about your search, you're going to look at a lot of places. Right from the beginning, setting up a system of recording, organising and tracking the masses of information you collect along the way helps your search. As difficult as it may be to imagine, a time is going to come when the properties you look at all blur into one another. Even if you do a lot of your research and information gathering via the internet (for more on this, see the following section) you're still going to be accumulating lots of bits of paper, in the form of brochures, newspaper lift-outs and print-outs from websites, as well as your own notes and sketches of floor plans. How are you going to store and organise all that information?

You can stuff everything into a document wallet, but you may be better off getting yourself a loose-leaf folder and a hole punch, or a display folder with plastic pockets in which you can file loose pages. At the beginning of your records, list your criteria. Then, for each property you look at, allow a page or two of ruled paper to write down some details about it, followed by brochures or print-outs on the property. Properties that you decide probably deserve a second look can get more space, where you can note to what extent they meet your criteria.

Place the following items in your search folder:

- ✔ Auction/sales results for properties that are comparable to the one you're seeking

- ✔ Brochures on individual homes that look promising

- ✔ Clippings from newspapers and property supplements

- ✔ Lists of homes that are open for inspection each week

- ✔ List of your criteria for the perfect home

- ✔ Page (ruled) for each home you're serious about, on which you note how well it fits your criteria

- ✔ Print-outs from real estate websites of properties that fit your requirements

Doing the research

To maximise your chances of finding the home that best meets your wish list, try to consult every possible source of information on properties that are on the market. That means you shouldn't just rely on the internet, convenient as it may be, or on referrals from a real estate agent. Be broad-ranging and open-minded in your search and you may well uncover a gem that no-one else has come across.

Don't be too anxious about missing out on the perfect property. You've got to be a bit philosophical when you're home hunting — otherwise, you set yourself up for despair. You can only do your best and cover as many bases as you can in the time you have available.

In this section, I discuss some of the main sources of information about properties for sale.

Looking at property on the Web

The internet has revolutionised home hunting. Instead of waiting with bated breath for the midweek and weekend newspapers to come out with the latest batch of available properties, home hunters can now plug in their preferences to a real estate website.

Real estate websites

The most popular real estate website in Australia is www.realestate.com.au (sourced from Nielsen Market Intelligence, September 2010). Another popular site is www.domain.com.au.

These sites include properties to buy, rent or share, as well as information and articles on home buying, renovation and the property market. Here you can search for properties according to suburb, price, type of property and number of bedrooms. Both websites also allow you to further refine these criteria by desirable local amenities such as schools, parks, entertainment and transport, and by property features such as air-conditioning, built-in wardrobes, and eco-friendly features like water tanks and solar panels. You can also register for email alerts (for free) and enter your preferences and — *voilà!* — a selection of properties that match your criteria is sent to you via email. If you like the look of any properties on these email alerts, you can click back to the website itself to get more information about them.

Most of the property listings on websites contain photos and a floor plan of the property. Some offer a 'virtual tour' that gives you a 360-degree view of rooms in the property, as well as a map that shows the property's location. You can zoom in on the address using the satellite view option on the map, which gives you a sense of what the surrounding neighbourhood looks like, what size the blocks are, and whether there are parks — or factories — nearby. Using StreetView or a similar facility, you can even see what the house or apartment looks like from the street, without the 'glamour-dressing' used in the agent's brochures and website photos. Sites also provide open-for-inspection times and the contact details of the listing agent, as well as a link to the website of the real estate agent handling the property.

If you like the look of a property, add it to the 'short list' or 'saved properties' function on the website or print out the information on it from the website, as well as the floor plan and map to file in your search folder (refer to the section 'Keeping track of all the information' earlier in this chapter).

Both realestate.com.au and domain.com.au allow you to create a shortlist on the website of properties you're interested in. On these two main websites, you can also keep track of what's happening to an individual property by returning to the short list. The short list may notify you that the property has been sold (and sometimes state the selling price, too). You may also see that some properties originally up for auction are now 'For Private Sale', which indicates that they have been passed in, and the vendors are now open to offers. (I discuss making offers on passed-in properties in Chapter 11.)

Apart from the listings themselves, real estate websites are a very handy resource for information about the property market in general, as well as information specific to the suburb or region you're looking at. 'Suburb snapshots' list the latest median prices for the suburb and the kinds of properties there, as well as demographic information on its population. These websites may also contain property market news as well as information about home loans and financing.

Websites of real estate agents

Most individual real estate agents also have a dedicated website, some offering a form of email alert. If you narrow down your search to a particular area served by a limited number of agents, this approach can be a good way of getting access to suburb-specific listings. While most real estate agents list their properties with one or both of the real estate websites discussed in the previous section, you may occasionally come across an agent with listings you can't find anywhere else.

DIY sites

Some vendors see the internet as a way to sell their property without having to use a real estate agent. They can do this via a 'do-it-yourself' property website (www.diysell.com.au is one example), or by placing a newspaper advertisement and including an internet address where buyers can find more information about the property. To cover those possibilities, you may like to use a search engine such as Google to search your chosen suburbs, adding 'property for sale by owner' to the keywords.

Perusing the property lift-outs

While property websites may well be your main port of call in your property search, don't neglect your local and metropolitan newspapers as a source of information and inspiration. A Saturday metropolitan newspaper is the best place to get information on properties that are open for inspection that weekend.

Newspapers also contain the odd little ad by sellers who aren't prepared to pay for glossy ads or a website listing. I found out about the house I eventually purchased through a small four-line ad in a metropolitan newspaper. The owner hadn't put up a 'For sale' sign outside the house, so I would never have known it was on the market if I hadn't scoured the newspapers every day.

After you narrow down your preferred location, checking the glossy property lift-out from the local newspaper is one of the best ways to get a feel for the kinds of property available in that area. The information in these lift-outs is usually organised according to the real estate agent rather than the suburb, but they often have more information on a property than do the metropolitan papers (but usually less information than the internet) as well as lots of colour photos. Local and metropolitan papers also send reporters to write up more detailed descriptions on selected properties.

Individual real estate agents, or groups of agents, often issue a weekly property guide to properties on the market in a particular area or region. These guides range from expensive-looking, glossy, bound books to newspaper-style handouts; you can usually find them in a rack outside a local real estate agent's office.

If you're looking for a bargain (and who isn't?), be aware that the more photos and information a property advertisement contains, the higher the vendor's expectation of the selling price. It can pay to look out for small advertisements that give the impression that the vendor hasn't wanted to spend too much money advertising. Potentially, that approach is the vendor's loss and your gain — the less competition from other buyers, the lower the price a property may be able to command.

Going through a real estate agent

If you want a real estate agent to help you, the best idea is to go in armed with a succinct description of the kind of property you're seeking, and a rough (but not exact) price range you can afford. Then ring back once a week or so and ask if anything is available that fits your criteria. Be polite and undemanding and you may come across an agent who is willing to help.

Be careful not to become the dumping ground for properties that the agent can't otherwise sell. Make sure you're using more than one firm of real estate agents and keep searching yourself at the same time. (For more information on dealing with real estate agents, refer to Chapter 4.)

One misapprehension of many home buyers is that all they have to do is ring up a few real estate agents in a particular area, tell them what they're looking for and then sit back and wait for the agent to get back to them with a selection of suitable properties. If you do this, don't be surprised if you don't get many calls from the agent. Calls from the agent are more likely if you have more money than the average to spend on a property.

Checking an area out for yourself

When you're on the hunt for a property, you don't want to leave any stone unturned — particularly the possibility that a property is out there that hasn't been advertised or listed with a real estate agent. Go ahead and drive around suburbs or particular streets that you like, just in case you spot a 'For sale' sign outside a suitable property you didn't know was on the market.

Sometimes you may see signs advertising a future auction or private sale. While vendors are unlikely to accept an offer before they draw out all potential buyers with a formal advertisement, you can always mention your interest. Perhaps they need to move in a hurry and would welcome getting a property off their hands quickly.

Word of mouth

You have nothing to lose by telling friends and co-workers that you're in the market for a new home. They may know of someone who wants to sell and who would be happy to negotiate a price with you without having to involve a real estate agent in the process. Friends of mine bought a house this way. The vendors saved several thousand dollars they would have had to pay out in commission and advertising fees, and my friends got a good price for the property.

However, don't always assume you're going to get a bargain by buying 'off the market'. Sometimes buying when you know how much other people would be prepared to pay for the same property is better. Neighbours of other friends of mine offered to sell them their house for 'a very good price'. A bit of research into the local market uncovered that the neighbours' asking price was no better than the prices being asked for similar properties on the open market.

Narrowing Down the Search

Much as you might want to look at every property with a listing on the market and which seems to meet your criteria 'just in case ...', the reality is that you can devote only so many hours in a week to home hunting, and only so many brain cells in your head to absorbing all the information about prospective properties. Your task now is to pare down the number of properties to a short list of those that you're seriously likely to consider when they're open for inspection.

You can separate the wheat from the chaff if you

✔ Drive by a property that interests you to check if the streetscape appeals to you, and how well maintained neighbouring properties are.

✔ Eliminate properties that clearly don't meet your 'must-have' criteria.

✔ Find out if shops such as newsagents and convenience stores are in the neighbourhood.

✔ Re-read property advertisements carefully to ensure there's nothing in them that doesn't fit your bill.

✔ See what public transport options are available to residents of the neighbourhood.

Paring down the properties

To prevent you wasting your time on unsuitable properties, it can help if you can tell from an ad or a photo whether a property meets your criteria. Some of a property's features can be quickly ascertained — you can usually find out easily enough whether a property has three bedrooms or a lock-up garage. Other features may require a bit more detective work.

I've been looking for months for a unit for my parents-in-law. They have some very specific requirements, including no shared walls with their neighbours. This feature isn't always easy to find in a unit and isn't something you can always see easily from a photo. I've learnt to recognise from the floor plan that a wall without windows is likely to be shared with a neighbour.

Understanding real-estate speak

You can glean other pieces of information from the language used in an advertisement: A house described as 'cosy' is probably small, for instance, and possibly very small. The same goes for 'compact'.

Other terms that need careful interpretation include:

- ✔ **Deceased estate:** A property description that includes the term *deceased estate* means the property is being sold as part of the estate of someone who has died. But the deeper meaning can be that the property hasn't been renovated for a long time, which could make it a bargain, or a 'renovator's delight'.

- ✔ **Deceptively spacious:** This little phrase means a property that looks small from the outside, and is probably small inside, but you may be able to cram more into it than you expect.

- ✔ **First home buyer's special:** This term is used to describe a property that is cheaper than most homes in the area. This may be because it is small, in a bad location or not in great condition, or that is only suitable for a single person or a couple.

- ✔ **Has potential:** The property needs a lot of work. Watch out for 'enormous potential' or 'huge potential', which indicate even more work is required to make it liveable!

- ✔ **Investor's special:** Somewhere you probably wouldn't want to live yourself! Sometimes this property is an apartment or a unit, and is generally at the lower end of the price range for similar properties in that area. Investors' specials could have an existing tenant, with a lease, so that it is not available to other occupants for some time.

- ✔ **Original condition:** Means unrenovated. This term suggests there just may be one or two remnants of the property's period style; they may be in poor condition.

- ✔ **Renovator's delight:** This description invariably means that the property is a complete dump that only the very brave handyperson should take on!

Doing the drive-by

As soon as you put together a list of possibilities from studying the ads, you can further eliminate properties by doing a drive-by. Your aim here is to look at the suburb, the general area and the street itself to get a sense of whether the area is an attractive, or at least an up-and-coming area. Check out what the neighbouring houses are like, and whether the area includes anything, such as a freeway or a factory within metres of the property, that could detract from it.

When you're doing your first drive-by, take note of important features in the neighbourhood:

The streetscape

Does the street boast shade trees and nature strips, or is it a concrete jungle? Are there parks nearby? Local greenery can make a huge difference to the character of an area. A street lined with trees is pleasing to the eye and somehow conveys a sense of affluence. If you've got a dog or kids, a park gives you a destination for walks and games.

If an area is somewhat lacking in the greenery department, don't let that put you off it entirely. Our street was rather bare of trees when we first moved in. Four years ago, the council widened the nature strips and planted fast-growing street trees. Their presence has already changed the feel of the area, making it a pleasant place to walk and linger.

Adjacent properties

Have a look at the neighbouring houses. What are their gardens like? Are they well cared for? Are the exteriors freshly painted or looking a bit tired? Once you're really interested in a particular property, you may like to stop and chat with a neighbour.

When you chat to a local, you kill two birds with one stone — you may well get inside information about the area and the house itself, and you may find out why the current owners are selling up. You may also get a feel for whether the people in the street are the kind you can drop in on to get a cup of sugar or whether you're expected to keep to yourselves.

Checking out trains, trams and buses

Even though Australians are deeply wedded to their cars, if you can find a home that has close access to a train station, a bus route, tram line or ferry wharf, you're availing yourself and any future buyers of the property of extra options for getting about. Nearby public transport means you and your family may only need one car, and, if you have children, they're going to be able to get around independently once they're old enough to travel on public transport on their own.

Strolling to the corner shops

Despite the fact that many families do a big weekly shop at a shopping mall, having easy access to a good, local mini-mart, convenience store or milk bar, where you can pick up a loaf of bread or a carton of milk on the way home, is a big plus. Having a nice cafe just down the street helps, too — although the existence of nearby cafes may well add to the purchase price of a home.

Assessing the Properties on the Short List

Now that you know a bit more about the properties on your short list, you may find it useful to draw up a kind of checklist to put in your search folder. Figure 5-1 is an example of the kind of report you can draw up for each property. To each report, add your own sketch of the floor plan or attach a print-out of it. Also add the advertisements that appear in the print media and, if they're available, paste in digital photos of the exterior and interior of the property.

Figure 5-1: Your personal property assessment report.

Property Assessment Report

Address: _____

Agent: _____ Quoted price: _____

Inspection times: _____

Comments/assessment and rating out of 10

- ✔ Street and streetscape (such as whether the property is in an attractive tree-lined street, is beside well-maintained period homes, has acceptable traffic levels; if traffic is fairly busy, make a note to come back to observe at peak hour) _____

- ✔ Shops, cafes and other amenities (such as whether the property is close to a good primary school, a convenience store, a main road, a large shopping centre within two kilometres and so on) _____

- ✔ Parks (such as having a big park with play equipment approximately five minutes' walk away) _____

- ✔ Public transport (such as a train into the city less than ten minutes walk away, a tram to the local shopping centre or close to the local milk bar) _____

- ✔ Style and exterior appearance of property (such as an Edwardian style — see Chapter 6 for more on architectural styles — having few original exterior features remaining, having an unsympathetic colour scheme and so on) _____

- ✔ Size and facilities (such as how many bedrooms, one bedroom that's quite small, large living areas, rooms that overlook the garden, a bathroom and kitchen that need a complete overhaul) _____

- ✔ Parking and storage (such as a fibro lock-up garage, one linen cupboard, no built-in wardrobes and so on)

- ✔ Garden (such as an attractive front garden planted with standard roses, a fairly small backyard dominated by one large tree and so on) _____

Figure 5-1: Continued

> **Overall assessment and rating out of 10**
>
> ✔ Does the property deserve a second inspection? _____
>
> ✔ What is your estimate of the likely sale price? _____
>
> ✔ Offer or bid made? Y/N _____
>
> - How much _____
>
> - Date _____
>
> - To whom? (individual agent's name) _____
>
> ✔ Eventual sale price: _____

Attending an Open for Inspection

You compile a file of information on a property, drive by it, check out the street and the area, and make your own personal assessment. If all this sparks your interest in taking matters further, take the next step — attend an inspection!

Working out a schedule of visits

Hopefully, you can cull your prospective properties down to a manageable number — visiting five open-for-inspection properties in one day is as many as most people can take in before everything starts to blur. So, with the list of the properties that are open for inspection over the next week (you find the list in the local newspaper), get out pen and paper to devise a schedule and plan your journey across town.

Most properties for sale have set open-for-inspection times — at least one on the weekend, and often one on an evening midweek. If you can't attend at the set times, contact the agent and request that they allow you to view the property at a time that suits you.

Most properties are open for inspection for half an hour. Depending on the time it takes to drive (or even walk) between them, you may be able to fit in two property inspections in half an hour. Make sure you have the street directory reference for each property you want to look at to maximise your chances of getting there on time.

Make a photocopy of the relevant maps in your street directory for each search day (or print out maps from an online source such as Google Maps). Mark with a thick, black, felt pen the properties you want to have a look at and the times they're open for inspection. You may also want to mark up the route you need to follow when driving between each property you intend to look at that day.

What to look for during an inspection

Think of an inspection as taking place at a couple of levels. The first is the whirlwind tour where you march from the front gate to the back of the house, taking a quick look at each of the rooms along the way. People often say they make up their minds about a house within the first five minutes or so, so by the time you get to the back of the house, you'll probably know whether the property deserves a second look. If you have time, you can start again at the front of the property, checking off its features against your criteria. Otherwise, make a note to yourself to attend a later viewing.

As you walk in the door at just about any property inspection, the real estate agent is waiting to take your name and contact details. Do you have to give those details? Yes. Under civil law, when an agent holds an open home inspection, they take responsibility for the home while they have it in their possession. There have been instances where burglaries or assaults have occurred in a property that has been open for inspection and the perpetrator has not been able to be identified due to a lack of information. Therefore, a buyer can be refused entry if they don't provide their name and contact details to the agent. If you're concerned about privacy issues, you can ask to write your name on a separate piece of paper that no-one else at the inspection can see. If you don't want the agent to contact you, you can tell them. But you may actually appreciate the agents following up with you to suggest other properties that might be suitable.

Sussing out the street appeal

Starting at the front gate, or the entrance to the apartment block if you're looking at a flat or unit, get a feel for whether this is the kind of home you'd be happy to come back to every day. Don't be too prescriptive — not every property needs a gate topped with a flowering arbour, or a smart funky lobby. The question you should be pondering is: Can I do something with this property?

Focusing on the floor plan

Changing how space flows through a property is a more difficult and expensive process than changing the colour of the walls or the fit-out of the kitchen. If the floor plan doesn't suit you, think of ways in which it can be improved. Remember that structural changes cost a lot of money, and also disrupt your life for possibly months on end. However, if you believe the property has possibilities, you may want to buy it to live in until you have the time or money to get it to work better for you.

Letting in the light

The ideal is to have a home where the windows in the main living areas face north. But natural light works differently in different houses. To get a clear sense of how light works in a place, visit it at different times of the day (if you can). If you're the type of person who spends a lot of time in your living area, you may want to be sure the property is a light and breezy place for most of the day, not just for a precious hour or so around the spring equinox.

Be open to possibilities to improve the natural light in a home. The house we bought originally had no north-facing windows. We were able to install two new windows that now flood our living area with light for most of the day.

Finding room for everything

If you're attached to particular pieces of furniture, is the property you're inspecting able to fit them all in? A friend of mine who collected antique and retro furniture went house hunting with a tape measure to make sure his larger pieces would be able to fit into the available space.

If space considerations are important, carry with you a note of the dimensions of your bigger pieces of furniture, so you can make a quick calculation and eliminate properties that clearly can't accommodate them without significant remodelling.

A requirement for properties to have suitable spots for certain pieces of furniture may significantly narrow your options in a particular area. You may need to make a hard decision: Either you start looking in a different area, which has bigger homes in a price range you can afford, or you cull your furniture collection.

Having plenty of storage space

If you can find a home with plenty of storage space, you're very lucky. While newer homes are more likely to offer plenty of storage, period homes are notoriously skimpy on built-in cupboards. Once again, though, you can look for potential storage spaces. Many older homes have fireplaces with room on either side for built-in wardrobes or bookcases.

Our home lacked built-in storage except for one rather shallow linen cupboard. The home did have a very high-pitched roof that we were able to later convert into an attic, now as big as a room.

Taking a Critical Look at a Property

When you find a particular property that fits most of your criteria, your best next step is to detach yourself emotionally and look for possible flaws. As perfect or pretty as a property may be, the house or unit may be hiding some major problems that can cost you money and cause you heartache down the track. While you may still go ahead and buy a property with a few blemishes, keeping your eyes wide open as you do it is to your advantage. For example, if you're negotiating a private sale, you may be able to use the information you glean about any problems in your haggling over the price.

If you have a parent or friend with some understanding of how buildings work, ask them to accompany you to an inspection. In addition to their knowledge, they're likely to be more objective than you are in drawing attention to a property's flaws and shortcomings.

While getting a building inspection report is a must before you make a serious offer on a property, you can do some preliminary investigations yourself before you go to the expense of employing a professional building inspector. (I discuss inspection reports in the next section.)

Some of the potential problems that a closer inspection can detect are

✔ **Building out of alignment:** Open and close a few doors and windows to check whether the house is out of alignment.

✔ **Cracks in walls:** Cracks may indicate subsidence in the earth under the house. Look carefully for cracks that seem to have been painted or plastered over.

✔ **Faulty or substandard wiring:** Check the electrical box near the front door. If the box and contents is ancient, it may mean the wiring and switches need replacing.

✔ **Plumbing problems:** Turn on a tap to see if you can detect water hammer or discolouration in the water.

✔ **Rising damp:** If you notice paint on walls flaking off and a musty smell in some rooms, you may have a problem with rising damp.

✔ **Tree roots causing damage:** Large trees planted too close to the building may mean roots can get into the sewers and plumbing pipes. Tree roots can also lift the foundations of the house.

Getting a Pre-Purchase Building Inspection Done

If you're seriously interested in a particular property, your next step should be to engage a reputable specialist to carry out a building inspection. If you buy a property through a private treaty sale, you can add a condition to the contract that makes the sale subject to a satisfactory building inspection report. If you plan to buy at auction, you need to arrange an inspection prior to the auction date. Given that building inspections can be fairly expensive, usually between $300 and $500, you can't have one done on every single property that interests you.

Find a building inspector by asking friends or neighbours for a referral, or by contacting:

✔ Archicentre (www.archicentre.com.au).

✔ Australian Environmental Pest Managers Association (www.aepma.com.au).

✔ Housing Industry Association (www.hia.com.au).

✔ Institute of Building Consultants NSW
(www.ibcnsw.com.au).

✔ Master Builders Australia (www.masterbuilders.com.au).

The building inspector provides you with a written report, pointing out faults in the property, whether they can be repaired and, if so, how much these repairs are likely to cost. The report should also highlight any unsafe or unauthorised renovations and extensions.

The following list covers some of the aspects of a property that a building inspection report addresses and comments on:

✔ Concrete paths

✔ Condition of guttering and roofing

✔ Evidence of any asbestos

✔ Evidence of council approval of building additions and/or renovations

✔ Evidence of termite damage

✔ Evidence of water damage

✔ Overall condition of doors, windows, cupboards, basins, sinks, taps and other fixtures

✔ Overall condition of mortar, plaster and paint

✔ Plumbing and drainage

✔ Roofing and wall insulation

✔ Star ratings for energy and water efficiency

✔ State of the fencing and/or retaining walls

✔ Structural integrity

✔ Ventilation issues

✔ Wiring and general electrical safety

Chapter 6

Buying a Piece of History

• •

In This Chapter

▶ Knowing the true costs of buying a period home

▶ Acknowledging heritage restrictions

▶ Looking at Australian housing styles

• •

*Y*ou're either the type of person who loves a home that has age and character, or you're not. Many people would far rather buy a property that incorporates modern standards and is newly plumbed and wired than one that has a quaint iron lacework verandah and a tiled fireplace in every room.

However, period homes have lots of charm and, moreover, people in Australia place a high value on property that has a sense of history. A 2004 study by Macquarie University showed that the prices of period homes — whether in cities or in country towns — increase faster than do non-period homes.

If you're interested in buying in a certain area — for instance, in the inner suburbs of an older capital city — you may not have much of a choice whether you want to buy a period home or not. Many suburbs are almost entirely built in one particular architectural style.

What constitutes a period home is changing, too. As recently as the mid 1990s, the term 'period home' referred mainly to properties built before 1910. Today we accept that properties built during the 1950s and 1960s have characteristics and attractions of their own. One day there may even be heritage restrictions on properties built during the 1970s and 1980s.

Buying a property with historical value can bring its own challenges. Apart having to deal with an old structure and outdated amenities — something you anticipated — you may have to deal with your local council. Some councils place strict restrictions on what you can and can't do to the exterior and sometimes even the internal structure of the property.

In this chapter, I discuss some of the problems you may face in buying and renovating a period home to a liveable standard, and also look at the characteristics of some of the more common period home styles found in Australia.

The Pros and Cons of Buying a Period Home

Advantages, disadvantages and idiosyncrasies are common themes for period homes. Heritage restrictions and costs of renovating are considerations as well. This section looks at the impressive and the doubtful aspects of buying an architectural style that captures your heart.

Impressive pros

Nothing is more impressive than a beautifully restored or renovated period home. The lofty ceilings of a Victorian home, the elaborate timberwork of a Federation-style home and the grand verandahs of a California bungalow have a character and quality quite beyond that of even the smartest modern designer building.

Modern homes never seem to show the attention to detail of a Victorian home's elaborate ceiling rose or the decorative flourishes of an Art Deco home. Even the roofs and brickwork of older homes often have features that give them a special character.

However, not only do older homes have character, they were often also built with a solidity that makes them longer wearing, more soundproof and more adapted to our climate than many modern homes. The fact that homes are still standing often 100 years after being built is a testament to the original high quality of the workmanship and the materials used. Older homes built in double brick or solid weatherboards keep their interiors cool in summer, and also insulate the house from noise. Wide overhanging verandahs protect the interior from harsh summer sun, while north-facing sunrooms capture the warmth of the sun in colder climates.

Also, period homes are usually located in established suburbs with attractive tree-lined streetscapes and many good local facilities. An architectural attractiveness is more evident (and more valuable) when expressed via a whole street full of period homes from around the same era. Period homes have a sense of history, too, of the lives of others who lived in the home and of the ways they changed the home to suit their needs and lifestyle.

Not-so-impressive cons

However, older homes do have some drawbacks. While the construction may be more solid than many houses built today, worth remembering is the fact that older homes were built before the introduction of many of the lifestyle comforts we now take for granted. Problems that may be presented by an older home include inadequate foundations on clay soils, ageing plumbing, wiring and heating systems, as well as floor plans suited to an age far different to our own. Many people buy a gorgeous older-style cottage only to find they need to spend thousands of dollars replacing cloth-taped electrical wires and cracked terracotta pipes.

If you fall in love with a property and are determined to make that property your home, steel yourself for the cost of replacing the ancient wiring and decrepit plumbing. Assuming your budget can stand it, however, updating your home's plugs and pipes is an excellent investment.

Living with the idiosyncrasies of a period home

Even if you renovate an old property, you may still have to live with some features that you can't change. Many single-fronted Victorian houses, for instance, have a floor plan that resembles a series of railway carriages — one room after another leads off from a narrow hallway. You may be able to open up the back of the house to create an open-plan living area, but you probably can't transform it into the centralised floor plan you may be dreaming of.

Now look at the characteristics of the building itself. Apart from out-of-date wiring and plumbing, which must be replaced for safety's sake, your period home may have some idiosyncrasies of its own. The original windows may be smaller than you like, the high-ceilinged rooms may be difficult to keep warm, and the beautiful solid timber original doors may not close as neatly as in a brand-new project home. While you may be able to change some of these features, others, such as the high ceilings and the imperfectly closing doors, you may have to learn to live with.

Dealing with Heritage Restrictions

Some local councils place restrictions on the changes and improvements you can make to a particular property. These restrictions are more common in inner-city areas of consistent period architectural style and some country towns that have a particular heritage style.

Heritage restrictions can be placed on a particular property, or on an area. A heritage restriction on a particular property indicates that the property has historical or cultural significance that makes it worth preserving as close to its original state as possible. Such a property may be listed with the state or national heritage listing — depending on its significance.

In most cases, an area rather than a particular property has heritage restrictions. (In Victoria, such restrictions are described as *heritage overlays*.) These restrictions delineate areas or places considered to have significant heritage values worth preserving. This significance may be a consistent streetscape of homes in a certain period style, or examples of unusual buildings constructed during a particular period.

Restrictions often only apply to the exterior of the building, in an attempt to keep the streetscape consistent; if your property is affected, you may not be able to build on or change the front of the property without council permission. You may also be required to make sure that things like verandah trimmings and fences are in keeping with the style of the other homes in the street, and to paint the exterior in colours that fit in with the period of the home. In many cases, you may not be allowed to add a second storey unless it is designed to be inconspicuous from the street.

The main issue for you to be aware of in keeping to heritage restrictions is to think about how any work you do to your home affects the streetscape. Any plans you put into council when you apply for development approval or a building permit need to address this issue in what is called a *viewline analysis*. This analysis covers drawings in plan (from above) and elevation (from the sides) that show whether the extension is visible from the street and what it looks like.

Some councils are happy for you to create a contemporary extension to a home in a heritage area as long as it is well designed and has a connection to the older home in some way — such as the materials used or the shape. Check with your local council's heritage adviser for guidelines on the design of extensions to a heritage-restricted home.

Some individual homes or streetscapes, however, are considered to be so historically or culturally important that councils place restrictions on how owners can alter or renovate the interiors. While no council would expect you to use a century-old bathroom or kitchen, in some cases, councils prohibit the demolition of parts of the property, and have rules on what materials you can use in your renovation to ensure that the character of the property isn't altered too dramatically. For instance, you may not be able to replace your slate roofing tiles with terracotta tiles.

Finding out whether a property is heritage listed or is in an area that has heritage restrictions should be part of your research. In most cases, the real estate agent should inform prospective buyers. If you suspect that heritage restrictions may apply, you may want to ask the question upfront. Check with your local council for the rules and restrictions that apply to heritage areas and heritage-listed properties in your area. Some councils are stricter in their restrictions than others.

If you're happy to live with them, heritage restrictions aren't necessarily a bad idea. A study carried out by the economics department at Macquarie University in 2004 found that heritage-listed homes in Sydney were valued, on average, 12 per cent higher than non-heritage listed properties.

Renovating your period home

Whether you need to toe the line of strict heritage-listing rules, or you would like to at least retain some of the character of the home in your renovations, you're best to carry out some research into the home's original style and characteristics. In some cases, you may be buying a property that has been less than sympathetically renovated in the past and you may want to return some of its original character and features.

Most local councils can supply guidelines on important exterior and interior features and colour schemes that apply to the housing styles in the area. Councils and local libraries may also have documents and historical photographs that may give you more information about your particular suburb or, if you're lucky, your actual street.

For more general information about housing styles and about restoring old homes, the National Trust or the Heritage Council in your state or territory can provide you with relevant publications. Some informative books and magazines that focus on particular architectural styles are available, as well as manuals on how to renovate with sympathy for the original style of a property.

Look closely at surrounding properties to get a sense of the features and colour schemes shared by the period homes in your area.

Unless your house is in an area of strict heritage restrictions, you don't need to slavishly follow a period style when you renovate. Some of the best renovations are those that integrate period elements of the original home — architectural forms, decorative motifs, colour schemes or building materials — into a contemporary style.

One council (Moreland City Council in Melbourne's inner north) points out that in altering a period home, you're adding a chapter to its history and that the connection between the new and the old is as important as the original home. Rather than trying to blend the new with the old seamlessly, it may be more aesthetically and culturally worthwhile to clearly distinguish the new chapter from the old — through some kind of visual break, like using a clearly contemporary design, or recessing part of a wall.

Restoring original features

Restoring a period home can be an expensive proposition, depending on how closely you want to recreate its original style. Painting a home in its heritage colours shouldn't cost much more than giving it a contemporary colour scheme. If you're lucky, the property still has many of its original features that just need some tender loving care — and several weekends of hard work — to return them to their former glory. Doors and window frames can be sanded back to the original woodwork, and carpets lifted to polish the floors.

When it comes to replacing or restoring features like ornate Victorian ceiling roses and Art Deco basins, costs can start to mount. Replacing things like original light switches, vents and pressed metal ceilings can soon add thousands to your budget. You may want to decide at the outset how faithfully you want to keep to the original style and features.

Specialist suppliers of already refurbished period fittings and furnishings have sprung up to cater to the growing demand for these products. Many of these suppliers also stock reproduction furnishings in various period styles.

Websites that specialise in resources for renovators of period homes in Australia include

- *The Period Home Renovator* (www.periodhomerenovator. com). This website has a list of resources and suppliers for renovators of period homes, information on different period styles and an archive of articles from its magazine.

- World of Old Houses (www.oldhouses.com.au). A great site full of information, ideas and links to anything to do with restoring and refurbishing old homes in Australia.

- *Trading Post* (www.tradingpost.com.au) or its print publications and the classified sections of metropolitan and local newspapers are another way of sourcing furnishings and fittings being sold by individuals who may be replacing their home's period features with something more modern.

- eBay (www.ebay.com.au) is another good source for second-hand fixtures and fittings.

If your budget is tight, look in second-hand building materials outlets for fittings and furnishings that may need some work to return them to their earlier glory. Sometimes you come across a property on demolition row with features around the same period as your own home. Talk to the demolition company before it starts smashing things up; you may also have to elbow your way past people collecting doors, windows and other furnishings to sell in the second-hand building material yards.

Unless your property is in a strict heritage area, or you're a stickler for detail, you don't need to ensure every furnishing and fitting is in its original period style. Just make sure the additions and fittings are consistent with the period; for example, use traditional materials, such as timber window frames rather than aluminium window frames in homes built before the 1930s.

Architectural Periods and Styles

Australia's historical housing styles grew out of styles imported from Britain and America and other colonies like India. In many cases, the imported styles were modified to adapt to the local climate and lifestyle. For example, the deep verandahs of the colonial and Victorian eras were a response to the harsh Australian sun, and the elevated Queenslander style was a response to the hot, muggy climate and frequent floods that beset that tropical state.

Different styles developed in response to new materials and also new mindsets. Houses became grander and more elaborately decorated as the Victorian boom reached its height, and then were pared down to greater simplicity after the housing crash of the 1890s. In the mid to late 1900s, modernist homes built with a framework of steel and using glass were able to create large open spaces.

In this section, I summarise the characteristics of each housing style. However, be mindful that during any period, regional variations of the theme occurred and many sub-styles and spin-off styles resulted.

Colonial style: 1788–1830s

New South Wales and Tasmania are the states to find examples of this very early style of Australian housing. The large deep verandahs on these otherwise simple low-roofed homes were adopted from the bungalows of India and proved well-suited to the local climate, providing an escape from the glare of the Australian sun. Many houses were built of timber boards or split logs and had mud or flagstone floors. Others were built of stone. While some originally only had two rooms, most have had rooms added over the years.

Ordinarily, the grander versions of the colonial style have survived. However, you may be lucky to find a cottage that has seen better days and that is likely to appreciate with some careful restoration. Features characteristic of this style include the following:

- ✓ Bluestone base with timber boards or split logs
- ✓ Fireplace with chimney
- ✓ Generally single storey
- ✓ Low verandah under low-pitched, single-hipped roof
- ✓ Mud or flagstone flooring
- ✓ Simple plan, sometimes only two rooms
- ✓ Stone window sills and louvre shutters

Georgian period: 1810s–1840s

The Georgian style stripped the features of the Colonial style back to perfectly proportioned simplicity. Built of sandstone blocks and using quality fittings like sash windows, panelled doors and carved woodwork, houses built in the Georgian period have an elegance that harks back to the Classical style of ancient Greece and Rome.

Most houses didn't have verandahs or eaves, and the windows were small and regular. New South Wales and Tasmania have some fine examples of Georgian homes (Hobart's Battery Point and Sydney's Rocks area have many beautifully preserved Georgian cottages).

Characteristic features of the Georgian style include the following:

- Corrugated iron roof

- Little use of verandah or eaves

- Sandstone or bluestone walls (occasionally rendered)

- Simple and symmetrical plan

- Small rectangular windows

- Timber windows and doors

Victorian styles

When you think of a period home, a building in the Victorian style (named after the queen who reigned over Britain from 1837 to 1901, not the state) is what comes to mind. There were actually three main periods of Victorian style: Early Victorian, 1840–60; mid-Victorian, 1860–75; and the late-Victorian boom style, 1875–92. Many sub-styles were built as well, including the Victorian Mannerist style, the Gothic Revival and the Italianate style of the 1880s.

The reason the Victorian period is so renowned is because the houses were built during a period of unprecedented prosperity brought on by the gold rush that started in the 1850s. That prosperity meant that home owners could afford to spend money on their homes, and wanted their homes to reflect their affluence and their success. Owners also used new materials to decorate their homes, such as cast-iron lacework used for verandahs and fences, and elaborate plasterwork mouldings on ceilings and cornices.

Early Victorian: 1840–60

Features of houses built in the early Victorian style include the following:

- Front of the building usually sited close to the footpath

- Limited ornamentation

- Pitched, hipped roof of slate or corrugated iron

- Often *terraced* (in rows)
- Red brick or block fronted (square-edged weatherboards)
- Simple, often single-fronted, design
- Tall, narrow windows placed in the middle of each room

Mid-Victorian: 1860–75

Features of houses built in the mid-Victorian style include the following:

- Decorative brickwork and elaborate lacework
- Large and elaborate cornices, ceiling roses and architraves
- Multi-framed windows
- Use of stained glass beside entry doors

Late-Victorian boom style: 1875–92

Houses built in the late-Victorian boom style (see Figure 6-1) feature the following:

- Complex paint and wallpaper schemes
- Grand, ornate appearance
- Intricate iron lacework and complex tile patterns on verandahs
- Multicoloured brickwork
- Towers and turrets incorporated into the building
- Use of triple windows and stained glass

The climate of ostentation and grandeur that climaxed in the late-Victorian boom style came to a sudden stop in the 1890s when Australia went into a severe economic depression that caused a housing crash. Many years passed before houses were again constructed on a mass scale.

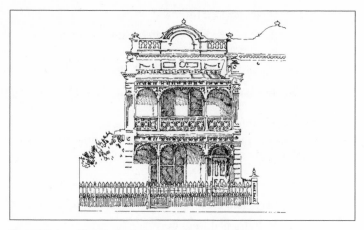

Figure 6.1: Late-Victorian style features an ornate appearance.

Source: What house is that? A guide to Victoria's housing styles, *second edition. Published by the Heritage Council of Victoria and the Building Commission, 2007. Illustrated by David Harvey.*

Federation or Edwardian style: 1901–16

Houses built at the beginning of the 20th century adopted some of the characteristics of the Victorian style, but stripped back their grandeur. This style was perhaps the real beginning of the Australian suburban style, with a more relaxed, centralised floor plan and an emphasis on the garden, even in the more modest versions of the style. Whole suburbs in Australia are made up of brick or weatherboard Edwardian-style houses; they're elegant without being too grand and lend themselves well to renovation.

Features of houses built in the Federation or Edwardian style include the following:

- ✔ Bay windows
- ✔ Complex roof lines
- ✔ Houses set back further from the street than Victorian homes

- Red brickwork or square-edged, bull-nosed weatherboards
- Return verandahs
- Stained glass in front windows
- Steeply sloping hipped roofs with wide eaves

Queenslander: 1880s–1940

Positioned high on stilts and surrounded by a large deep verandah that is often enclosed by lattice panels or roll-down canvas blinds, the Queenslander is an ideal adaptation to a hot tropical climate. The style changed and evolved over the years, but has always retained the airy grandeur that is now highly sought after in most Queensland coastal towns and cities. The Queenslander lends itself beautifully to renovation, although watch for termites.

Features of Queenslanders include the following:

- Extensive verandahs often enclosed with latticework
- Freestanding and elevated on stilts
- High-pitched corrugated iron roofs
- Light, timber construction

Californian bungalow: 1916–1940s

The basic style of the Californian bungalow was imported from America, but it acquired its own particular Australian suburban style. These houses are usually single storey, with a low-pitched roof and large pillars that support a front verandah and give the house a rather heavy solid appearance. Living areas were generally at the front of the house, with the kitchen and laundry tucked away at the back; for renovators determined to create a living area that flows out to an entertaining area in the backyard, this can create a bit of a challenge. Californian bungalows do lend themselves to being extended, and the creation of a second storey.

Features of Californian bungalows include the following:

- ✓ Exposed rafters and beams showing from under the roof
- ✓ Front doors often decorated with leadlight
- ✓ Interior plan generally featuring a central hallway
- ✓ Large masonry pillars alongside a wide front porch
- ✓ Rustic appearance; materials with a rustic, natural look
- ✓ Living areas at the front of the house and the kitchen and laundry at the back
- ✓ Shallow, low-pitched roofs
- ✓ Windows with small panes and arranged in casements

Early modern: 1915–1940s

Early modern styles (see Figure 6-2) include Art Deco, Spanish Mission, Mediterranean and Dutch Colonial. These buildings are the beginning of a more modern style that would evolve into the brick veneer suburban home. Houses are often on single-storey blocks set well back from the street, with side driveways and expanses of lawn with narrow garden borders. They're usually built of brick with contrasting detailing around porches, windows and chimneys. Many early apartments and flats were built during this period and are today much sought after for their stylish design, large rooms and Art Deco ornamentation.

Features of early modern styles include the following:

- ✓ Brick or rendered walls
- ✓ Chrome details on stairs, lights and handles
- ✓ Curved corner windows and porthole windows
- ✓ Simple block shapes
- ✓ Terracotta tiled roofs

Spanish Mission homes feature colonnaded verandahs, and Art Deco homes feature textured and/or patterned glass in the windows.

Figure 6-2: Early modern style features simple block shapes.

Source: What house is that? A guide to Victoria's housing styles, *second edition. Published by the Heritage Council of Victoria and the Building Commission, 2007. Illustrated by David Harvey.*

Modernist: 1945–70

Once scorned by period home buyers, many modernist homes are now becoming prized for their bold geometric style and their open living plans. While these homes can range from modest suburban bungalows to architectural landmarks, they tend to share a few characteristics that set them apart from the average brick veneer suburban home.

Modernist homes (see Figure 6-3) have square proportions tending to the horizontal, flat roofs, vast expanses of glass and a stripped-back style that verges on the austere. They're often well designed for the modern family with plenty of light and good access to the outdoors.

Modernist homes feature the following:

- ✔ Design tending to the horizontal
- ✔ Occasional bold curving elements
- ✔ Vast expanses of floor-to-ceiling windows
- ✔ Walls made of geometric shapes
- ✔ Use of natural materials such as stone and timber mixed with steel and glass.

Figure 6-3: Modernist style features geometric shapes.

Source: What house is that? A guide to Victoria's housing styles, *second edition. Published by the Heritage Council of Victoria and the Building Commission, 2007. Illustrated by David Harvey.*

Renovating a period home with sensitivity and flair

Here's how to renovate a period home with style:

✔ Don't 'over-restore' a period home. Aim to retain the original character of the house rather than making a perfect reproduction of the period style. Perfectly restored homes can look sterile.

✔ Try to use materials that were in use when your house was built, even if they're modern versions of original fittings. Avoid using aluminium-framed windows in a Victorian or Edwardian home, for instance.

✔ Paint the home in colour schemes known to have been used on houses of your period.

✔ Even if heritage restrictions limit what you can do to the front of the home, you can still often create a more modern rear extension or design an unobtrusive second storey extension.

✔ Make rear extensions sympathetic to the period in which your house was originally built. These additions don't have to be lavish copies. In many cases, you can adopt a quite contemporary addition that successfully includes a reference point to the original style of the home.

Chapter 7

Renovator's Dream
(or Nightmare)

● ●

In This Chapter

▶ Settling into your 'renovator's delight'

▶ Finding out what's involved with making alterations

▶ Doing the renovation work yourself

▶ Hiring architects and building designers

▶ Finding a builder to do the work

▶ Deciding whether to live on a building site

▶ Borrowing the money to pay for your dream

● ●

*C*ount yourself lucky if you find a property that doesn't require too much work to make it lovable as well as livable. Even if the property you find does happen to fit your needs and style fairly closely, you're most likely going to want to put your mark on it, even if only to freshen it up with a paint job.

A home that requires a fair bit of work on it is generally cheaper to buy than one that has been freshly renovated; you can sometimes find really rundown homes for an absolute bargain. Some people simply love the challenge that the blank canvas of a so-called renovator's dream represents. However, renovating is a lot of hard work and there are many considerations you need to take into account before you jump into buying a home that needs a great deal of work.

In this chapter, I look at some simple improvements that can make your home more livable and lovable, and I also discuss the different ways in which you can approach the job of undertaking more extensive renovations.

Tackling a Renovator's Delight

When a home is advertised as a 'renovator's delight', the description often indicates a property that would probably be best knocked down altogether. Unless you have money to burn on a full-scale renovation, avoid these kinds of properties if you're a first home buyer!

Preferable is the 'live in now, renovate later' type of home. You may still have to put up with sagging floors, an ancient bathroom and poky rooms, but as long as the property is basically livable, you can renovate in stages as you get the money together. Ideal is a home with superficial ugliness but structural soundness, and that has a working bathroom and kitchen.

Making the place livable

Simply ripping up all the carpets, polishing the floorboards and painting the walls and ceilings in a light, neutral colour have instantly improved many a gloomy and musty home. If you can get these jobs done before you move in, you make life much easier for yourself. Having to move everything out of a room in order to paint or sand the floors is a major hassle best avoided if possible.

When horrible is delightful

The house my husband and I bought was a classic ugly duckling. Even the removalist shrieked when he looked down the hallway towards our new kitchen area. The sight of orange-patterned tiles on the floor and walls, brown wood-veneer cupboards, an ancient stove and a torn floral blind was hardly enhanced by the ugliest light fitting imaginable. But all this horror was superficial. Over the next couple of months, we lifted the floor tiles, painted the cabinets and wall tiles, and tossed the floral blind and the awful light fitting into the skip, making the house bearable until we could afford to renovate properly.

Two of the most important rooms in the house are the bathroom and kitchen. Some ideas for improving them are as follows:

- **Bathrooms:** The bathroom often needs more drastic work if the layout and fittings are out of date. However, re-tiling, and replacing the old basin with a new vanity unit immediately gives the room a lift. Just replacing a tired exhaust fan can reduce damp in a bathroom.

- **Kitchens:** If they're basically functional, changing the cabinet doors or repainting the doors, if possible, can improve kitchens. Use tile and laminate primer on laminated or wood-veneer panelled doors to give them a surface that can be easily painted over. Semi-gloss or gloss paint works best on kitchen cabinets.

  Replace tiles, or paint them over by using a tile primer product first. A very worn and stained bench top may need replacing. A stove that looks ugly and out of date can still work fine — just give it a good scrub inside and out. If it really needs replacing, buy something that can eventually fit into the swanky new kitchen you plan to build in the future.

As soon as you give the whole place a new coat of paint, it may well start looking fresh enough to live in for a few years without further major expense.

In colder southern states, one of the quickest ways to improve the feel of an old and dilapidated home is to install a good heating system. My husband and I eventually installed hydronic heating in our home during our final renovation and wished we had done it years ago, instead of shivering in poorly heated rooms.

Progressing from livable to lovable

As soon as you're in the position to spend some money renovating your home, you can start thinking about ways in which you can improve it structurally.

Before you start dreaming about your stainless steel kitchen or the study perched in a tower on top of your house, be aware of the very real possibility of *overcapitalising* — which occurs when you spend more money on your home than it is worth.

A general rule is to spend no more than 50 per cent of your home's value on a renovation. This rule presumes that property rises in value by around 10 per cent a year, so if, for instance, you spend $225,000 renovating your $450,000 home, you can expect to break even on your outlay within four or five years.

The 50 per cent rule doesn't take into account the probability that your home increases in value as a result of the renovation, but overestimating the effect of a renovation on the value of a property is too easy. Even a very good renovation is likely to add no more than 20 per cent to the value of a home; this is partly because the biggest component of a property's value is its land value rather than the building, and partly because buyers don't value renovations quite as highly as do sellers.

Some renovations can add more value to a home than others:

- **Adding a bathroom:** Having an extra bathroom, especially an ensuite, may add 50 per cent of its cost to your home's value. Two bathrooms have become a must-have for most families and even for couples.

- **Making outdoors entertaining:** An inviting area outside with paving and landscaping can return twice its cost to the value of your home. What you're in effect doing is creating an extra room at a fraction of the cost. Make sure the area has shade from hot sun and shelter from the rain, and add an attractive table and chair setting.

- **Maximising light:** Bringing more natural light into a home by adding windows and skylights definitely adds value to your home well beyond the outlay. People love light and bright homes.

- **Opening up the house:** Creating an open-plan living area at the rear of the home that flows on to your outdoor entertaining area can be an expensive but undeniably appealing improvement to any home. Without skimping on style and quality of material, try to find lower-cost ways of opening up rooms to the garden. You may be able to turn a bedroom at the rear of the house into a living area by installing French doors, for instance.

- **Painting:** Freshly painted walls, ceilings, doors and window frames add far more than their cost to the value of your home.

> ✔ **Refurbishing kitchens and bathrooms:** Clean and
> attractive kitchens and bathrooms usually return their cost
> to the value of your home. Don't spend too much, though,
> on luxury and high-end fittings and appliances. Aim to
> spend no more than 10 per cent of the purchase price of
> your home on all wet areas.

Planning the Job

Renovating a property can range from giving a few cupboards a
fresh coat of paint to building a whole new extension. In between
these two projects are myriad jobs that involve both skilled and
unskilled work, including some that can only be carried out by a
qualified tradesperson.

For structural work and work that costs more than a certain
amount (the value varies between states and territories), you
need to get hold of various permits (called building licences in
the Australian Capital Territory and Western Australia) from
your local planning authority, which means getting plans drawn
up, either by an architect, a designer or a draftsperson.

Obtaining the necessary permits

You may think that your home is your castle and you can do
whatever you want with it (a main reason for wanting to own
your own home in the first place). Local government authorities
don't agree. Yes, you can hammer as many nails as you like
into the walls, and paint feature walls in alternating purple and
orange, if that's your idea of a colour scheme, but whenever you
want to make any changes to the structure of your home, you
have to go to your local council and get permission.

The rules that apply to permits and approvals vary not just from
state to state, but also from local council to local council. Check
with your own council on how their system works, and find out
as early as possible in the process. Getting permit applications
through can take time, sometimes months, and you don't want
your job held up because you're waiting for your approval to
come through. Your local council's website almost certainly has
information on council's requirements.

Building permits

Ordinarily, any jobs that involve some kind of structural work require a *building permit*, also known as a 'building licence', 'construction certificate', 'building consent' or 'building approval'. A building permit demonstrates that the planned work adheres to the Building Code of Australia and is structurally safe and sound. The Building Code of Australia sets out the standards for all new building work (including renovations) in Australia.

If you're renovating as an owner–builder, you need to apply for the permit yourself. If you're using a builder or architect to project-manage your renovation, they make the applications on your behalf. You normally need to provide detailed plans and drawings, so if you have designed the renovation yourself, a qualified draftsperson must draw it up in a form that is acceptable to your local council. Look for draftspersons in the *Yellow Pages* or local newspaper. (I also discuss draftspersons in Chapter 9.)

Other information and documents you may need to provide in order to obtain a building permit include the following:

- **Copy of your title:** The title proves that you're the owner of the property.

- **Land survey:** The survey determines the exact location of your property's boundaries, the size of the land and any easements that may affect where you can construct an extension or new building.

- **Soil and footings report:** A geotechnical engineer carries out this report to determine what kind of footing or slabs are required for extensions and second-storey additions.

- **Structural engineer's report:** This report recommends whether footings or a concrete slab system is required, based on the findings of the soil and footings report. Required for extensions and second-storey additions.

- **Proof of insurance:** Always have these documents ready.

Some local councils have their own in-house building surveyors, but many now delegate the job to private building surveyors. Your local council may be able to give you a reference to a local surveyor. Otherwise, you can find a building surveyor through the Australian Institute of Building Surveyors. The Institute's website (www.aibs.com.au) has links to offices for each of the states and territories.

Planning permits and development approvals

For bigger jobs you may also need a planning permit or development approval. A planning permit isn't always required — in many case, you don't need one if the total land you hold title to is above a certain size, for instance. If you do need a planning permit, you need to get it before a building permit can be issued.

If your home is in an area that has heritage restrictions or has some other kind of Special Building Overlay (SBO), such as for land that is subject to flooding, you may need to apply for a special permit (refer to Chapter 6 for more information on heritage-listed properties).

Your plans may be affected, depending on whether the proposal fits in with the local neighbourhood character, does not contravene restrictions on building heights and has an approved setback from the street. (I discuss council's requirements further in Chapter 9.)

Problems getting your application through council

Some renovation applications are more straightforward than others. Anything that impacts on a neighbour's use of his or her land is more difficult to get through council. Rules are designed to ensure that your neighbour isn't imposed upon too much by your grand plans to renovate your dream home.

 If your renovation includes anything complicated, you're better off working with an architect or building designer who is familiar with the way the rules work in your local government area. These professionals have a good idea of whether what you want to do is even possible, or whether your plans can be presented in a way that can convince your local planning authority that they're going to work.

Planning authorities do refuse planning applications. If that happens, you have the right to appeal. At that point, you may find going to a professional town planning firm that can produce a professional document and even go to court on your behalf to argue your case, if necessary, worthwhile. In some cases, though, you need to go back to the drawing board to find a different way of achieving your renovation that is going to be more in line with what your local council is happy with.

Getting the work done

You can carry out renovations in a variety of ways. The method you choose often depends on how big the job is, your own particular skills and the amount of time you have available.

In the following sections, I describe the four main ways in which home renovations can be undertaken. Basically, you can:

- Do all or most of the work yourself.
- Hire a builder to project-manage and take responsibility for the work.
- Hire an architect or designer to organise and administer the whole project, including the contractors.
- Manage the project yourself but get contractors in to do most or all of the work.

Doing It Yourself

A spate of television programs on renovations has convinced many people that they can turn their ugly duckling of a house into a swan in just a couple of weekends. While you can do plenty of jobs yourself to improve the look of your home, be aware that most renovating jobs are not nearly as easy as they may look on television.

If your renovation is going to cost more than a certain amount, you officially become an owner–builder (see the section 'Becoming an owner–builder' later in this chapter for details; amounts vary from state to state). Being an owner–builder makes you legally responsible for the work you carry out. In many states, you need to get a permit to become an owner–builder; you may also be required to do a short owner–builder course. (See Chapter 9 for further information on the requirements for owner–builders.)

Deciding whether you're up to the job

Keep in mind that you need skills and good equipment in order to do much more than the most basic jobs of painting and tiling. And if you think that doing the work yourself saves you money, don't forget that tradespeople and builders get discounts on the materials and fittings they buy in bulk. Remember also that if you take time off from your day job to carry out the renovation, you need to cost your own loss of income against the money you may save by not paying for someone else's labour.

I discuss the responsibilities of the owner–builder in the context of building a new home in Chapter 9, and some of the recommendations in that chapter are relevant here. You also need to ask yourself the following questions if you're considering embarking on a DIY renovation project.

Do I have the skills?

Even though you don't need to be qualified to carry out many renovation jobs, such as tiling, painting, or building cupboards or shelves, each of these tasks requires expertise to create a professional-looking result. You can acquire those skills by doing a short course, but don't underestimate the time and effort involved. You may just waste the cost of your materials and your time if you end up with what is clearly a home-done job. While you may be able to live with the result, you may need to get a professional in to patch up your handiwork when you come around to selling your home. You're also liable to fix up any defects if you sell the home for up to ten years of doing the work.

Do I have the time and patience?

Renovating, even if you just need to paint some cupboards or put up some shelving, takes time and patience. Are you prepared to sacrifice your weekends and every other spare daylight hour sanding and scraping and hammering? You also need to think about whether you have the kind of personality that can persist with difficult and often fiddly jobs. For some people, the stress on themselves and their families can make doing-it-yourself a false economy.

Am I prepared to take on the legal responsibilities?

If you're doing anything more than a very basic job, you're responsible for getting an owner–builder permit, getting planning and building approval from council, and ensuring a safe workplace for any tradespeople.

Do I need to take out insurance?

If the renovation is worth more than a certain amount (the amount varies from state to state), you need _home warranty insurance_ (known in some states as _home indemnity insurance_) when you come to sell your home (home warranty insurance is discussed later in this chapter). Many states require you to take out public indemnity insurance to cover possible injury of tradespeople and others working on your renovation. Be aware also that your existing home insurance may not cover your construction work until it is completed. In that case, you may want to take out *construction risk insurance* sometimes called a *builders all-risk policy*, which covers the main risks during the construction process — including damage by storm, fire or vandalism.

What about health and safety issues?

Working with tools and certain materials and substances can be hazardous to your health. You need protective clothing and equipment for yourself and any contractors. You also need to ensure that other people who enter your home are protected from hazards. If the property has evidence of lead-based paint or asbestos, you must get professionals in to deal with it.

Check the following websites for your state or territory WorkCover authority, where you can find information on the minimum safety standards required for your worksite:

✔ Australian Capital Territory, www.ors.act.gov.au/WorkCover

✔ New South Wales, www.workcover.nsw.gov.au

✔ Northern Territory, www.worksafe.nt.gov.au

✔ Queensland, www.workcoverqld.com.au

✔ South Australia, www.workcover.com

✔ Tasmania, www.workcover.tas.gov.au

✔ Victoria, www.workcover.vic.gov.au

✔ Western Australia, www.workcover.wa.gov.au

Do lenders lend me money for a DIY renovation?

If you need to borrow money to pay for a renovation, be aware that lenders can be reluctant to lend to an owner–builder. Your renovation is their asset, too, and they need to be convinced that you are going to complete the renovation in a professional way that adds rather than detracts from your property's value.

Becoming an owner-builder

Each state and territory has different rules about what you need to do as an owner-builder. Here are the rules as they stand at time of publication of this book. However, the rules change often, so check with your local building or planning authority before you start any renovation work.

Australian Capital Territory

An owner-builder must obtain a licence for any work that requires building or development approval — that is, any work that involves changing the external appearance or structure of a home. In order to obtain the licence, the owner-builder needs to have successfully completed an owner-builder course or examination within the last five years. Owner-builders are responsible under the *Construction Occupations (Licensing) Act 2004* for up to ten years for any building work they do. The licence and application fee is $203.

New South Wales

Owner-builders need to obtain a permit for any work on a dwelling that requires development approval and where the market value of the labour and materials is greater than $5,000. For work that has a value of more than $12,000, you must also show evidence that you have completed an approved owner-builder course or can satisfy equivalent qualifications. Approved course providers are listed on the NSW Office of Fair Trading website (www.fairtrading.nsw.gov.au). The application fee is $151.

Northern Territory

Owner-builders need to obtain an owner-builder's certificate for renovations and extensions valued at more than $12,000. To apply for an owner-builder certificate, you must provide the Building Practitioners Board with a completed declaration stating that you have read and understood the Owner-Builder Manual, and also provide a copy of a Land Title Office search and a completed owner-builder certificate application form. The application fee is $200. The owner-builder must also obtain an Owner-Builder Home Building Certification Fund policy of insurance before commencing prescribed building work, protecting any future owners of the property against financial loss for a period of ten years.

Queensland

Owner–builders must get a permit for work on their own property valued at $11,000 or more. One of the owner–builders on the title must complete an education course before lodging your application. A list of approved course providers is available on the Building Services Authority website at www.bsa.qld. gov.au. Courses vary in price and duration.

South Australia

Owner–builders are required by law to meet the same legislative requirements relating to building work as licensed builders. You must obtain a Development Approval before starting building work, notify the council at the completion of the building work, and submit a signed Statement of Compliance to the relevant authority that issued the Building Rules Consent.

Tasmania

Any work you do as an owner–builder valued at over $5,000 requires you to be registered by the Director of Building Control. To register you need to have read the *Owner–Builder Kit* published by Workplace Standards Tasmania (www.wst.tas. gov.au). The Director of Building Control must verify the eligibility of the owner–builder before a building surveyor can issue a Certificate of Likely Compliance. You are legally responsible for the work for at least six years after it is completed.

Victoria

Owner–builders must obtain a Certificate of Consent from the Building Practitioners Board in order to obtain a building permit to carry out domestic building work that costs more than $12,000. You must ensure that the work meets building regulations, standards and other laws, and arrange for building inspections as required by law at particular stages of the building work. It is also recommended that owner–builders complete an owner–builder education course.

Western Australia

Owner–builders are required to obtain a licence for works where the costs of labour and material exceed $20,000 from the Builders' Registration Board (BRB). As an owner–builder you are responsible for the standard of the building work and structural soundness of the building for at least six years after the work is done. In order to obtain the licence, you must fill out a statutory declaration form (available from the local council and the BRB's website at www.brb.org.au) together with a fee of $126.

Owner–builders must also take out home indemnity insurance (see next section).

Owner–builders can find more information on owner–builder courses and on their responsibilities, and the web addresses of the relevant state and territory bodies, in Chapter 9.

Taking out home warranty insurance

As an owner–builder, you must take out *home warranty insurance* (sometimes called home indemnity insurance) in the event that you sell your home within six and a half years of building it or completing renovations that total more than $12,000 in labour and materials. This insurance protects future buyers of your home from any defective work that was carried out during building or renovating. In New South Wales and Queensland, you need to do an owner–builder course before you can get home warranty insurance.

Keep all your documentation and certificates, because the insurer may need to see copies of the following:

- ✔ **Certification in relation to all plumbing and electrical work:** Certificates are issued by the relevant state authority to confirm the work adheres to state standards.

- ✔ **Copy of title of land and a current rates notice:** These documents show that the owner–builder owns the property that is now for sale.

- ✔ **Copy of the building permit:** The permit applies to the particular renovation.

- ✔ **Experts' reports:** These reports indicate the quality and completeness of works undertaken by you as an owner–builder. These experts may include a building surveyor, an architect or an engineer.

- ✔ **Final inspection certificates:** The local council issues these certificates to confirm that the work has been completed according to the contract and to the standards required under the Building Code of Australia.

- ✔ **Statement in relation to the use of second-hand materials and in relation to incomplete works:** Insurers prefer that all materials used in a renovation are new and that the work is complete before granting insurance. However, they may grant exceptions as long as you make clear which materials are second-hand and which aspects of the work aren't yet complete.

Calling in qualified tradespeople

Only qualified tradespeople are permitted to carry out certain work. Plumbing is one, and anything to do with electricals is another. In both cases, the plumber and the electrician need to provide you with a certificate guaranteeing the safety of the work.

A professional should also do structural work that involves knocking down walls or creating a new structure as part of an extension. For other work, such as building kitchen cabinets, tiling a shower cubicle and even polishing floors, you may theoretically be able to carry out the work yourself. But these jobs require either such precision or they're so labour intensive, such as in the case of polishing floors, that you may be better off getting an expert in to do the work.

Not all tradespeople are happy to work for owner–builders. Some complain that owner–builders are poorly organised and difficult to work for. In some cases, tradespeople charge more to work for an owner–builder than they would to work for a professional builder.

In most states and territories, you need a written Domestic Building Contract for work above a certain value of labour and materials that you hire a tradesperson to carry out. You can get these contracts from legal stationers, the Housing Industry Association (www.hia.com.au) or the Master Builders Australia (www.masterbuilders.com.au). Both these bodies are involved in regulating the building and construction industry in Australia and can provide references to qualified builders and access to documentation like contracts.

Domestic building contracts can be used for work like concreting, paving, plastering, re-stumping, painting, fencing and landscaping.

The contract should include the following:

- ✔ A detailed description of the work, materials and appliances to be used
- ✔ An itemised price list, including GST
- ✔ The percentage of the deposit to be paid
- ✔ The payment schedule

    ✔ A start date

    ✔ A finish date

Do not pay a deposit until work has commenced and do not make any *contracted stage payments* (also known as *progress payments*) before a stage is complete, even if you receive an invoice.

Make sure you receive *completion certificates* from tradespeople including electricians and plumbers that show that their work complies with current safety standards. The relevant state authority for that trade issues these certificates, and they should include a description of the work and licence details of the tradesperson.

Acting as project manager

One option if you want to 'do it yourself' is to act as the project manager and hire contractors to do all of the specialist work. In this case, you're still officially an owner–builder and, as such, you're liable for responsibility for the work as a whole. However, you can farm out responsibility for specific pieces of work to contractors. You can still also do some of the non-skilled work yourself, like sanding, painting and varnishing, thereby saving money.

As *project manager*, you're responsible for all the financial, regulatory, legal and safety issues associated with your renovation work. Taking on this responsibility requires management and administrative skills, as well as the time to ensure that every part of the process is carried out smoothly and efficiently. (See Chapter 9 for more information on project managing.)

Hiring Designers and Project Managers

Sometimes what you need to do to improve a home is clear. Putting in a new window or knocking out a wall may be the obvious solution to bringing in more natural light or opening up a space. Sometimes you may have a more problematic situation that requires a creative solution, or you may need to extend the home, either outwards or upwards, in order to create more rooms or more space. When you have a complex job on your hands, hiring professionals to do the design work for you, or to take on the project management, may be a good solution.

Resolving complex renovation situations

Using a professional designer, such as an architect, interior designer or a building designer, can be especially helpful if there is anything complicated or controversial about your renovation. Designers are skilled at shaping space and at finding solutions to problems in ways that are as aesthetically pleasing as they're functional. If they do a lot of work in your particular location, they're also likely to have a good understanding of how the local planning authorities work, and what needs to be done to get your permit application through the various bureaucratic hoops.

You can hire a designer just to draw up the plans, which you can then use as owner–builder and project manager. Or you can get the designer to take on the whole job from beginning to end. (For more information on choosing and working with an architect or building designer, see Chapter 9.)

Architect and/or designer fees cost around 10–15 per cent of the cost of the whole job, so engaging these professionals may be a more expensive option than doing the building or even project managing the renovation yourself; however, you may save yourself a lot of the stress and effort involved in doing it yourself.

Another way of seeing the light

When we decided to extend our home to create an extra bathroom and laundry, we envisioned a utilitarian narrow box down the side of our house. Our architect managed to create a beautiful new space that incorporated a whole wall of storage and was flooded with light to become a focal area of our home.

Handing over the project management

Architects and building designers can design your renovation around your needs, and they can also manage the whole project, including organising planning and building permits, supervising the builder and tradespeople and ensuring the work is completed right through to the final sign-off. (See Chapter 9 for more on handing over project management.)

You can also get a builder to project manage the whole job for you. The builder hires, coordinates and supervises all the contractors, and ensures that the job stays on schedule and is completed to an agreed standard of quality.

Hiring a Builder

Having a good builder helps smooth the many complications that are often part of a renovation, so shop around for someone you can trust as well as someone who can do the job within your available budget.

A recommendation from friends is probably the best way of finding a good builder. People readily tell you if they've had a bad experience with a builder, and are also happy to recommend someone who has been good. Sometimes the little things can make a difference. For instance, it can be difficult to deal with builders who are surly and uncommunicative, no matter how professional and perfectionist they are in their work.

An architect or building designer may also recommend a builder he or she has worked with successfully in the past; however, you may still want to seek out quotes from one or two other builders as well. (See the next section for more tips on getting a quote.)

You can also contact your state or territory Master Builders Australia (www.masterbuilders.com.au) or the Housing Industry Association (www.hia.com.au) to get recommendations of builders in your area. Ask each builder to give you the contact details of previous clients so you can phone them and ask them about their experiences with the builder. If you build up a rapport with some of the previous clients, you may be lucky enough to get invited to their home to have a look at the work they had done and so be able to form your own opinion of the builder.

Getting a quote

Ideally, you should get a quote from three different builders. The quote should be as detailed as possible, including information about the materials, fittings and appliances to be installed if, for instance, you're having a kitchen renovated. Make sure you give each builder exactly the same requirements — the same design and specifying the same materials — so you can make an accurate comparison between each builder's quote.

Be aware of the difference between a quote and an estimate. An estimate is often lower than a quote, because a quote builds in contingencies and possible blow-outs. Unless you specify the exact fittings, appliances and materials to be used, the builder may give you a quote based on the cheapest items, which may not be what you want.

While going with the least expensive quote may be tempting, taking the cheap way isn't always sensible. Just as important are the quality of the builder's work, and the nature of your relationship with the builder. Someone who is working at cut-price rates isn't necessarily going to be happy working for you, and may be reluctant to make any changes to the plans as soon as they start the job.

Sometimes a builder may try to talk you into becoming an owner–builder, telling you it can save you money. In some cases, they may do so because they're unregistered and uninsured or don't want to take on the responsibility of taking out home warranty insurance themselves (refer to the section 'Taking out home warranty insurance' earlier in this chapter). You should only become an owner–builder if you're prepared to take on the full legal responsibility for building your home and managing the contractors and tradespeople yourself.

Signing the contract

Make sure you're happy with a particular builder and have checked out their work and the satisfaction of previous clients before you sign the contract. A contract is a legally binding document and it can be a messy business trying to extricate yourself from your agreement if you realise that the builder isn't going to do the job to the standard you had hoped for.

Standard building or home improvement contracts are generally supplied by your state or territory Master Builders Association or Housing Industry Association. The contract sets out the following in detail:

- ✔ The work that is required
- ✔ Details of fixtures and fittings
- ✔ The anticipated construction schedule
- ✔ The total contract price
- ✔ The deposit required
- ✔ A schedule of progress payments to be paid at each stage of construction

Have your solicitor check over the details of the contract before you sign it to ensure you have legal recourse should you and your builder have any disagreements.

Any variations you make to the contract subsequent to signing may be expensive because the builder may have already ordered materials or fittings. Try to think of everything before you sign. You may also like to write into the contract a mechanism by which you can make variations.

Living Through the Building Process

Because a renovation necessarily involves meshing a new structure into an existing one, with all its quirks and flaws, a renovation often takes a lot longer than building a new home from scratch. Invariably, you're going to want to make changes to the original plan as you go along. Delays due to bad weather, sick contractors and tradespeople or supplies that just don't turn up can also drag out the job well beyond the scheduled completion date.

Any number of factors can slow down a renovation. For example, when we had renovations carried out, the plumber discovered that the sewerage system into which the new shower outlet emptied needed to be completely replaced, and the carpenter found that the floor of the original building was sloping and had to be replaced to match the level of the floor in the new extension.

If you're managing the job yourself, expect the delays to be even worse. Unless you're a gun coordinator and able to put the pressure on contractors to keep to their schedule, you may not be able to get the job moving along as snappily as an architect, project manager or builder can.

Depending on how big your job is, be prepared for a long relationship with a whole range of tradespeople.

Moving out until the dust settles

Even the smallest renovations can be disruptive. Having walls painted and floors polished usually requires you to empty those rooms, for instance. Then there's the dust and the fumes, not to mention encountering the tradespeople while you're eating your cornflakes. Tradespeople generally start work just as you've dragged yourself out of bed in your pyjamas to put the coffee on, so you need to be prepared to drop some of your inhibitions, too.

Unless you can move in with friends or family while you're renovating, renting adds to your renovation costs. You may also find it difficult to find short-term accommodation at a reasonable price.

If you have a big job that involves a builder and decide to rent while you're renovating, you can add a penalty clause to the contract to the effect that the builder is obliged to pay the cost of extra rent if the job isn't completed by the scheduled date.

Staying put during renovations

The advantages of staying home during renovations are that you don't have to pack for a move and you can keep a close eye on progress. You soon know if the electrician doesn't turn up for three days in a row, holding up the rest of the work. At each stage of the work, you need to make decisions; being able to discuss progress on-site with the builder, even if you only have 15 minutes in the morning before you rush off to work, makes life easier for everyone.

Being practical and staying serene during renos

Staying home during renovations doesn't have to be unbearable as long as you're flexible and resourceful. We used a camp-stove, a microwave and our laundry sink while our kitchen was being renovated. Later, when we renovated our bathroom and laundry, we visited friends and neighbours to use their shower, and hooked the washing machine up to an outside tap.

Coming back each day to a home that has improved even just a little is an exciting experience. Even if you're not doing the work yourself, you get to be part of the process of creating a new space.

Funding Your Renovation

Unless you've made enough extra payments into your mortgage to be able to redraw on the loan to fund your renovation, you need to apply for a loan to fund it. The way in which you fund your renovation may depend on the amount of work you want to have done to your home.

Renovations can fall into two categories:

- ✔ **Small renovation:** If the renovation is a small one — say, less than $25,000 — you may be able to extend your home loan, as long as you have built up enough equity in the property to keep your loan-to-value ratio below 80 per cent. (If the ratio goes above 80 per cent, you have to pay mortgage insurance, which can add several thousand dollars to the loan.) You could also obtain a personal loan to fund a small renovation, although interest rates are higher on these than on home loans.

- ✔ **Large renovation:** Getting funding for larger-scale renovations probably requires refinancing your existing loan, which means closing down your existing loan and re-establishing a new loan at the higher level. Your lender may need to revalue your home to ensure that you have enough equity to cover an extension of the loan.

Lenders usually also need to see detailed drawings of your plans, as well as evidence that you have the necessary building and planning approvals. In addition, you may need to pay establishment fees as well as valuation fees to refinance the loan.

Given that you may need to make progress payments to your builder or contractors, you need to organise how to make these regular scheduled payments beforehand with your lender. Some lenders offer specific construction or renovation loans that have a provision to make progress payments built in. (Chapter 10 has detailed information on obtaining a home loan.)

Chapter 8

Nice and New

. . . .

In This Chapter

▶ Looking at homes on a housing estate

▶ Deciding whether to take the house-and-land package

▶ Checking out display homes

▶ Building your dream home

▶ Having your home built by a project builder

▶ Exercising caution with off-the-plan apartments

. . . .

*P*roperty is one of the few things that most people are happy to buy second-hand, even if they're not averse to the idea of a newly built home. If you want to live in something that is completely and utterly brand new, rather than fit into someone else's hand-me-down, you have a couple of options, both to do with location.

Families buying house-and-land packages or project homes that deliver a spanking new dwelling and an extremely comfortable lifestyle for an often quite reasonable price are rapidly populating the fringes of the cities and many regional towns.

Closer into the centre of town, you may be able to find newly built 'in-fill housing', generally in the form of townhouses or units. Move further into the inner suburbs and the city centre and you may be in the market for a flash new apartment in a high-rise, multi-unit development.

In all of these cases, you're relying on what's known as a *volume builder* or *project-home builder* to build your new home. As the names suggest, these are builders who mass-produce dozens and sometimes hundreds of similar houses or units, and are therefore able to keep prices to a minimum. That means you generally have a limited range of designs and finishes to choose from, although you can sometimes get variations for an additional cost. You also have limited control over the actual building process, so you need to make sure you're happy with your arrangement with the builder before you enter into a contract.

In this chapter, I discuss what you need to look out for to make sure you get what you want from a house-and-land package, or a project home. I also look at how not to get burnt buying a unit or apartment off the plan.

Buying Into a Housing Estate

The concept of the housing estate goes back to the early part of the 20th century when entire Australian suburbs were created by developers who mass-produced homes for families. AVJennings is a particularly famous developer of housing estates and has become synonymous with the house-and-land package, although today dozens of similar developers and project-home builders are available to choose from.

The advantages and disadvantages of a housing estate include the following:

- **Advantages:** Buying into a new housing estate can be a relatively low-cost way of getting into the property market. Because the land, usually on the fringe of the city, is relatively cheap and the houses are constructed by volume builders, developers can keep prices down. As a result, you often end up with a level of luxury and a size of house that first home buyers who want to live closer to the city centre can only dream of.

- **Disadvantages:** One major downside of buying into a new housing estate is that you may end up living a long way from your place of work and also from your family and friends. Because the area is just newly developed, it may suffer from a lack of facilities, especially public transport, and it can be several years before trees and shrubs grow large enough to soften the sea of roofs.

  The size of the block can also be very small compared to the size of the house being built, which means that the building can take up most of the land. Sometimes driving to the outskirts of the city to find that the backyards of the houses built there are smaller than the backyards of properties in the supposedly more cramped inner suburbs is rather depressing.

Checking out an estate

When you're looking for a home in a new housing estate, remember to apply the same criteria as if you were looking for an established home anywhere else, particularly when it comes to the location. For your home to increase in value over the years, it needs to be in an area that is attractive to other home buyers. Avoid estates that have been poorly planned and are far away from industrial and retail centres.

When you're looking at a new housing estate where some of the homes have already been built and construction of the rest of the estate is evidently going to be under way for some time to come, envisaging how the whole estate is eventually going to look and work as a community isn't easy.

Brochures and marketing materials, as well as display homes, give you some idea of the overall look the developer is aiming for. You can also ask the consultant working for the development company if you can look at the long-range plans for the community, such as plans for schools, shops, public transport and other facilities. Double-check with the local council as to whether the developer's plans have been approved. You may also want to contact the local road traffic authority to find out about any planned road developments for the new estate.

Landscaping is an important part of any housing estate. The faster the barren streetscape is softened by trees and garden greenery the better. Many new developments sell blocks of land with strict guidelines (imposed either by the developer or the local council) that dictate how home owners should plant out and landscape their front yards. While this approach may be restrictive, it does ensure that the area has a pleasant and consistent landscape in years to come.

Look for a housing estate located near a local attraction, such as a national park, a reserve, a beach or water. If the marketing materials make much of the rural setting, do some research with the local council to find out whether the vista of fields is likely to be built out by further housing in years to come.

When you're assessing a housing estate for its suitability, take the following things into account:

- ✔ Child care facilities
- ✔ Entertainment, especially for younger people

✔ Libraries

✔ Medical facilities

✔ Parks and playgrounds

✔ Public transport

✔ Restaurants and cafes

✔ Schools, including pre-schools and kindergartens, primary and secondary schools

✔ Shopping facilities; not just a general store, but easy access to good supermarkets and other speciality stores like newsagents and chemists

✔ Sporting facilities, such as sports grounds, gyms, tennis courts, swimming pools

✔ Universities in the area

Be careful of buying into an estate that only has one exit onto a main road. You're likely to spend your mornings banked up with everyone else at the single set of traffic lights trying to get out of the estate to work, school or the shopping mall.

Studying the developer

Most housing estates are created by a developer, or sometimes a consortium of developers that may include a state government body as well. They then sell blocks to individuals and may sell or outsource particular blocks to other project or volume builders to build individual homes. The developer draws up the master plan for the estate and determines the landscaping and what kinds of amenities are provided. Sometimes these landscaping and amenities guidelines are developed jointly with the local council.

Each developer may have a particular style of development and style of homes. When you're looking at a particular estate, it might be worthwhile doing some research on the developer. Find out how long they have been in business and how many house-and-land packages they have sold. Visit other developments they have been involved in. Drive around and think about whether this is the kind of place you would be happy to live in.

Developers almost certainly have a website that gives background to their projects and their developments. Naturally, the information on a developer's own website tends to be rose-tinted, so you may want to conduct further investigations, such as doing an internet search on the company name. You may find out if there has been any bad publicity about any of the developer's projects, especially regarding court cases in which the developer was involved. If the developer issues annual reports, you may want to obtain the latest report to get further information on the company.

You can also ask the developer to give you the names and phone numbers of three clients that you can contact to ask how satisfied they have been with the service they received and the quality of the work that was carried out on their homes. While the developer may push only very satisfied customers your way, you're at least given an opportunity to ask them questions and get a sense of whether they were really happy. Talking to owners of properties at least five years old is likely to give you a better insight into the quality of the buildings and their finish. Cracks in the walls, for instance, may be evidence of faulty footings, while peeling paint or rickety windows may reveal poor quality materials and shoddy work practices.

The House First or the Land?

As soon as you decide on a housing estate, you have a couple of choices as to how you get the home of your dreams built. You can either buy the land first and then get a project-home builder to build a house on your land, or you can choose a house from the range offered by the developer, who ordinarily offers you the choice of a couple of different blocks on which to build the house. This option is usually known as a house-and-land package, and is generally the cheapest option.

Getting the land first, then the house

If you buy land from the developer and then have a house built on it, you usually have to pay a 10 per cent deposit on the land and then pay the balance in full before the builder can start building your home. While the house is being built, you probably also need to make progress payments to the builder at various stages of construction.

You generally have to choose from a selection of builders who have been approved by the developer and who build houses from an approved set of designs. Even when you are able to engage your own builder, many land estates have design guidelines as to the styles, materials and finishes allowable.

The advantages and disadvantages of this approach are as follows:

- ✔ **Advantages:** The upside of buying land first and then building the house is that you only have to pay stamp duty on the undeveloped land and not on the house. Why? Because you only pay stamp duty on the transaction, not on the 'improvement' you make on the land by building the home. The savings can be considerable; in Victoria, for example, you may pay only around $3,800 stamp duty for a piece of land that cost $150,000, but if you buy a house-and-land package worth $350,000, the stamp duty rockets up to as much as $14,000. (This does not take into account the grants and bonuses you may be eligible for as a first home buyer.)

- ✔ **Disadvantages:** You can end up with two mortgages, one for the land and one for the house itself. Sometimes, though, you can negotiate with the developer to allow you to delay your payment on the land until you start building so you can roll the loans for both land and house together into one mortgage. You then also have to pay your full whack of stamp duty (refer to 'Advantages').

By engaging a builder yourself to build on your land, you take more responsibility over the building process than if the developer engaged the builder to build on their land. (See Chapter 9 for information on building your own home and dealing with builders.)

Taking the package

The good thing with the house-and-land package approach is that it generally involves a fixed-price contract, so you know exactly how much you're up for and when you need to pay the balance. The other positive is that after you pay your deposit, usually around 5 per cent, you generally don't need to pay any more until the home is built. This can be a good way of buying the home if you're paying rent.

The downside to this scenario is that you have to pay stamp duty on both the land and the house. The developer may also add a margin to the cost of the package to cover the interest costs on the land and the building materials. A house-and-land package may therefore be a more expensive proposition than buying the land first and then having the house built on it, but that difference is balanced out by the fact that the final purchase payment of the house and land is deferred until you're ready to move in.

Looking Behind the Facade of the Display Home

Get ready to spend your weekends nosing around display homes. Display homes not only give you a sense of how a particular floor plan looks and how the space works, they should also give you a sense of the quality of the materials and the quality of the builder's work.

If you're planning to buy a house-and-land package in a particular estate, visit the display homes there. These homes have probably been built by a number of different project builders that have been contracted by the developer of the estate.

If you want to buy the land first and contract a particular volume or project builder to build your home, ask the builder where you can visit their display homes. Most builders have display homes dotted around the suburbs, either in their own display villages or within new housing estates.

Display homes you visit are often the top of the range for that model. If you want to have a look at lower-cost homes, check the builder's website or brochures. Lower-cost models may be smaller and have fewer rooms; the quality of finishes and materials may also be lower than those that you see in the display homes.

While in some cases you can ask to have variations made to the standard floor plans and finishes, be aware that this could add quite a bit to the total cost. Volume builders can keep costs down because they're mass-producing more or less identical homes, and if you want to make a lot of changes they charge accordingly.

Knowing about inclusions

When you're looking around a display home, don't assume that you're going to get everything you see. You need to check the list of inclusions to find out what you get and what you don't get along with your home — you may get a surprise at what's on the list and what's not.

> ✔ **Items that are usually included:** These items may include tiling in wet areas, hotplates and oven, bathroom fittings, a heating system and a hot-water service.
>
> ✔ **Items that may not be included:** Very often the dishwasher isn't included, even though space is left for the appliance. Fences are generally not included and often neither is the driveway. Curtains, blinds and light fittings are normally not included.

Note that many developers point out in the fine print that they can vary the inclusions and even the floor plan without notice.

Deciding on some optional extras

You may have to pay for some inclusions that are optional. They may include the following:

> ✔ Air-conditioning
>
> ✔ Carpets
>
> ✔ Clothes line
>
> ✔ Curtains or blinds
>
> ✔ Driveway concrete or paving
>
> ✔ Fences
>
> ✔ Landscaping
>
> ✔ Light fittings
>
> ✔ Security screens
>
> ✔ Wall and ceiling insulation

As a way of differentiating themselves from other builders, some builders offer these optional inclusions as 'standard'. Invariably, however, you have to pay extra as a result. Check whether you can add these features yourself; you may find it costs less.

Upgrading to a better model

Housing estate developers and project-home builders are slick operators used to dealing with hundreds of hopeful buyers just like you. While the good operators take note of your needs and suggest something that falls within your budget, many try to talk you into upgrading to a higher-end model.

When you're buying in an area of grand homes, feeling pressured into spending a few thousand dollars extra to get something a bit more palatial is easy. But be aware that you have to service that bigger loan, and that adding an extra walk-in robe or bathroom may stretch your ability to make those monthly repayments.

Getting finance through the developer

Many of the bigger developers have arrangements with banks and other lenders and may offer to arrange finance for you to buy one of their house-and-land packages. You may even still see promotions along the lines of 'No Deposit? No Problems!' that suggest you don't need to come up with a deposit. These arrangements generally presume that you use your first home owners grant money as a deposit, and often also require a family member to act as guarantor.

Taking finance into your own hands

A house-and-land package company told friends of mine they would take care of their home loan. Based on this assurance, my friends were happy to be talked into upgrading the model and fittings on the house they had chosen, confident they would be able to get a home loan through the company to cover those extra costs. After making their choice, they were astonished to hear that the company's finance company had refused their loan application.

'We had just assumed that we'd get the money because it was being organised in-house, so we let them talk us into applying for a more expensive loan,' they said. Taking matters into their own hands, they applied for a home loan themselves, adjusting their budget to the amount the bank was prepared to lend them. 'At least we then knew exactly how much we could afford.'

Instead of first choosing a home and then arranging the finance to pay for it, you may be better off getting a loan independently and then choosing a house that you can afford based on what the lender is prepared to let you borrow.

Your Dream Home: From Plans to Completion

You've picked out the house design, you've decided whether you want the Nova or the Heritage or the Ventura, you've agonised over the colour scheme: That's the easy part. Now you've got to make sure that all the really important stuff — getting your home built properly, legally and to your requirements — is carried out.

Obtain copies of the plans and the specifications, and engineer and site reports, and review them carefully. You may consider having an independent architect review them as well.

The sequence of events is usually as follows:

1. **Builder correlates the house design with the block of land.**

   Before anything else happens, the builder should make sure the design of the house fits properly on your block of land, and that the land has all the connection points for power supply, phone lines and plumbing. The builder should also get an engineer to determine the correct slab/footing system for your site, and then arrange for site clearance.

2. **You sign the building contract.**

   When you're happy with the plans and specifications, you're asked to sign a building contract, which contains all the information about the property, a schedule of finishes and a list of appliances and fittings. This list should be quite a detailed one that includes the make and model number of each item.

3. **You wait for building approval from council.**

   After the approved plans are received, you've arranged your finance and the builder has organised their construction insurance, construction can begin.

4. **You keep informed of progress during construction.**

   Speak with either the construction manager or the building supervisor on a regular basis. If you engage a builder to build on your land, the contract specifies how the progress payments are to coincide with particular stages of the construction.

5. **You make regular inspections.**

   As construction proceeds, you're entitled to walk through your new home to make sure the finish and quality of work are of the standard you expect. Some developers contact you after settlement to check that all is in order.

Project Building

If you already have a piece of land, or perhaps you're planning to knock down the property you already live in, you may want to contract a project builder to build your home. If you've visited a display home, the quality and the style of a certain builder's designs may have impressed you.

Project builders may be a little more flexible in their designs than are the volume builders that construct homes on new housing estates. Project builders tend to be more expensive as a consequence, but the cost isn't nearly as much as it would be if you commissioned an architect to design a one-off project. The advantage of having a project builder is that you have more control over the design and the building process.

Apart from having better control over the project, the process is similar to that outlined in the preceding section. You need to agree on a contract that covers all the inclusions, has distinct progress payments at various stages of construction and ensures that all the necessary surveys and planning is carried out and building permits obtained. (For more information on the process of building your own home, see Chapter 9.)

Buying 'Off the Plan'

In one way, buying an off-the-plan unit or apartment isn't too much different from having a house built for you, based on what you have seen in a display home. However, when you're having a house built on a housing estate, you at least have a piece of land, and you can get a sense of the location and the kind of facilities you're getting.

An off-the-plan apartment is located in a building that isn't even constructed yet (unless the apartment is a conversion of an existing building). The quality and facilities of the building — as much as the apartment itself — determines how happy you're going to be living there.

You can benefit from stamp duty savings in some states if you buy an off-the-plan apartment. This has long been the case in Victoria, where stamp duty is payable on the value of the land and building at the date of the contract of sale, so as long as construction hasn't started yet you only pay stamp duty on the value of the land. New South Wales has also recently introduced an initiative under the Home Builder's Bonus program where, if you purchase a new home off-the-plan for up to $600,000 before the start of construction, you pay no stamp duty.

Be aware, however, that if the sale takes place after construction has commenced, you have to pay stamp duty on the value of the work that has been completed. (For more on stamp duty, and stamp duty concessions granted to first home buyers, see Chapter 2.)

You have a lot less control over the design and construction of a unit in a multi-unit development than you do over a house being built just for you, so getting as much information as early as possible before you make any decision is important.

Imagining your home from a glossy brochure

A glossy brochure, and even a display unit, can make things look great, but pretty pictures don't guarantee that the end result is going to be an exact replica of an artist's impression. When you buy off the plan, you must carefully read the contract and take note of the inclusions, especially of any fittings or furnishings that the contract says may vary.

The golden fleece

That an artist's impression of a proposed building can be misleading was very vividly depicted in one of the apartment buildings built in Melbourne's Docklands area. Hundreds of people bought into one building on the basis of an artist's image that showed the building glowing like gold and towering above the horizon. When it was built, the golden exterior had somehow transformed itself into a dull brown that, as one angry buyer complained later, 'Couldn't even be described as bronze'. The colour was described, in fact, as a much more offensive shade of brown. Other buyers of off-the-plan units in the building complained that interior surfaces and fittings did not match the impressions from the brochure or display units. In most cases, the complaints of buyers have been dismissed on the basis that the contract made it clear that the final product might sometimes differ from that advertised.

You would do well to get the advice of a solicitor right from the beginning if you're considering buying off the plan; you don't want to get involved with a dubious scheme. The companies that build large-scale developments have deep pockets and can afford to pay expensive lawyers to fend off complaints from unhappy customers.

Finding out everything you can

To get a sense of the kind of work the development company produces, ask if you can visit some examples of their previous apartments. You can learn a lot about their approach to design and, most importantly, the quality of their work just by opening and closing a few doors and windows and knocking on a couple of walls. If the apartments look poky and poorly laid out and the materials feel flimsy and cheap, don't bother.

Apart from the slick design and stunning views the brochures show you, other factors are just as important. Look out for the following when considering an apartment:

- ✔ **Air-conditioning:** In some developments, air-conditioning is provided on a floor-by-floor basis rather than to apartments individually. The floor-by-floor system isn't great if you have to share your air with a next-door neighbour who smokes, or you're confronted with the smell of boiled cabbage in the hallways.

✓ **Body corporate or owners' corporation fees:** These are annual fees that cover the cost of maintaining any public areas such as lobbies and lifts, as well as swimming pools and gyms, and the cost of security guards and concierges. The fees can add up to several thousand dollars in some developments, so you would be wise to find out beforehand to avoid unpleasant surprises.

✓ **Car parking and storage:** While most large-scale developments have a basement car park, don't take it for granted. Check how many spaces you're entitled to. If you're a two-car family, or you're living with a friend, you need spaces for both cars. Also check additional storage options. Given the compact size of many apartments, having access to storage — often in the form of a storage cage in the basement or car park — can be a great way to store larger items. Also check on security in the car park.

✓ **Neighbours:** You're going to be living in fairly close proximity with others in your building, so you want to know whether they're the kind of people you could live with. Have a look at the brochures for clues on whether the building is aimed at young groovy types, or whether the marketing material is targeting busy professionals who may not be interested in sharing the time of day in the lift.

✓ **Privacy:** Can people see in easily, either from the street or from other apartments? Are you expected to provide your own curtains or blinds?

✓ **Soundproofing:** One of the biggest complaints about apartments is the lack of soundproofing. There's nothing worse than being forced to listen to the more intimate aspects of your neighbours' lives. Ask the developer how well the building design deals with the issue.

✓ **Views:** One reason to buy into a high-rise development is to get a great view. However, make sure you really are getting the view you assumed was yours, and that you're not going to be looking out at the apartment block next door. Also do some research with the local council into proposed developments nearby to make sure your stunning water view isn't built out in years to come.

Chapter 9

Building from Scratch

• •

In This Chapter

▶ Choosing the perfect block of land

▶ Finding the right designer

▶ Moving from drawing board to building site

▶ Building your dream home

• •

*T*he ultimate goal in life for some people is to build their own home on their own piece of land. Not a house-and-land package, nor a project home or someone else's idea of what a home should look like, but their own custom-built home, built to their requirements and using their ideas.

You can build your own home in one of three ways:

✔ You can engage an architect to design your home to your specifications and project-manage the actual construction, organising all the administration and coordinating the builders and tradespeople right up to completion.

✔ You can design the home yourself, with the help of a draftsperson if necessary, and engage a builder with whom you coordinate the tradespeople.

✔ You can design and build your own home yourself, with a little help from your friends if you have a high level of technical expertise or know people who do.

Building your own house can be enormously rewarding and enormously challenging, but you need to be prepared to put in the time and money. In this chapter, I discuss all the factors you need to take into account when making the decision whether or not to build your own home.

Starting with a Block of Land

Much the same criteria apply to finding a good block of land as apply to buying a home (refer to Chapter 5 for advice on finding the right home). You want somewhere you're not only happy to live but which also grows in value over the years. Finding the right block isn't just about falling in love with a particular piece of land; you need to consider how well the location serves your and your family's needs. Does it have the kind of facilities you're going to need over the years, such as shops, schools, sporting facilities and access to public transport?

If you're buying in the country or an area that is newly established, be mindful of how much it is going to cost to connect the block to water, telephone, electricity and gas, as well as the sewerage system.

Don't take a selling agent's word that you're going to be able to build where and what you want to. Check with your local council whether you're restricted in any way in building a home on the block you have in mind. The following are examples of some not uncommon situations:

- ✔ Check out blocks in areas that seem well established but may have restrictions on the size and number of bedrooms that are allowed. You can pay a fortune for some coastal blocks, for instance, only to find that a limit of two bedrooms is in place on the block because of septic tank systems.

- ✔ Find out what the council's regulations are concerning new buildings when you're thinking of buying in a rural or newly established area. Some blocks are zoned rural and strict rules apply to them, such as how close you can build to other dwellings.

- ✔ Find out whether any heritage restrictions apply in an area, which could prevent you from building that ultra-modern townhouse you dreamed of. (Refer to Chapter 6 for information on heritage restrictions.)

- ✔ Look out for possible caveats or covenants on the land if you buy a vacant block in town — they may prevent you from building more than two storeys, for instance.

Assessing a block of land

The ideal block of land is relatively level, thinly wooded and not subject to flooding. The block should preferably already have connections to water, power, telephone and sewerage. Ideally, the block is in a regular shape and is easily accessible for construction vehicles.

You may get a bargain price on a steep, heavily forested block of land, or one that is miles from any sealed roads, let alone sewerage or power connections. However, you need to remember that it may cost you more in the long run when you have to deal with the inevitable problems caused by lack of services.

The following are some factors you should consider:

✔ **Easements:** In already established areas, parts of a block of land may be set aside so that essential services such as water and sewerage pipes can be connected throughout the suburb. These areas are called easements and are generally buried well below the ground. However, you're restricted in how you can build over or near them.

✔ **Position:** Is there a view from your block that influences your decision on where you want to build? Are there trees or buildings that may cut out your sunlight? Ideally, you want to position your home so that you capture the winter sun for warmth and have shelter from the summer heat, and it is easier to achieve this if your block has a north–south alignment. You can, though, design your home so it is aligned to the north even if it is on an east–west configuration.

✔ **Soil type:** Some types of soil are easier to build on than others. Sand is easier to excavate than clay, but may require side support. Rocky soil can be expensive to excavate. Clay soil is prone to subsidence and the installation of stiffened slabs or deep strip footings to avoid soil movement may cost a lot.

Pole positions

Some amazing homes have been built in Australia to adapt to difficult conditions. One of the more famous is the pole house on the Great Ocean Road in Victoria, which is set entirely on an enormous pillar that rises up from the land for 30 metres and is reached by a walkway across the crevasse. Other houses around the country are built into the sides of hills, or are set on stilts above flood plains.

Working with a less-than-great block of land

What if your block of land is steep or swampy or has awkward access? You can deal with all these problems, for a price.

Getting around these flaws in a block of land requires a certain amount of ingenuity and usually a lot of money, due to the cost of engineering, materials and specialist architects. You need to balance out the lower cost of buying a less-than-appealing block of land with the higher cost of building on it. You may also be motivated by the attractions of owning land in a particular area. An interesting and innovative property, built well and designed to overcome the challenges its site presented, may command as good a price down the track as a more conventional property on a standard block.

Designing Your Dream Home

If you buy a house-and-land package or a project home, you may be able to make a few changes here or there, but generally you have to stick fairly closely to a given home design. When you design your own 'custom-built' home, you get to decide for yourself what it is going to look like and how it is going to meet your family's needs. You also have input into other design considerations, such as energy efficiency, water recycling and use of natural light.

Other design issues may include

- ✔ Building around trees or other natural features
- ✔ Creating cool, shaded areas for outdoor living in summer
- ✔ Including extra-large entertaining areas for extra-social families
- ✔ Making the best use of views
- ✔ Providing storage space such as wardrobes, cupboards and shelving

Finding someone to turn your vision into reality

Unless you're a trained designer, you need to find someone who can turn your ideas into professionally drawn-up plans for submission to your local council's planning department, to builders and to any other tradespeople who are working on your new home.

Depending on how much input you personally want to make into the process, you can

- ✔ Engage an architect to convert your ideas and aspirations into their vision.
- ✔ Hire a building designer to take a more practical view of your ideas.
- ✔ Get a draftsperson to draw up your fairly well-formed designs.

Harnessing an architect's vision

Architects combine an in-depth knowledge of the building process with a creative and holistic approach to designing your home — thinking about issues like the best way to use your land, how the building is to be oriented to the sun, how to maximise natural light, how to plan for space and traffic flow, privacy, climate control and environmental factors.

Architects can help you with the following:

- ✔ Choosing a builder
- ✔ Designing and planning
- ✔ Designing the interior
- ✔ Landscaping the surrounding ground
- ✔ Managing the building budget
- ✔ Selecting a site
- ✔ Selecting and managing the project team
- ✔ Undertaking feasibility studies

Architects in Australia need to complete a six-year degree course in order to belong to their professional body, the Royal Australian Institute of Architects. Architects are held to a strict code of professional conduct and are required to undertake continuing education to keep them up to date with current professional standards.

Hiring an architect to design and manage the construction of your new home adds between 10 and 15 per cent to the cost of an average construction project. While you may baulk at adding that extra cost to an already expensive construction job, it may well be more than compensated for by the architect's ability to make the whole building process run more smoothly. An architect may also add more value to your property in the longer run, by creating a building that is well-designed, energy-efficient and of a high construction quality.

Homes that can be advertised as 'architect designed' can sometimes command a higher price than volume-built homes when selling time comes.

You can find a great deal of information on how to find and work with architects if you go to the website of the Royal Australian Institute of Architects (RAIA) at www.architecture.com.au and click on 'Community', or go straight to www.findanarchitect.com.au. Also, check out the link on that website to the RAIA's building advisory service, Archicentre, at www.archicentre.com.au. Recommendations from friends are another good way to find an architect.

Deciding on a building designer

Building designers are usually less highly qualified than architects, having completed a two-year diploma or less to be entitled to practice. However, they do have to register with their state or territory building practitioners' board and are subject to codes of professional conduct.

Building designers may be more inclined than architects to design homes from the client's point of view and to take a more practical approach to their task. Most are also less costly than architects. You may not always get cutting edge design (though some are just as innovative as architects), but they may be perfect for less complex projects.

The Building Designers Association of Australia has a website set up to help people find a designer in New South Wales, the ACT, Tasmania and South Australia (www.findadesigner. com.au). Look for Victorian building designers on the website of the Building Designers Association of Victoria (www.bdav. org.au), and those in Queensland and the Northern Territory at the website of the Building Designers Association of Queensland (www.findabuildingdesigner.com.au). While the website of the Building Designers Association of Western Australia (www. bdawa.com.au) doesn't offer a 'find a designer' service, it does provide phone numbers you can contact to find a designer in your area. You can also find a building designer in your area through the *Yellow Pages* under 'building designer'. Friends are another good source of referrals to building designers.

Getting a draftsperson to draw your design

You hire a draftsperson if you don't require any external design input at all. While a draftsperson has tertiary qualifications in drafting plans to paper, their knowledge and design abilities are much less than those of an architect. The rates charged are consequently much cheaper than those of a building designer or architect. You can find a draftsperson in the *Yellow Pages* or in your local newspaper.

Given how crucial the design is to the success of a building project — not just aesthetically, but also in terms of its structural and functional quality — skimping on paying for good design at this stage doesn't pay off in the long term.

A good architect or building designer can also help navigate you through the planning process and any dealings you have with local government bodies.

Choosing an architect or building designer

When you reach the stage where you're ready to engage a professional to design your home, ask yourself a few questions when you're assessing their suitability:

- ✔ **Does the architect/designer suit your project or, more likely, does your project suit the architect/designer?** Architects and building designers have specialties. Some are interested in very contemporary projects where they're allowed to make an artistic statement with the building; that may not suit you. Others are specialists in higher-density dwellings, while some may not be interested in working on anything other than large-scale homes. Ensure that whoever you engage is comfortable to work within your budget and won't pressure you into spending more than you can afford.

- ✔ **What is the architect/designer's other work like?** Seeing other projects that the architect or designer has worked on can give you a feel for their style and for the quality of the work they have supervised. You should also ask them for contact details of previous clients. If previous clients were happy with the experience, they're sure to tell you — and you're sure to get a fair idea if they weren't.

- ✔ **Is the architect/designer available?** Good architects and designers are usually busy, which means they may not be available for a while to work on your particular project. How long should you be kept waiting? If they're so busy they can't fit you in for months, they may also have trouble keeping their focus on your project.

- ✔ **Do you get on?** When you're building the house of your dreams, you want to work with someone who has a similar approach as you to homes and lifestyle, or who can at least empathise with you. You're likely to be spending quite a lot of time together and going through what can often be quite an ordeal together. So find someone you feel you can talk to and that you feel you share something with.

Other questions of a more practical, tangible nature include the following:

- Does the architect/designer have the appropriate licence or professional registration?
- Does the architect/designer provide services other than preparing the design and working drawings, such as

  - Site inspections (to ensure characteristics of the block and its environment are fully considered)?
  - Sketches of the elevations (three-dimensional side views of the house as it is to look when the work is completed)?
  - Preparation of tender documents (if the job is to go to tender)?
  - Preparation and lodgement of documents (including plans) for local government approval?
  - Checking for easements and the location of utilities (such as sewerage pipes) that could affect the siting and design of any renovations?

- Does the architect/designer use a standard contract? If so, obtain a copy and read it carefully before signing.
- How much deposit does the architect/designer require before they commence work?
- How is the architect/designer's fee calculated (for example, is it a percentage of the project's budget, a flat fee or an hourly fee)?
- What procedures/costs apply if you wish to vary the plans after they're completed?

A good architect or building designer gets you to talk about what you and your family need for your home to function effectively. They should also find out what you like aesthetically. Here are some ways you can help the process:

- Think ahead to your family's future needs and build in some flexibility.
- Don't be too fixed in your ideas. It may be more useful to talk in terms of what you're aiming for rather than volunteering your own fully formed ideas.

> ✔ Do be upfront about your budget. What you can afford to
>   spend determines what kinds of concepts and schemes
>   your architect or designer can come up with.

Moving from Concept to Contract

You've made all the necessary checks on skills, experience and
work quality and have engaged the services of an architect or
building designer. Following your initial interview, you have
detailed discussions with her which lead to plans being drawn
up, which in time are finalised.

Drawing up the concept plans

Your architect or designer comes back to you with concept plans
based on your input and their survey of your site. These initial
sketches might include a floor plan and drawings that show how
the finished building is going to look from various angles (known
as elevation drawings).

During these discussions, you get a sense of whether your
architect or designer has listened clearly to your initial brief
and responded to it creatively and functionally. You can talk
through changes at this point, or if you're really unhappy with
the approach, you can reconsider your choice of architect or
designer. To brief more than one architect or designer to
prepare concept plans before you're confident to engage them
for the project isn't unusual.

Developing the design

When you're happy with the concept plans, your architect or
designer works up more developed designs that go into further
detail about the materials and fittings you want to use, and
that can thus be used to get a more accurate idea of budget.
Sometimes you can use a quantity surveyor to estimate the
costs of the project.

Finalising the plans

The final plans are the blueprint for the construction of your
house. They're the plans that are submitted to your local council
in order to obtain building approval and are used by the builder

and contractors who work on your house. The final plans are also used in the tendering process to get accurate quotes from contractors, subcontractors and quantity surveyors.

Signing contracts and project managing

If you've hired an architect or designer, you may also have asked him to supervise the construction of your home. Getting an architect or building designer to project-manage adds to your costs, but it can also save you a great deal of stress and even money in the long run.

Whether you or your architect does the project management, you have to agree to and sign the builder's contract. The builder's contract is the agreement between you and the builder that covers in detail the work the builder is to carry out, the building timetable and information about materials and fittings. The contract also sets out what you need to pay at different stages of the construction.

You can negotiate with the builder what you would like to add or remove from the contract. Some people write in a clause that penalises the builder if they don't finish the job on schedule. The builder may also specify the mechanism to deal with any variations to the plans; for example, if you decide to add a window after construction starts.

Given that a contract is a legal document that becomes binding as soon as you sign it, if you have no previous experience of building contracts, you may want to get your solicitor to review it beforehand.

For more information on choosing a builder and managing the project yourself, refer to Chapter 7.

Building a Home of Your Own

If you have some expertise in building yourself, you have contacts in the building industry and have the skills and confidence to organise other tradespeople, building your own home may be a viable proposition. Whether doing it yourself works out cheaper than getting a builder in to do the job for you is another question.

Some of the things you need to consider are the following:

- Tradespeople are expensive and you can save money by doing much of the work yourself, especially tasks that don't need specific skills such as tiling, laying wooden floors, bricklaying, painting and plastering. (Plumbing and electrical work can only be done by a licensed tradesperson.)

- If you have to take time off work while you're working on your home, you lose income from your regular job.

- If you squeeze the work into weekends or evenings, the job can take a lot longer than if builders were working full-time on the job.

- As an owner–builder, you have more control over the quality of the work and the costs of materials and fittings.

- Builders and tradespeople add a margin of between 8 and 20 per cent to the costs of materials and fittings.

- Builders and tradespeople are often able to get substantial discounts on materials and fittings because they buy in bulk. This discount can often be as much as 50 per cent.

You may find getting a home loan for a home you build yourself more difficult. Talk to a couple of lenders before you launch too deeply into your plans to avoid disappointment on this level. See Chapter 10 for all your home loan options.

The responsibilities of the owner–builder

As an owner–builder, you have the same responsibilities as a professional builder does. You're responsible not just for the actual construction of the home, but also for fulfilling all the legislative requirements that may apply in your state or territory. Refer to Chapter 7 for full details of the requirements of each state and territory.

You almost certainly need to get an owner–builder permit or licence. Check with your state or territory's department of consumer affairs or building services department for other requirements. Ordinarily, owner–builders in any part of Australia are responsible for the following:

- ✔ **Certificates for specific works:** You must obtain certificates certifying that specific works such as waterproofing and pest treatments have been carried out to the appropriate standard.

- ✔ **Council permits and approvals:** You're required to obtain all necessary council permits and approvals, such as development approvals, planning permits and building permits.

- ✔ **Financial requirements:** You need to ensure that everyone — including subcontractors and suppliers of materials — is paid on time.

- ✔ **Home warranty insurance (also called home indemnity insurance):** This insurance protects anyone who buys your home in the future from defective work carried out in the process of building or renovating. Owner–builders need to take out this insurance themselves and it is compulsory in all states and territories. Refer to Chapter 7 for further details on home warranty insurance.

- ✔ **Insurance:** Owner–builders are advised to take out Construction Risk Insurance (also called Builders All Risk Insurance), which covers construction projects in the event of fire, theft and vandalism and also for public liability.

- ✔ **Occupancy certificate:** The *occupancy certificate* (also known as *final inspection certificate* or *completion certificate*) is issued by your building surveyor to show that the work meets the standards set by the Building Code of Australia and that the building is ready to occupy.

- ✔ **Safe working environment:** Owner–builders are obliged under the Occupational Health and Safety Act to provide a safe working environment for any subcontractors, and for anyone else — such as family or friends — who work on your home during the construction process. Contact your state or territory WorkCover authority (refer to Chapter 7 for contact details) for more information on the minimum safety standards you need to comply with.

- ✔ **Tax:** Subcontractors and suppliers charge you GST on their materials and services. Ensure you factor these extra costs into your budget. *Note:* As an owner–builder, you can't claim back the GST.

✔ **Trade licences:** You're responsible for ensuring that your builder, as well as any plumbers, gasfitters and electricians you use, is properly licensed with the relevant state or territory authority.

Each Australian state and territory can provide you with important information about your responsibilities as an owner–builder, as well as useful tips and guidelines:

✔ Australian Capital Territory: Planning and Land Authority, www.actpla.act.gov.au

✔ New South Wales: Office of Fair Trading, www.fairtrading.nsw.gov.au

✔ Northern Territory: Building Advisory Services Branch, www.nt.gov.au/lands/building

✔ Queensland: Building Services Authority, www.bsa.qld.gov.au

✔ South Australia: Planning SA, www.planning.sa.gov.au

✔ Tasmania: Department of Infrastructure, Energy and Resources, www.wst.tas.gov.au

✔ Victoria: Consumer Affairs Victoria, www.consumer.vic.gov.au

✔ Western Australia: Builders' Registration Board, www.builders.wa.gov.au

Looking at your options

You can operate at three different levels as an owner–builder, depending on your skills and expertise, and the amount of time you have available.

✔ **Level one:** You build everything yourself (except in areas where licensed tradespeople are required by law, such as electricians and plumbers).

✔ **Level two:** You do some of the work yourself and oversee the project through to completion, but hire subcontractors or tradespeople to do part of the building work (such as framing or roof tiling).

✔ **Level three:** You don't do the building yourself, but you act as the project manager, where you organise all the materials and subcontractors (including perhaps an accredited builder) to build your home.

In each of preceding scenarios, you take on the responsibility for financing the construction, paying for insurance, supervising the work and all the legislative requirements.

Taking a course for owner–builders

In some states and territories, you're required to do an approved owner–builder course and apply for home warranty insurance before you can get an owner–builder permit. Check with your state or territory's department of consumer affairs or building services department for a list of approved courses.

Most other states and territories also offer owner–builder courses. These courses are less about the technical aspects of building than about project management issues, budgeting, estimating, scheduling and dealing with relevant authorities during the building process. Owner–builder courses are often provided by TAFE colleges or adult education centres. They usually run over a couple of days, or can be done by correspondence. Course costs are in the region of $100 to $300. (For more information on owner–builder courses, refer to Chapter 7.)

Getting council approval

One of the most onerous tasks when you're building or renovating your own home is applying for council permits. Depending on the scale of your proposed building, you may require a development permit, a planning permit or a building permit (and sometimes all three).

Be aware that meeting council's requirements and getting the application approved can take time, sometimes a long time, especially if the proposal is likely to meet objections from neighbours. You may want to allow several months, and even a year, for the planning process to go through council and for you to obtain final approval to commence work.

If your development application is a complex one, or carrying out these kinds of administrative tasks isn't your cup of tea, you may want to outsource the work to a town planning firm that specialises in preparing planning submissions (look in the *Yellow Pages* under 'town planners'). Building surveyors can also help navigate you through the process of getting permits for the actual construction. Getting help with a complex development application may add several thousand dollars to the budget, so you may want to get a quote from two or three firms. Ask for examples of successful applications and appeals, and for details of how they managed the process to success.

(Refer to Chapter 7 for more details on meeting your local council's requirements.)

Getting on with tradespeople

As an owner–builder, you have a close relationship with the tradespeople and contractors who work on your home. You're, in effect, their boss, and you need to develop the management skills to make sure they do the work properly and within the proper time frame. Things can get especially difficult if some tradespeople rely on others to complete a task so they can get on with their work; for example, the tiler can't start work in a bathroom until the underfloor plumbing is finished. You don't want to have people charging you an hourly rate while they hang around for several hours waiting for someone else to get their job done.

Every trade has its own jargon and way of working. If you're going to be an owner–builder, learning the terms and the processes associated with each trade can help you to talk intelligently about what someone is doing at any time (see the earlier section in this chapter, 'Taking a course for owner-builders'). Having tradespeople come up to you and start talking about flashing and bargeboards can be very embarrassing or intimidating if you have no idea of what they're talking about. (Chapter 7 has more information about dealing with builders and tradespeople.)

Part III

Borrowing For, Buying and Protecting Your Home

Glenn Lumsden

'Sold! Sold to the lady whose husband has just collapsed.'

In this part ...

*F*or many people, particularly first home buyers, the thought of the word *mortgage,* let alone the sheer number of loan options, is intimidating. In this part, I help you to cut through mortgage-related jargon and choose the best type of loan for you and your lifestyle. I also cover the pros and cons, and processes, of buying at auction or by private treaty sale. And I guide you through the final steps to owning your own home, including considering the contract of sale and what to look for, exchanging the contract and deposit, and the all-important key stage, settlement. The motivation to complete this technical process appropriately may convince you of the importance of getting a good solicitor or conveyancer to help.

Chapter 10

Climbing Aboard the Mortgage Merry-Go-Round

. . . .

In This Chapter

▶ Knowing what a mortgage entails

▶ Checking that you can get a loan

▶ Finding the best loan for you

▶ Choosing the best lender for you

▶ Looking at non-conforming loans

▶ Viewing your credit file

▶ Looking at non-bank lending options

. . . .

*U*nless you receive some kind of windfall — an inheritance or a lottery win — get ready to acquire a rather large loan along with your new home. The Real Estate Institute of Australia, a major source of real estate data and statistical research, supplies figures related to housing affordability. The average home loan in Australia for first home buyers is around $283,000 and, if you live in New South Wales, the amount is more like $300,000. (However, in this book I have assumed the typical first home costs $450,000, so I have also assumed the typical first home loan, at 90 per cent of that amount, to be $405,000.) Because you may be paying your loan off for a long time, be prepared to become as familiar with your new mortgage lender as you plan to become with your new neighbours.

You may have already worked out how much you think you can afford to borrow — based on your income and living expenses, as well as on how much you've already saved. (Refer to Chapter 2 for more help on the costs of buying your home.) You may also want to think about what kind of loan you want.

Home loans come in various shapes and sizes and can offer features that can make them more user-friendly and flexible, or sometimes just more expensive.

This chapter looks at how a mortgage works and the smorgasbord of loans available to select from. You also learn what you need to do to qualify for the loan you want. And, if it all looks too difficult to deal with yourself, you can find tips on how to get the best from a mortgage broker.

Understanding How a Mortgage Works

You may remember from the board game 'Monopoly' how you can borrow money from the bank by taking a mortgage against one of your properties. You turn the card over and you can't charge other players any rent until you pay back the money you owe to the bank. That scenario from the game is a pretty accurate picture of how a mortgage works. Except, in real life, you take out the mortgage against your property as soon as you buy it (and you can rent out a property even if it is mortgaged to a lender).

Taking, say, $450,000 as a typical cost for a first home, few people have that kind of money available upfront to buy their home. However, lenders are prepared to give you the money upfront in return for taking ownership of the property itself as security (as well as you paying lots of interest of the amount they loan you).

Most people tend to interchange the words 'mortgage' and 'home loan', but the mortgage part actually indicates via a written contract the ownership that the lender has over your home as the security for the loan. That ownership is reflected by the fact that the lender holds the title to your home until you pay off the last cent of your home loan.

For some people the fact that a lender owns most of their home is a depressing thought, and their main aim in life is to pay off their mortgage as quickly as possible and get the title to their home into their own bottom drawer where it belongs. But you can also think of paying off a mortgage as just one of the normal expenses of life, like the telephone or food bill.

Having a mortgage is certainly better than paying rent because, while rent goes up over time, your repayments on a home loan eventually decrease and the part of your home that you own (the equity) increases.

Qualifying for a Loan

Lenders make a lot of money from home loans. Over the life of your home loan you may be paying back as much again in interest as you originally borrowed — not to mention the upfront and ongoing fees levied by the lender to cover administration and other loan servicing costs. But, for lenders, the main concern is to ensure they're not creating 'bad debts' by taking on borrowers who may not be in a position to pay back their loan.

If you default on your payments, the lender has the option to *foreclose* on your home (acquire your home, which is the security for the loan and why they own the title to it). However, this onerous and sometimes expensive step is one that most lenders would rather avoid.

Lending criteria

In order to establish whether you're a reliable and upstanding person of sound reputation and therefore, financially speaking, safe to lend to, lenders look at a number of different criteria:

- ✔ **Your ability to service the loan:** Lenders look at your income and your expenses (living expenses plus any other loan repayments) to determine whether they think you can afford to service a particular size of loan. They also take into account the number of dependent children you have.

- ✔ **Your assets:** Your new home is probably going to be your biggest asset, but a lender wants to know what other assets you may have accumulated in order to get a sense of what you're doing with your money. Your assets include items such as a car, furniture, tools and equipment, collectables and a share portfolio.

- ✔ **Your credit history:** Lenders look darkly on instances where you have failed to make a repayment on a loan — including a credit card. They may also take note of instances where you have failed to pay bills or consistently paid bills late.

Never having had a personal loan or a credit card before you apply for a home loan isn't always beneficial when applying for a home loan. A good record of having made loan repayments on time is an important guide to how you're likely to approach paying off your home loan.

✔ **Your job stability:** Ordinarily, you need to have an employment history with a single employer for at least 12 months to qualify for a loan.

If you're planning to change jobs in the near future, you may want to get your home loan first and then go job hunting.

✔ **Your liabilities:** These little gremlins are your debts, such as car and personal loans and what you owe on your credit card, all of which you need to continue repaying along with your mortgage after you buy your new home.

Even if you have a small debt on your credit card, or you pay it off in full each month, the lender is interested in its maximum limit, not the amount you have outstanding. That maximum represents possible financial commitments that may compete with your home loan in future. If you have credit cards with a high maximum limit that you don't use very much, you may want to consider closing them before you apply for a home loan.

✔ **Your savings history:** Most lenders want proof that you have been able to save 3 to 5 per cent of the expected purchase price of your new home. This amount needs to be supported by a genuine savings record showing that you have saved over the past three to six months, rather than money you have been given or have managed to scratch together in a month or so.

Savings can be in the form of

- A savings account into which you have made regular deposits.

- A term deposit you have held for at least six months.

- Land or an investment property.

- Managed funds or a share portfolio.

- Voluntary superannuation contributions that are above and beyond the compulsory contributions your employer makes on your behalf.

Avoiding mortgage insurance

You may only need to show proof of being able to save 5 per cent of the expected purchase price of your new home to get a loan, but unless you can come up with 20 per cent of the purchase price, you have to cough up a few thousand more dollars to cover the cost of mortgage insurance. Mortgage insurance protects your lender from the risk of your defaulting on your loan. The insurance premium is added to your loan establishment costs when your home loan is more than 80 per cent of the expected purchase price of your new home.

If you can manage to pull together 20 per cent or more, you can save yourself a lot of money.

While lenders want proof that you can save around 5 per cent of the property value yourself, they're not quite so fussy about how you get hold of funds beyond that. To save yourself the cost of mortgage insurance, you may want to ask family to lend you enough money to take your total funds over the 20 per cent mark. Even if you have to pay it back quickly, you're going to save yourself several thousand dollars in mortgage insurance.

 Unfortunately, lenders don't take into account rental payments as proof that you have the capacity to pay off a home loan — even if you have paid your rent on time for years and years. That approach by the lenders means that even if you pay, say, $2,000 rent a month, you need to save another $2,000 a month for six to nine months or so in order to save 3 to 5 per cent of the purchase price of your $450,000 home.

Providing documents to your lender

When you put in your application for a home loan, the lender is likely to ask you to supply some or all of the following documents:

✔ Proof of income, including

- Two or three recent pay slips.

- Two years of tax returns.

- Proof of any other income, such as rental income or Centrelink payments.

✔ Proof of ongoing employment via a letter from your employer showing

- The date you commenced employment.

- The basis on which you're employed — part-time, full-time or casual.

- Your average weekly or monthly income.

✔ Proof that you have saved 3 to 5 per cent of the expected purchase price of your new home over a three- to six-month period. This proof may be in the form of bank statements or shareholding certificates and must be in the name of at least one of the borrowers.

✔ Proof if you have received a gift of money from family or a friend to help you buy your new home. You may need the person making the gift to sign a statutory declaration that states that the gift is non-repayable.

Choosing the Home Loan That Suits You and Your Hip Pocket

Learning about the many types of home-loan options, so that you choose the one that suits your lifestyle and growing needs, is important if you're to be a long-term happy home owner.

To fix or not to fix

One of the first decisions you need to make when choosing a home loan is whether to get a *fixed-rate loan* (the interest you pay is fixed at a certain rate for a certain period) or a *variable loan* (the interest you pay varies according to the rate in the marketplace).

Fixing the rate on your home loan means that you know exactly how much your repayments are going to be every month for as long as you've fixed the rate for. Even if interest rates go up generally, you can count on making the same repayments. Conversely, if interest rates go down you're stuck with paying more than everyone else on variable rate loans for as long as you've fixed the loan. Property investors often like fixed-rate loans so they can budget exactly for their borrowing costs against their rental income.

How the RBA rules your mortgage life

Home loan interest rates, sometimes called mortgage rates, are related to the *cash rate* that is set by the Reserve Bank of Australia (RBA). The cash rate is the interest rate that banks pay or charge to borrow funds from or lend funds to other banks. Mortgage lenders then add a margin — ordinarily around 1.5 per cent — to this rate in order to make a profit.

One of the main roles of the RBA is to ensure that inflation doesn't get out of hand. Setting the cash rate is one important way the RBA aims to control inflation. When the economy is sluggish and people aren't spending, the RBA lowers cash rates to encourage people to borrow more, and thus spend more. Higher spending leads to higher demand and can push up prices for products and services. If prices run too high, this leads to inflation, and as soon as inflation gets too high people can no longer afford to spend. When the economy is running too hot, the RBA raises cash rates to try to contain the boom by slowing borrowing and thus spending.

All this tinkering with interest rates and the economy has a direct effect on you the home owner. When the RBA raises the cash rate, the banks follow suit and mortgage rates go up and, if you have a variable-rate loan, you get a rise in your monthly repayments. Drops in the cash rate are less instantly, but usually fairly quickly, passed on by the banks in the form of lower mortgage rates. Interest rates have been relatively low for the last five years. However, these low interest rates encouraged people to take on debts around double that of 1990. That scenario means that even when interest rates rise by a couple of percentage points or so, the effect is much more dramatic than when rates rose by 5 per cent or so during the 1980s.

This intimate connection between inflation and interest rates may make you as the new home owner much more interested in the state of the economy than you have ever been before. The RBA determines interest rates with a quarterly review in February, May, August and November each year. For more information you can check out the RBA website at www.rba.gov.au.

Most Australian home owners prefer to have a variable rate on their home loans — even though variable rates can move up or down without much warning. At one time, in 1989, the variable interest rate moved up to around 17 per cent and stayed there until March 1990, gradually dropping to 10 per cent by 1992. Since June 1996, rates have stayed below 10 per cent, averaging 7.2 per cent. But while they have been as low as 5.5 per cent, they've also been as high as 9.75 per cent. So you have to be prepared for anything. People are always speculating whether the Reserve Bank of Australia (RBA) is about to lift rates, and every now and then an economist comes out with a menacing prediction that interest rates are going to rise back up again to double figures.

Although the figure varies over time, at any one time less than 5 per cent of Australians have fixed loans, compared to about 65 per cent of New Zealanders and 80 per cent of those in the United States. This reluctance to fix seems to be partly a cultural thing — perhaps Australians like to bet that rates are more likely to go down than up.

Fixed-rate loans are also more restrictive than variable-rate loans. One of the biggest issues is that you can't make extra repayments above a certain level on a fixed-rate loan. That may mean that if you want to pay your loan out early — say, if you get an inheritance or some other kind of windfall — you can't do so without paying a penalty.

Some fixed-rate loans don't give you other features, like being able to redraw on the money you've paid in. Many aren't *portable* — don't let you transfer the loan across to another home if you move.

Splitting the difference

Every time the RBA decides to lift the interest rate, thousands of people rush to fix their home loans. And for a number of periods over the past five years the interest rate on some fixed-rate loans has actually been lower than the variable rate. A scenario such as that means fixing at least some of your loan can make sense.

Splitting your loan — where some of it is in a variable rate loan and some in a fixed-rate loan, lets you have a bet each way. You know exactly how much you need to repay each month on your fixed-rate loan for however long you fix it for. If the variable rate goes up, you also have the comfort of knowing that at least some of your loan is quarantined at a lower interest rate.

By having some of your loan in a variable rate you can take advantage of the possibility that interest rates could go down. You're also able to make extra repayments on the loan when you can. And you can benefit from features and facilities like being able to redraw on your loan.

You can split your loan by taking out two separate mortgages on your home — either with the same lender or two different ones. You can split the loan in half, or in any proportion you like. Some lenders allow you to link one of the loans to a *mortgage offset account*, in which the interest earned on your savings account offsets the interest charged on your mortgage.

Introductory illusions

When you're buying a new home, the prospect of paying a lower interest rate for the first year or so is very tempting. Many lenders offer so-called introductory or honeymoon rates that promise lower repayments for the short term — ordinarily a year, but sometimes for longer. These loans can either be variable rate loans that move up or down 1 or 2 per cent lower than the rates on standard home loans, or a lower rate fixed-rate loan.

After the honeymoon period is over, introductory-style loans often revert to a higher-rate loan than a standard variable loan. In some cases, they can be as much as a percentage point higher. Over the life of your loan that difference can add up to a much higher interest bill than if you took the normal variable rate to begin with. Look at the *comparison rate* that all lenders must include in any home loan advertisement or schedule of interest rates to get a truer picture of the average interest rate over the life of the loan. The comparison rate takes into account the interest rate (including the interest rate the loan reverts to after the introductory period is over) as well as fees and charges relating to a loan, and reduces it all to a single percentage figure. (This figure is often in the fine print, so get out your magnifying glass.)

No-frills variable

If you want the absolute cheapest form of home loan, investigate a *basic variable loan*. This type of loan is really a variable home loan at a more attractive rate because you don't pay for the extra bells and whistles you can get with a standard variable loan.

As the name suggests, what you get is a straight-out loan that you're expected to pay back each month (or fortnight), with interest. You don't have access to loan portability, or get an offset or a redraw facility (see the following section for an explanation of these features). What you do get is an interest rate that is often one-half of a per cent lower than the standard variable loan. Sometimes you don't even have to pay a *mortgage establishment fee* (also called an *application fee*), which is the fee charged by the lending institution to cover its costs in processing your loan and preparing your mortgage.

A basic variable loan is good if you're more concerned with price than with the flexibility and features you can get with a more expensive standard variable loan.

The downside of taking out a basic variable loan is that sometimes you can't transfer the loan when you move home.

Standard variable vanilla

The so-called *standard variable loan* (the rate applied by the lender to its premium product) generally offers a number of optional features, which means you can tailor the loan to your needs. This loan type may offer these features:

- **Extra repayments:** Lets you pay extra funds into your loan account without any penalty. Can be on a regular basis or on occasion when you have spare cash to put into the loan. The best way of reducing loan interest.

- **Loan portability:** Allows you to transfer the loan when you move to a new property without having to break and re-establish the loan.

- **Offset facility:** A savings account linked to your mortgage, so that the interest earned on your savings offsets the interest charged on your mortgage. This feature may save interest on your loan.

- **Redraw facility:** Allows you to redraw any funds that you pay over and above your required monthly repayments.

- **Salary credit facility:** Allows you to pay all your salary into the loan and draw on it as you require.

The more features that are on offer by a lender in a standard variable loan, the higher the interest rate and the higher the account-keeping fees are likely to be.

Line of credit loans

A *line of credit loan* is potentially an endless revolving loan that you can keep drawing on up to 80 per cent of the value of your home (the 80 per cent level is the point at which mortgage insurance kicks in, something you're best off avoiding). The idea is that you pay all your salary and other income into the loan account, and you redraw on those funds to cover your living expenses. These loans are usually operated in conjunction with a credit card. You pay for everything on your card, and then each month you redraw on your line of credit to pay off the credit card. You may also have an associated transaction account that gives you access to cash.

Theoretically, this process can reduce the total interest you pay because your pay sits in your account for a full month before you pay off the credit card. If you have a credit card that pays rewards, you can get the benefits from that as well.

Lenders who advocate line of credit loans often show charts that demonstrate the financial benefits of using this system. However, critics of this type of loan point out that little difference exists between this system and making extra payments into your home loan. A financial danger to keep in mind, too, is that you can keep drawing to the limit on the loan and never actually pay the home loan off. Line of credit loans are, in fact, interest-only loans, and if you only ever make the minimum repayment, you may never pay off the principal.

Features and facilities can add one-half of 1 per cent and sometimes more to the interest rate on a basic home loan. Make sure you're able to use and take advantage of the features you pay for. Do some maths to work out whether you're better off making extra repayments, for instance, rather than paying your salary into your loan and redrawing on it to pay for living expenses.

Going professional

A *professional home loan package*, at its basic level, gives you a discount on the interest rate on the loan — ordinarily around one-half of 1 per cent and often up to a percentage point off the standard variable rate. So-called professional packages were once reserved for people like doctors and lawyers asking for loans above around $250,000. These days few home loans come in at less than $250,000; and lenders care little about how you earn your income for you to qualify for a professional package — as long as your income is at least $50,000 for a single, and $80,000 for a couple. (*Note:* This amount varies between lenders.)

Most professional packages also offer additional benefits, such as no mortgage establishment fee, no fees on offset transaction accounts or credit cards that are part of the 'package', as well as discounts on insurance and other banking products.

The catch is that you pay an annual fee — often a few hundred dollars a year. But even accounting for that extra expense, you're likely to save money. On a $405,000 loan, every one-half of 1 per cent reduction in the interest rate saves you around $150 a month. Add to that amount the savings on credit card and transaction fees, and you're likely to be ahead around $2,000 a year, even with an annual fee of $300.

Lenders may or may not offer you a professional package when you make inquiries about taking out a home loan. Ask if you qualify. Each lender has its own rules and eligibility criteria.

Shopping Around for Your Lender

Understanding how to get a good deal on your mortgage loan from your lender is just as important as the type of home loan (refer to the previous section 'Choosing the Home Loan That Suits You and Your Hip Pocket') because, to you as a home owner, your mortgage repayments are typically your biggest monthly expense.

With literally hundreds of mortgage lenders out there, how are you possibly going to work out which one is going to be right for you? Much of that process depends on whether you see a mortgage as a stand-alone part of your financial affairs or, as so many people now do, as the core product of them all.

Stand-alone mortgage

You can look at a mortgage just as a big loan that you make monthly (or fortnightly) payments into. If this method is your preference, you can set up a regular payment from your existing deposit or transaction account, and apart from that you don't need to have much to do with it. In this case, you probably don't care too much who your mortgage is with, as long as it has a low interest rate, low-cost establishment and ongoing fees, and the loan features (refer to the section 'Standard variable vanilla' earlier in this chapter) you need, such as the ability to carry it with you if you move to another property.

A couple of financial research companies provide comparative information on home loan lenders. InfoChoice (www.infochoice.com.au) has a Home Loan Selector that offers a list of available home loans according to a set of criteria you choose. RateCity (www.ratecity.com.au) has information on home loans that includes interest rates, establishment and ongoing fees. CANSTAR CANNEX, a supplier of research and analysis on financial services, provides the information. RateCity also has a star-rating system that lists home loan products according to whether they represent 'superior', 'exceptional' or 'strong' value.

The mortgage as the core of your finances

For many people, the mortgage represents the centre of their financial affairs. Many mortgages allow you to redraw on additional payments you've made, making them a kind of savings account in reverse. Your mortgage loan can also be connected to transaction accounts, credit cards, high-interest accounts and even other investment products such as *margin loans* (which allow you to borrow to invest in the sharemarket using shares or managed funds as security for the loan) and *share-broking facilities* (which allow you to buy and sell shares). This interrelationship between accounts results in a mortgage that is the core product in a web of accounts.

To banks and other financial institutions, connectedness between accounts is the ultimate scenario. After you spend the time to set everything up with one financial institution, moving the whole show over to another lender can be too time-consuming to contemplate. That linkage then makes you something of a captive customer. Therefore, you need to make sure that you get the best deal possible before you tie yourself into this kind of arrangement.

Getting pre-approval

Before you go out home hunting, organising a pre-approval of a loan amount from your chosen lender is important. Not only can you be confident that you qualify to get a loan, you can also have a clear picture of exactly how much you can borrow and therefore spend on a new home. When you arrange this amount, remember to take into account the other costs associated with buying a home, such as stamp duty and legal fees.

Don't make a contract binding until you receive written confirmation of final loan approval. Pre-approval doesn't guarantee that the lender is going to lend you money on a particular home. Lenders lend you only as much as they believe the home is worth on the open market. If they believe you have offered too much for a home, they may refuse the loan or offer you a smaller loan based on their own valuation.

If your approach to your financial affairs is to use your mortgage as the core product, you should choose a lender that offers not only the cheapest rate. As well, the lender needs to be one that you're happy to have a long-term financial relationship with. When you use your mortgage this way — that is, as the basis for your day-to-day banking — your banking life is a lot easier if your lender's other financial services and customer service are of a high standard.

You may be paying your salary into a mortgage with a redraw facility from which you can transfer funds into a savings account or credit card account, as well as pay bills online. In that arrangement of accounts, you need the benefit of a well laid out and functional internet banking facility. Also, if you have a linked credit card, it should offer low annual fees, a reasonable interest rate (although you probably want to pay off the balance each month) and a good rewards program to boot.

If you already have a savings account or credit card with a financial institution you're happy with, approach it with your plan to take out a home loan and ask the lender what kind of package the financial institution can set you up with. Make sure you shop around, and be prepared to move your savings account if that is required. Even though other considerations may be important, you should always haggle for the best deal.

In most cases, lenders desperately want your custom, and you may be surprised how flexible they can be when they're looking at the possibility of losing a long-term customer.

 The core-product approach for your mortgage lends itself well to the 'professional packages' offered by many lenders today. For more information on this loan type, refer to the section 'Going professional' earlier in this chapter.

Who's who of mortgage lenders

Australians can choose to borrow money for a new home from a number of different organisations at different levels of banking. The major lenders are

- ✔ **The 'big four' banks:** ANZ, Commonwealth, NAB and Westpac still lend most of the mortgages in Australia, with around 80 per cent of all owner-occupied loans approved between them. They source their funds from customers' savings and deposit accounts as well as international sources. They can provide integrated banking packages that include transaction offset accounts, credit cards and insurance.

- ✔ **'Second-tier' banks:** These banks include BankWest, Bendigo, Adelaide Bank and other regional banks that also offer integrated banking packages, and sometimes more personalised service and more flexible arrangements and features.

- ✔ **Credit unions:** These offer low rates and often don't charge ongoing fees. Many credit unions offer fully-featured banking packages.

- ✔ **Building societies:** These were the original home lenders. Many still offer the best deals in home loans.

- ✔ **Mortgage managers or originators:** *Mortgage managers* or *originators* act as intermediaries between non-bank lenders and borrowers. They source their funds from investors and mortgage trusts rather than from customers' deposits. A mortgage originator may appoint a mortgage manager to manage and administer the loan throughout its life.

- ✔ **Mortgage brokers:** *Mortgage brokers* offer home loans from the lenders they're accredited with (called a panel of lenders). Mortgage brokers manage or administer the loan process up to settlement on behalf of the borrower. (See the following section for more on mortgage brokers.)

While a mortgage involves a lot of money, the lender's money is at risk rather than your own. This arrangement means that if by some chance the lending company collapses, your equity isn't at risk. Unfortunately, you don't get out of paying your home loan off either. Instead, a lender's loan book, which is a very valuable asset, is likely to be taken over by some other loan company and you have a different company name on your monthly repayment notice.

Choosing the right mortgage broker for you

A mortgage broker can give you access to a variety of home loan products. Around 4,000 mortgage brokers are in business in Australia. These businesses can range from one-person outfits, to medium-sized local firms, to giant national companies such as Mortgage Choice.

Because anyone can set up a business as a mortgage broker, training standards and personal qualifications can vary widely. Brokers may receive bad press from time to time, and not all of them may act as professionally, impartially or comprehensively as they like to make out. The broker who acts in a businesslike way, though, can be a lifesaver for people who don't have the time or the inclination to comb through the dozens of possible home loan options.

Because mortgage brokers may have an inside understanding of how lenders assess home loan applications, they can be invaluable if you have any doubts over whether you're likely to qualify for a loan. If you apply straight to one lender and you're knocked back, applying to other lenders can be more difficult. A mortgage broker can point out problems with your application from the outset and advise you on ways you can improve on your chance of getting a loan.

How a mortgage broker works

Mortgage brokers give you access to a range of home loan products from a range of lenders. They need to be 'accredited' by the lenders on their list, which requires that they prove to the lenders their ability to properly advise on that product.

When the mortgage broker successfully places you with a lender, the lender pays the mortgage broker an upfront commission, and also often pays an ongoing commission to the broker.

If a mortgage broker asks you to pay an upfront fee to arrange your loan, steer clear. Charging you an upfront fee is against the law in some states.

Commissions can add up to several thousand dollars over the life of your mortgage, so the broker is well compensated for his effort. Indirectly, the mortgage broker's costs are added onto your loan as well. Make sure your broker works for his money.

Questions to ask a mortgage broker

Don't be afraid to ask the mortgage broker questions to get the information you need. Begin with this list:

- ✔ **How many lenders do you provide access to?**

- ✔ **How do you research and rate the lenders and their loans?**

- ✔ **What are your qualifications and experience?**

- ✔ **Are you a member of the *Mortgage & Finance Association of Australia* (MFAA)?** The MFAA is the representative organisation for all mortgage and business finance lenders in Australia — banks and other mortgage lenders as well as mortgage brokers. Membership is voluntary, but using a broker who is a member gives you the assurance that she has promised to adhere to the association's professional and ethical standards, that she has professional indemnity insurance and that you have recourse to an independent dispute resolution service (the Credit Ombudsman Service Limited — see the sidebar 'Resolving a dispute with your lender or mortgage broker') if something goes wrong. Brokers who are members of the MFAA are only too happy to advertise the fact.

- ✔ **What types of commissions do you receive?** By law, mortgage brokers must disclose all commissions in dollars.

- ✔ **Do you rebate some of the commission?** (This rebate saves you money.)

- ✔ **Do you charge a fee?** Some mortgage brokers charge by fee for service, claiming this procedure makes them more independent. Mortgage brokers shouldn't charge fees as well as receive a commission.

- ✔ **Can you provide a formal comparison of the loans you recommend, including the dollar cost of upfront and ongoing fees, and the *average annual percentage rate* (AAPR) that applies to the amount borrowed?** The AAPR gives a more accurate account of the cost of the loan because it adds the loans fees, costs and charges to the loan rate

✔ **What service do you offer after the loan is settled?**

✔ **Do you belong to an independent complaints scheme?**

✔ **What are you going to do in the event of a dispute between myself and the lender?**

Critics argue that mortgage brokers don't provide access to some of the cheapest lenders — such as credit unions and building societies — partly because these financial institutions don't pay them commissions. If after you do your research you find a credit union with a better rate than the lender your broker has recommended, ask why you should go with that lender rather than the credit union.

Deciding to change your mortgage lender

Theoretically, you can change your lender if you're not happy with the service, or you feel you can get a better deal elsewhere. This is known as *refinancing*, and what it means is that the new lender 'buys' your loan from your former lender. (Remember that lenders make a lot of money from the privilege of lending you money.) However, you do need to be aware that lenders often charge *exit fees* if you leave, especially if you leave within the first few years of your home loan.

Resolving a dispute with your lender or mortgage broker

If you have a dispute you can't resolve with your lender or mortgage broker directly, you can contact the independent Credit Ombudsman Service Limited. This service is free and allows consumers an alternative to pursuing legal avenues for resolving a dispute. You can find this service and file an online complaint at www.creditombudsman.com. au or phone the consumer line 1800 138 422.

Exit fees are also known as switching fees, early termination fees, early discharge fees or deferred start up fees and were originally developed as a way of cutting down the initial costs to borrowers of establishing a home loan. Exit fees generally only apply if you change your loan within three or four years of establishment. However, complaints about high exit fees led to the federal government amending its National Credit Code legislation in 2010. The law now limits these fees to the recovery of a lender's loss caused by the early termination. Lenders can't use exit fees to discourage borrowers from switching their loan or to punish them for doing so.

For mortgages established after 1 July 2010, if you think you have been charged an exit fee that is 'unconscionable or unfair', you can complain to your lender. If needed, you can then take the dispute to the lender's External Dispute Resolution Scheme, complain to ASIC, and/or challenge the fee in court proceedings.

At the time of writing, the federal government has announced they intend to ban exit fees altogether. However, some warn that this may result in costs being recovered in higher interest rates or through fees charged to everyone rather than just those who decide to change their lender in the first three or four years of the loan.

 Check the loan contract before you sign it to see what exit fees will be charged and at what point of your home loan they are phased out. Remember to also check how the loan compares on other factors, such as interest rates and other fees, as well.

When You're Not the Standard Mould

Lenders prefer to minimise the financial risk to themselves by lending to people who fit a narrow set of criteria — people who are employed by a company or institution on a regular salary basis, have been in their jobs for a year at least and who earn more than the average wage.

Potential borrowers who make lenders nervous because they don't meet the standard criteria include people who

- ✔ Are older than 40 years who may not be able to service a 25-year loan once retired
- ✔ Are self-employed

✔ Earn more than half of their income through commissions

✔ Have a history of changing jobs regularly

✔ Have a history of not paying loan repayments or bills on time, or who have defaulted on a loan or bill

✔ Have an employment history with the one company for less than a year

✔ Have recently immigrated to Australia

✔ Haven't been able to save 10 per cent of the projected purchase price of their new home

If you fit any one or more of the preceding descriptions, you're going to find getting yourself a home loan more difficult. Since the global financial crisis (GFC), Australian lenders have tightened up considerably on their lending to people who fall outside the regular criteria. That's even though Australia's system is quite different to the American system that led to the mass defaults on home loans there.

This tightening up of credit doesn't mean you won't be able to get a loan at all. You just have to work harder to convince lenders that you're not a credit risk — for example, by being able to demonstrate a longer savings history. Unless you want to pay interest rates up to 5 per cent above regular rates, you may also need to bring a higher deposit to your purchase.

Accessing no-doc and low-doc loans

If you're self-employed, lenders usually want to see several years of tax returns as well as any financial reports, financial statements and pay slips if you have them. Gathering all this documentation can be difficult, especially if you've been in business for just a year or so.

One way of getting around this dilemma is to apply for either a *low-doc* (low-document) or a *no-doc* (no-document) loan. With these kinds of loans you're not required to supply financial documents to prove your income. Instead, you fill out an income declaration form stating your income and assets in a process called *self-verification*. Most low-doc lenders also require you to have had an Australian Business Number (ABN) for at least 12 months.

Low- and no-doc loans are available through several lenders —
including some of the bigger names such as ANZ, Westpac, AMP
and St.George Bank. You can choose from fixed or variable rates
and can often get features like redraw and *portability* (taking the
loan with you when you move home) as well as the ability to
make extra repayments.

The downside, apart from higher establishment fees and interest
rates that are generally about 1 per cent higher than mainstream
home loans, is that if you borrow more than 60 per cent of the
value of the property you may be required to take out mortgage
insurance as well. This can add several thousand dollars to
the cost of buying your home. (Borrowers of mainstream home
loans don't have to take out mortgage insurance for loans under
80 per cent of the valuation of the property.)

Sometimes lenders reduce the interest rate to the standard
variable or fixed rate after a certain time period — often three
years — provided you make all the repayments on time. Other
lenders may give you a lower interest rate as soon as you're able
to provide the required number of tax returns.

A low- or no-doc loan is not the same as a credit-impaired or
non-conforming home loan. These have different qualifications
and rules as you can see in the following section. Some loans do
provide for the possibility that you are both credit-impaired and
self-employed; these loans usually involve even stricter lending
criteria and even higher interest rates and fees.

Looking around when your credit is impaired

One of the biggest obstacles against getting a home loan is
having a history of bad debts — unpaid loans, regularly late
repayments or bill payments, or a bankruptcy. In these cases,
the former credit provider or biller may have lodged a *payment
default* (or black mark) on your credit report. When you apply
for a loan, the lender may refuse your application based on
that default.

Sometimes you can appeal this decision by explaining to the
lender how the default came about. But given the fall-out from

the GFC — which was largely caused by American lenders' over-generous (and perhaps foolhardy) practice of lending money to people who did not fit the traditional criteria for home loans — Australian lenders have become more likely to stick to their refusal than give you the benefit of the doubt.

However, specific *credit-impaired* or *non-conforming loans* are designed to cater for just this kind of situation. These loans are generally provided by specialist lenders rather than regular banks. As with low- or no-doc loans, these loans have stricter lending criteria than regular home loans and charge higher interest rates and fees. Even when going through the specialist lender, you may need to make a trade-off between the amount you borrow and the interest rate you pay. The difference between borrowing 90 per cent rather than 60 per cent could be a 2 per cent higher interest rate, for example.

To apply for a non-conforming loan you generally have to provide full financial documentation. Loans are available for credit-impaired borrowers who also lack full financial documentation, but they have even stricter requirements and higher interest rates again. At the time of writing, one such lender is charging 12.99 per cent for the highest level of credit-impaired borrowers who want to borrow more than 70 per cent of the value of the property they want to purchase (compared to the standard home loan rate of about 7.5 per cent).

Even though you may be unhappy having to pay higher interest rates than a mainstream loan, paying off such a loan is one of the best ways to establish or rebuild your creditworthiness in the eyes of mainstream lenders. Many borrowers use this source of finance as a way back to ordinary borrowing. Check to see if the lender offers discounts on the interest rate if you build up a record of on-time payments. Look for a loan that either reduces the interest rate each year that you stay in the loan or that automatically converts to a standard variable loan after two years.

Non-conforming home loans by their nature represent a higher risk of defaulting to the lender. The lender usually requires a higher interest rate and may charge extra fees and have other requirements to compensate for that higher risk.

If you're not approved for a regular loan because the lender isn't convinced of your ability to make the repayments, you're unlikely to be able to cover the even higher repayments required by a non-conforming lender. You may be better off waiting until your income is higher and you're better able to service a loan, rather than getting yourself into a difficult financial position.

Understanding Your Credit File and What to Do about a Bad One

Anyone who uses credit or has applied for credit in the last seven years has a credit file. The file is held by a personal credit reporting agency and is used by credit providers to assess your ability to repay a loan or credit.

A credit file doesn't have a score or a rating. It may include information about

- ✔ Accounts overdue by more than 60 days where a credit provider has tried to contact you by letter

- ✔ Applications for new accounts or loans

- ✔ Bankruptcy orders

- ✔ Defaults and court processes such as claims, summonses and judgments for a limited time

- ✔ Previously listed overdue accounts that have been settled or brought up to date

Credit applications and defaults are deleted after five years and serious credit infringements and bankruptcies are removed after seven years from the date of listing.

If you've had an overdue account reported, it remains on record even after you pay it in full. All overdue account listings remain on file for five years. The fact that an account has become overdue and then been paid, becomes part of your credit history.

Each credit provider has its own lending criteria. Your loan application may be rejected on the basis of a history of unpaid bills, insufficient income or a combination of reasons. If your loan is rejected on the basis of your credit record, you must be notified in writing.

You can correct your personal details held on file by writing to the credit reporting agency. To update your credit record — for example, to note that an overdue account has been paid — you need to contact the relevant credit provider and ask it to notify the reporting agency. If you believe a record isn't yours or isn't accurate, you need to write to the credit provider and request it to investigate the matter.

You can get a copy of the complete details of information kept on your file from the websites of personal credit reporting agencies such as Veda Advantage (www.mycreditfile.com.au) or Dun & Bradstreet (www.dnb.com.au). Both of these agencies will provide you with a copy of your credit file free within ten business days. You need to provide proof of identity, including the name of the organisation to which you last applied for credit. If you need your credit report more quickly, a payment of $30 to $40 ensures you receive it within one business day.

For more information on correcting your credit file and improving your credit rating, see *Debt Repair Kit For Dummies* by Anthony Moore and Steve Bucci, Wiley Publishing Australia Pty Ltd.

Bypassing the Banks Altogether

If you want to avoid borrowing through lenders altogether, another option is available. *Vendor finance* is, as the name suggests, a loan arrangement provided by the person or company that owns the home you want to buy. You pay the owner, or vendor, back in the form of instalments, with the idea being that you get to own the house down the track when you have either paid it all off, or are able to get a regular home loan to pay off the balance of what you owe to the vendor. The instalments you pay include an 'interest' payment that is typically 1 or 2 per cent higher than commercial interest rates. You may also need to pay an upfront deposit.

For people who aren't eligible for a home loan any other way, this arrangement can seem like a godsend. But a few major pitfalls exist that you need to know about before you take up this option.

One problem is that the purchaser doesn't legally own the property until all the money owing to the vendor has been paid. If the vendor still has a mortgage against the property, and defaults on the loan, theoretically you could lose the home you thought you had been paying off. To ensure this can't happen you are wise to get an Instalment Contract drawn up that includes a caveat on the property to safeguard your interest.

Many vendors of such properties also charge a premium not just on the interest but also on the market value of the home. That premium could be as high as 20 per cent. That means that the property has to significantly rise in value before you have enough equity in the house to refinance the loan through a regular lender, thus locking you in to a high interest loan perhaps for some years.

Make sure you get good legal advice before you enter into any kind of vendor finance arrangement.

Chapter 11

Going, Going, Gone: Buying at Auction

. . . .

In This Chapter

▶ Understanding the pros and cons of auctions

▶ Recognising the limitations of relying on advertised price ranges

▶ Knowing all about the auction-day process

▶ Making an offer after the auction

▶ Making an offer before the auction

▶ Reviewing and signing the contract

. . . .

*1*n Melbourne, Sydney and, to a lesser extent, Brisbane, auctions are the accepted way of conducting a property sale, especially in the inner suburbs. As a buyer in those cities, you can spend much of your weekends as a participant in the very intense human drama of putting your hand up for a property that your heart is set on. More often than not, you walk away after witnessing another bidder beat what you can afford to pay — until the day you yourself are the successful bidder.

Auctioneers thrive on and promote this emotional intensity. Their role as selling agents is to encourage competition among potential buyers to push up the price as high as possible; the auction provides the perfect stage setting for that process. Very skilled auctioneers are in huge demand for their expertise at entertaining and, at the same time, manipulating a crowd to create a sense of desire and urgency for a particular property. Their art is to make bidders fear they're likely to miss out on the opportunity of a lifetime if they don't put in one more bid.

For potential buyers like you, the urgency of the auction process can create some pitfalls. Bidding in such a pressure-cooker situation isn't always conducive to making good decisions about such a large purchase. In the heat of the moment, bidding an amount that is more than you can really afford, or putting your hand up for a home that isn't suitable for your needs can be all too easy. A cooling-off period doesn't feature with an auction (see Chapter 13 for more on cooling-off periods) so, if yours is the winning bid, you may well regret that exuberance for years to come.

In this chapter, I look at the tricks and traps associated with auctions and look at ways you can maximise your chances of successfully and sensibly making the winning bid.

Assessing the Pros and Cons of Auctions

The frenzy associated with auctions, as well as some rather dodgy practices, such as *dummy bidding* (bids by people who have no real intention to buy the property, and which are now banned in most states and territories), has put many people off the idea of even attending an auction.

But you can prepare for some positive aspects of auctions that are often overlooked. One is the fact that bidding on a property takes place in an open and transparent market. (In a private treaty sale — see Chapter 12 — you may never know the amount of the offer the selling agent is asking you to beat.) Yes, at auction, the auctioneer may do all he can to inflate the selling price, and individual bidders may go above the price they'd originally been prepared to pay but, in the end, the price goes no higher than the market allows.

You can see this factor in practice when the market comes off the boil. In that situation, having auctions with only one person bidding and just the neighbours looking on isn't unusual. In this situation, it's common for the property to be passed in because the vendor isn't satisfied with the amount being offered.

A lacklustre auction may be disappointing for the vendor, but it can put you, the potential buyer, in a very strong position. You know exactly how much the market is prepared to pay for the particular property, and can proceed with your negotiations on that basis.

Estimated Selling Prices and Other Half Truths

One thing you learn very quickly about a property going to auction is that the price quoted in the advertisement bears very little relationship to what price a property eventually sells for — or, indeed, the price the vendor is really prepared to sell for.

Some auction advertisements give a price range described variously as an 'estimated selling range', 'buyer enquiry range', 'price guide' or 'quoting range'. Some quote a starting price or one 'in excess of' — although quoting this way is now prohibited in some states.

When you're looking at prospective properties, these price guides are useful to give you some sense of whether a property is likely to be in your price range. But they're not much help if the price range given is very wide. For example, a price range given as $400,000 to $550,000 is not much help if you're a buyer with a budget of $450,000. To ensure that price guides are useful, some states, such as Victoria and South Australia, have instituted codes of conduct that require the top of an estimated selling price range to not be more than 10 per cent higher than the bottom figure: For example, a house can have a quoted range of $400,000 to $440,000. Victoria has also recently banned the practice of properties being advertised as 'price plus'. Fair Trading New South Wales has also promised a review of pricing practices to deal with concerns about misleading advertising practices.

Be sure a property is likely to be within your price range before spending money on a building inspection report (refer to Chapter 5).

Even with the tighter price advertising codes, it is important to remember that the actual price on the day may still be higher than the top end of the range. The actual price may be 20 per cent more than the top quoted price in the range, and on occasions can be 50 per cent more. At the top end of the market, prices on occasion have been nearly double those quoted.

In some cases, the difference between the quoted price and the eventual sale price has been so wide that it has led to accusations of 'underquoting', which suggests that agents are deliberately quoting a low price to draw in prospective bidders, even though they suspect the property is likely to sell for a lot more.

Agents argue that they can't possibly second guess what the market demand is going to be for any one property, but too often you find out that the vendor's *reserve price* (the price below which a vendor isn't prepared to sell) far exceeds the prices quoted in the advertisement for the property. Even though vendors decide on a reserve price for their property independently of the agent, they base that price on information the agent gives them during the selling process. The real estate industry has acknowledged the problem of misquoting and has accepted new laws that can fine agents found to be deliberately misquoting.

To get around new legislation, many agents are now advertising properties without any price at all, sometimes listing them as 'price on application' (POA) instead. This gets around the problem of underquoting but means buyers now need to contact the agent in order to get a sense of whether the property is likely to fit their budget. Remember that the verbal price an auctioneer gives you is likely to be no more accurate than an advertised price.

 Seasoned home hunters know instinctively to add a margin to any quoted prices. If your top limit is $450,000, you may be better off looking at properties that are being advertised at between $400,000 and $420,000. A property advertised with a price of $450,000 may well go for $500,000 or more.

Understanding Auction Day

An auction is a piece of theatre that has its own rules and conventions. The auctioneer must follow certain procedures:

- ✔ The conditions of sale have to be read.
- ✔ The market must be opened to bidding.
- ✔ The vendor must be consulted at some point to see whether the reserve price has been reached.

Depending on the skill of the auctioneer, all these elements of the show may be conducted in a way that adds to the sense of excitement surrounding the auction.

Sometimes, the auction takes place in an auction room as part of a number of auctions of individual properties. Sometimes, the auction takes place onsite at an individual property. In that case, the auction usually starts with a half-hour or so open-for-inspection time to give prospective buyers a last opportunity to fall in love with the home and to inspect the paperwork. Then the auctioneer herds everyone out onto the street in front of the home, or under a verandah or inside a room if the weather is inclement.

Introducing the property

Whether onsite or in an auction room, the auctioneer reads the conditions of sale, trying to extract as much marketing opportunity as possible from the otherwise dry document. Then he gets his chance for a final spruiking of the property, launching into a sales spiel about the property, its potential and the features of the local area.

The bidding war

Now the real action begins. Sometimes the auctioneer offers a starting bid for someone to accept, sometimes someone in the crowd is ready to put up a hand with a first bid. Bidding can then go higher, either as a result of individuals offering a higher price or by the auctioneer throwing a price to the crowd in the hope someone accepts it. If the bidding starts to slow, the auctioneer may reduce the increments — lifting the price by $5,000, for instance, instead of $10,000. Bidders can also reduce the increments if they wish, although the auctioneer has discretion to accept a reduced bid or not.

Vendor bids

While dummy bidding (refer to the section 'Assessing the Pros and Cons of Auctions' earlier in the chapter) has been prohibited in most states and territories, the vendor is still allowed to bid. In most states, the identity of the bidder acting for the vendor must be declared before the auction commences, and each time the vendor bid is made. Only auctioneers or other identified and legally permitted persons are allowed to make vendor bids at auction on behalf of the vendor.

Bidding rules and regulations

The rules on bidding at auction vary between states and territories. Check out your state or territory for the current status:

- ✔ **Australian Capital Territory:** You must register as a bidder, giving the real estate agent at the auction your name and address and showing proof of your identity. You will be given a bidder's number. Dummy bidding is illegal. The agent can make one vendor bid on behalf of the vendor so long as the actual bid is clearly identified as such.

- ✔ **New South Wales:** If you're a buyer at auction, you must register with the agent before you bid, showing proof of identity and address. The agent will record your details in the Bidders Record and will give you a bidder's number. Dummy bidding is illegal. One vendor bid is allowed and it must be clearly identified by the auctioneer as such.

- ✔ **Northern Territory:** Vendor bids are permitted. No restriction on the number of vendor bids applies so long as the auctioneer announces the vendor bid before or while the bid is being made. Bidders aren't required to register and dummy bids are not specifically prohibited, but an auctioneer must not engage in conduct that is fraudulent or misleading.

- ✔ **Queensland:** If you want to bid, you need to register with the auctioneer before the auction starts. The auctioneer will give you a unique identifier, such as a numbered paddle. Vendor bids are allowed to be accepted up to the reserve price, so long as they're announced by the auctioneer in the conditions of sale at the beginning of the auction. It is illegal for auctioneers to engage in dummy bidding or take false bids after the property is on the market.

- ✔ **South Australia:** You must register as a bidder by providing the agent conducting the auction with your details and proof of your identity. If someone else bids on your behalf, you need to provide proof of your identity plus a signed document authorising them to bid on your behalf.

The vendor can make three bids up to the reserve price, but the auctioneer must announce each as such. Dummy bidding is illegal.

✔ **Tasmania:** Vendor bidding is allowed up to the reserve price as long the auctioneer clearly states to the people assembled for the auction that the owner or a person acting for the owner may bid for the property. Each vendor bid must be announced as such. Dummy bidding is illegal. Bidders don't need to register.

✔ **Victoria:** Vendors are allowed to make bids up to the reserve price but this must be made clear to other bidders at the start of the auction. Bidders don't need to register. Dummy bidding is illegal in Victoria.

✔ **Western Australia:** Vendor bidding is permitted. The auction form must specify whether the seller is to be making bids and how many. Bidders don't need to register. Dummy bidding isn't outlawed, but the Real Estate Institute of Western Australia's code of conduct bans the practice of agents pitting dummy bidders against genuine home buyers.

In many states and territories you have to register with the auctioneer before you are able to bid. But don't worry if you change your mind during the auction about bidding for the property — just because you register doesn't mean you have to bid.

On the market

A pause in the bidding can create an opportunity for the auctioneer to consult with the vendor to find out whether his reserve price has been reached. This may be the first time the auctioneer discovers what the vendor is really prepared to sell the property for. If the reserve has been reached, the agent emerges to tell the crowd, with a grandiloquent flourish, that the property is now *on the market* or *will be sold today*. This means that the property definitely is to be sold to the highest bidder from here on. This moment is also the signal for some potential buyers to enter the bidding.

Passed in

What happens if the vendor doesn't get her reserve price? In that case, the property goes back to the crowd for further bidding and if the price still doesn't reach the vendor's reserve, the property is announced as being passed in. At this point in the auction process, the last bidder can go in to negotiate directly with the vendor in the hope that a price can be struck that is acceptable to both. If after those negotiations the vendor still isn't happy, she can either take the property off the market or put it out to sale by negotiation. Such properties are often re-advertised as For Sale.

Tactics to beat the auctioneers at their own game

An auction can be a very foreign environment, especially if you're wanting to purchase your first home at your first auction. To give you a sense of how a property auction works and to build your confidence, visit a couple of auctions — even if you don't plan to bid for the property. The more auctions you attend, the more confident you're going to feel when your turn comes to bid for a property.

Tactically speaking

After having a building inspection done on a property that friends of mine were keen on, the subsequent report showed that the house was lined with asbestos. After the auctioneer had given his spiel, they put up their hands and politely asked if the auctioneer would inform the crowd about the asbestos problem. The new information unnerved both the auctioneer and some potential bidders who hadn't done their research. Our friends were able to buy the house at a price they felt took account of the extra expense to remove the asbestos safely.

You can improve your chances of success at an auction and enjoy the process. Here's how:

- Research the property and local market prices so you know exactly how much the property is worth.

- Read the contract before you attend the auction so you're fully aware of any issues or problems with the property. (For more information about contracts, read Chapter 13.)

- Take someone with you who has no emotional interest in the property and who can remind you of your bidding limit.

- Stand at the side of the auction where you can see the other participants.

- Remain calm and unemotional during the bidding — especially as you come close to your bidding limit — to avoid sending a signal to other buyers that you've nearly run out of money.

- Make an early high bid that can knock the confidence of the other bidders who presume that you have money aplenty and that they can't compete. (*Note:* Such a bid can push the price higher than necessary.)

- Wait until near the end of the bidding to put in a final killer-punch high bid, which can have a similar effect.

- Make bids in smaller increments — say, $2,000 rather than the $5,000 the auctioneer wants — which can suggest to the crowd that the bidding is nearing its peak, and can slow down the tempo of the auction as a result.

- Stop when you get to your bidding limit and/or the limit of what you believe the property is worth.

- Stay away from the auction if you don't feel confident that you can bid unemotionally. Ask a trusted friend or family member to bid for you. You can also engage a buyers' agent to bid on your behalf (refer to Chapter 4).

- Make sure you have your chequebook with you to cover the 10 per cent deposit if yours is the winning bid.

You make the winning bid — now what?

At the final successful bid the auctioneer announces: 'Going once, twice, three times ... SOLD!'

If you're the final bidder, you need to pick yourself up off the floor and make your way to the vendor, where you sign the contract of sale and hand over your cheque of 10 per cent of the purchase price, or whatever figure you're able to negotiate. Until you sign your name, you don't have a legally binding contract between you and the vendor, so the faster you can get on and leave your autograph, the better.

While you're talking to the vendor, you may also want to try to negotiate other aspects of the purchase. Would you prefer a longer or shorter settlement period, for instance? In some states, 90 days may be the norm, but the vendor may have already bought another property and appreciate being able to move within a month or so. You may also negotiate whether certain items — say, floor coverings or even furniture — can be included in the price.

Making an Offer after a Property Is Passed In

If a property is *passed in*, meaning that the final bid was below what the vendor was prepared to sell at, the person who makes the final bid may be invited to go to the vendor to negotiate a price that is closer to the vendor's reserve price. If that person is you, you have no obligation to agree to any price (even the price of your final bid), in which case the property goes back on the market or is withdrawn from sale.

But if just a couple of thousand dollars brings you to the asking price, and this amount is still within your budget, you may well decide that the amount is worth the negotiation. This moment, too, may be the point to ask if the outdoor entertainment suite you've so admired can be included with the price or to lock in a very long settlement period so you have plenty of time to sell your own property.

If you're not the final bidder, but you want to be part of the negotiations, you can ask the real estate agent to include you in the negotiations. In that case, the sale becomes a private treaty sale (see Chapter 12) and all bidders are asked to put in their best offers to see which offer is closest to the reserve price.

If you buy a property on the day of an auction as a result of negotiation after it has been passed in, you don't get the benefit of the cooling-off period that applies in all states and territories except Western Australia to purchases made through a private treaty sale. If you want more time to inspect the property, waiting until the next day to put in your offer may be worthwhile. That way you have a few days to make the necessary checks. (*Note:* In Victoria, you don't get a cooling-off period if you buy three days before or three days after an auction.)

Making a Pre-Auction Offer

You may wonder if making an offer on a property before it goes to auction gives you an advantage of any kind. If the vendors are nervous about the prospect of the auction or are anxious that the auction may not be successful, you can be in luck. But, ordinarily, vendors who go to the effort and expense of advertising and organising an auction are keen to go through with it.

If you decide to make a pre-auction offer, and you make a good offer, the vendors may presume that the planned auction is going to flush out even higher offers. Or they may accept your offer, simply because it is higher than their original expectations. In either case, you would have been better off attending the auction and getting the property at a lower price.

If you're keen to purchase a property pre-auction, make the offer in writing, including your offer price, the date, your name and a deadline by which you want a response to your offer. And word the note so that the agent is clear that if you don't receive a response, you're not going to attend the auction.

Be aware that if you make an offer by signing a contract of sale and the vendor also signs the contract, you have entered into a legally binding contract to buy the property. (For more information on contracts of sale see Chapter 13.)

In Victoria, contract notes — a short form of the final contract containing basic information needed for the transaction, such as the price and amount of deposit — have traditionally been used to formalise an offer. Although these contract notes were legally binding, many buyers and sellers may have been under the impression that they weren't. Contract notes have now been phased out, to be replaced by the full contract document; however, some agents may still be using them.

Signing (After Reading) the Contract

Hopefully, you have time to carefully study the contract before you attend the auction so, when you're successful at the auction, you're not going to find any nasty surprises in it. The contract includes details of the terms and the conditions of the sale. It includes the amount of deposit required, the settlement date and any chattels that are included with the property, such as carpets, light fittings and dishwasher. The contract is a legally binding document, so you need to fully understand your obligations before signing.

You don't get the benefit of a cooling-off period when you sign a contract of sale at an auction. This means you can't change your mind — because you decide the property isn't quite what you want, because you haven't got the finance, or because you find something in the contract you're not happy with. You're expected to closely read the contract before you attend the auction.

You can find more information about the contract of sale and the settlement process in Chapter 13.

Chapter 12

Making an Offer: Buying Through a Private Treaty Sale

In This Chapter

▶ Understanding how a private treaty sale works

▶ Considering other home-selling options

*M*ost homes in Australia are bought and sold by *private treaty sale* (around 75 per cent according to the Real Estate Institute of Australia). This type of sale means that the *vendor* (seller) decides on the price at which the property is marketed for sale. The *purchaser* (buyer) either agrees to the price or begins negotiations by offering a lower amount.

This chapter looks at some of the differences between private treaty sales and auctions (refer to Chapter 11 for all about buying at auction). I explain the ways in which you can successfully negotiate a private treaty sale. I also look at a couple of the variations on private treaty sales.

Checking Out a Private Treaty Sale

Buying or selling a property by private treaty lends itself to negotiation. The vendor is looking for the highest possible price and, in many cases, a private treaty sale can work a bit like a slow-motion auction to get to that price. That is, offers (bids) come in and move back and forth between the vendor and purchaser. This can take place over a matter of hours, and sometimes days, weeks or even months, rather than in a one half-hour auction session with other bidders in front of the property.

You make an offer via the selling agent handling the sale. When the vendor is happy with an offer price, she asks the agent to notify the buyer of her acceptance. At that point, contracts are signed and exchanged.

In the case of a *private sale* (where a vendor doesn't use a selling agent — see the sidebar 'Understanding the private lingo' later in this chapter), you negotiate directly with the vendor.

The process of a private treaty sale can seem more straightforward and less stressful than purchasing your home at an auction because

✔ You're not forced into making a decision in a brief, pressure-cooker situation.

✔ You can make an offer at your leisure.

✔ You decide on a price that you think is reasonable.

Sometimes, though — for example, when buyers are competing for a particular property — a private treaty sale requires more skill and negotiation tactics than an auction.

Negotiating a price

With a private treaty sale, the *list price* (advertised price) is often the top price that the vendor hopes for (whereas with a sale by auction, the listed price is generally the starting point). You can start negotiations by offering a price lower than the advertised price and, during negotiations, you can move your offer upwards as the vendor moves his price down towards a point you're both happy with.

A straightforward negotiation can work this way:

1. **You offer a lower price than you're actually prepared to pay for the property.**

   For instance, the property is advertised at $470,000. You're actually prepared to pay $450,000 for the property, but you start by offering $430,000.

2. **The vendor comes back with a counteroffer.**

   In this example, perhaps the vender offers to sell for $460,000.

3. **You make another offer and the vendor makes another counteroffer.**

   You offer $440,000, but the vendor suggests $455,000.

4. **You make another offer and the vendor comes down further.**

   You offer $445,000. The vendor offers $450,000 — your initial price plan.

5. **You accept the price and the property is yours.**

A more complicated negotiation develops when other people are interested in the property, too. The agent is obliged to inform you if someone else puts in an offer that exceeds your own, although he doesn't have to tell you how much the new offer is for. In that case, you need to put in your best offer and hope for the best.

Negotiating doesn't have to be fraught with difficulties. Follow these suggestions:

- ✔ **Start negotiating by offering a realistic price that shows you're serious about buying the property.** If you offer too low a price, the selling agent may not pass on the offer to the vendor if the vendor has asked not to be told about offers below a certain price. Alternatively the vendor may come back with the original price. From your research into similar properties in the area (refer to Chapter 5), you have an idea of how much properties similar in size and condition are usually worth.

- ✔ **Understand your position as the purchaser.** When you begin negotiating a private treaty sale, you have no clear knowledge of how many other people are interested in the property and how much they're prepared to pay. If the selling agent tells you they have a higher offer, you could ask to see it in writing but they aren't legally obliged to show you.

✔ **Negotiate with the agent.** Even if you have an option to deal with the vendor rather than the agent, using the agent may better help your cause. Vendors can have unrealistically high expectations of what their property is worth, and their selling agent can give them guidance on whether they should concede a little in the money stakes.

✔ **Stick to your plan.** The art of negotiating includes working out a starting price and a finishing price. Be prepared to walk away if the vendor's final offer isn't acceptable to you.

Beating down the price

When you're negotiating a price on a property, try to keep your enthusiasm for the property to yourself. Even when you're very keen, maintaining a 'take it or leave it' approach is important, especially when you're getting close to your top price.

While you may find keeping your emotional attachment to a property in check a challenge (especially when your dreams already place you sipping a glass of wine beside 'your' fireplace), an agent who senses your enthusiasm may emphasise that many others are interested in the property in a bid to get you to offer a better price.

You can withstand a ploy by the agent to get a better deal for the vendor when

✔ **Your research on the area (refer to Chapter 5) gives you a fair idea of how much the property is worth.** So, with this information at your fingertips, you can point out to the agent why the property isn't worth more than you're offering.

✔ **You know how much you can afford to pay.** Be prepared to walk away, reminding yourself that there will be other properties that will fit your criteria just as well.

You may find that the agent comes after you suggesting that the vendor is considering the price after all.

Some buyers are scathing about the faults and flaws with a property in an attempt to convince the agent, and the vendor, that the property is worth less than they hope to sell it for. There is nothing wrong with making the vendor aware that you

know about the problems with their property and to give them the opportunity to adjust the price accordingly. But doing this to the point of rudeness is counterproductive. The vendor has a choice whether to accept an offer or not, and some vendors aren't particularly keen to sell the home they've put years of hard work and love into to someone who clearly doesn't appreciate the property.

You can investigate how keen the vendor is to sell. Ask the selling agent the following questions:

- ✔ Why is the property on the market?
- ✔ Has the vendor already bought another property?
- ✔ Is the sale due to separation or divorce?
- ✔ Is the vendor in financial difficulty?

Be clever about how you interpret the selling agent's answers to these questions. For instance, be aware that you represent an opportunity for the agent to spin a story about how if you were to offer a certain amount, the vendor would probably accept the offer, and then use your firm offer as a platform to tell another buyer a similar story. Regardless, you may be able to 'read' the agent's responses to get some idea as to the truth.

Making an offer

When you want to make an offer, in some states you need to put it in writing, often by filling out and signing a particular form. In New South Wales, Queensland and Victoria as well as the Northern Territory and the ACT, you can put in a verbal offer, but it will be taken more seriously if it is in a written form. If the vendor agrees to your offer and any conditions you put on it, in most states and territories you both sign and exchange the contract document and the agreement becomes legally binding (subject to a cooling-off period, which I discuss in detail in Chapter 13).

Understanding the private lingo

You may come across the term private sale rather than private treaty sale. A private sale is a sale that doesn't involve a selling agent. However, many property advertisements use this two-word shorthand even if an agent is involved.

You can be confident that a property is for sale by negotiation (private treaty sale) if the advertisement:

✔ Gives a single price rather than a range.

✔ Uses the words For Sale without a mention of an auction date and time.

You follow the procedure set down in each state or territory:

✔ **Australian Capital Territory:** Buyers can make an offer verbally, unless the agent stipulates that it must be in writing. Agents may have a particular form, or may be happy with an email. Agents are legally obliged to communicate all offers to vendors, although the vendor can ask, in writing, not to be notified of offers below a certain price. When the vendor accepts the offer, she sends a contract and other documentation to a buyers' solicitor. This contract becomes legally binding when it has been signed by both the buyer and the vendor and exchanged.

✔ **New South Wales:** Buyers can make offers verbally, via email or even write them on the back of a paper napkin, and agents are required to communicate all offers, unless the vendor stipulates that it has to be in a certain form, or above a certain amount. (The vendor can also ask not to receive any offers that contain certain conditions added by the purchaser, such as 'subject to finance approval'.) However, the more serious the offer looks on your part the more seriously the vendor is likely to take it. An offer doesn't become binding until both you and the vendor sign and exchange the contract after the vendor accepts your offer.

✔ **Northern Territory:** Buyers can make verbal offers, and all offers must be communicated to the vendor. But a vendor's agreement to your offer is not legally binding until you both sign and exchange a Contract of Sale, available through the NT Department of Justice — Consumer Affairs.

✔ **Queensland:** Though verbal offers are possible, agents are only legally obliged to pass on written offers (in the form of a Contract of Sale) to vendors. When you make an offer, the selling agent provides you with a PAMD Form 27c Disclosure to Buyer and a Contract of Sale with a Warning Statement attached. This informs you of your rights under the contract, including when the cooling-off period starts and ends, and advises you to seek independent legal advice and a valuation before signing the contract. The form also provides special warnings with regard to house-and-land packages.

Negotiations on price or terms and conditions can still take place after the initial offer is submitted to the seller for consideration, and buyers can choose to withdraw their offer at any stage before the seller signs the contract.

✔ **South Australia:** Buyers must submit a Contract Note, which includes their name and contact details, the offer amount, settlement date and any conditions, and is signed and dated. The offer is not legally binding until the vendor also signs the Contract Note.

✔ **Tasmania:** Buyers should make an offer in writing, generally using the Law Society/REIT (Real Estate Institute of Tasmania) Contract of Sale provided by the agent. You can also exercise your right to ask your lawyer to draw up your own offer document. The agent is morally obliged to pass on any offers, but may not do so if an offer is less than the amount stipulated by the vendor. The contract becomes legally binding when the vendor signs it to show he agrees to your offer price and your terms and conditions.

✔ **Victoria:** Buyers can make offers in verbal or written form. However, if you want the vendor to take your offer seriously, it helps to fill out, sign and submit the Contract of Sale available from the agent, as well as offer a deposit. The agent is legally obliged to pass on all offers, verbal or written, to the vendor, unless the vendor has given written instructions not to. The contract becomes legally binding when both parties sign and date the agreed price and any terms and conditions, and exchange the documents.

> ✔ **Western Australia:** Buyers must fill out and sign a Contract for the Sale of Land by Offer and Acceptance ('O and A') form to put in a written offer. The agent produces the necessary form when you suggest you would like to make an offer. The agent presents the offer to the seller and the seller may counter, accept or reject the offer. The real estate agent has an obligation to inform the seller about all offers, although the seller can decide whether she wants to be presented with them all. The offer becomes a legally binding contract when the vendor signs the O and A form to show she agrees to your offer price and your terms and conditions. There is no exchange of contracts.

The agent can ask you to pay a *holding deposit*. This amount of money isn't the same as the deposit paid when you exchange contracts (see Chapter 13 for more on contracts of sale). A holding deposit is a small amount of around $1,000 and, depending on what arrangement you and the vendor agree to, is ordinarily refundable if you don't go ahead with the purchase within an agreed period of time.

Paying a holding deposit isn't common practice in all states, but it is a signal that you're serious about a property. The seller may still consider other offers because placing a holding deposit doesn't secure the property for you.

The rules and procedures for putting in an offer may change. Please check with your state or territory Real Estate Institute or consumer affairs department for the latest rules.

Putting conditions on your offer

When you put in an offer in a private treaty sale, you have the opportunity to write conditions into the offer. If the stated conditions aren't met, you can pull out of the sale.

The following are some conditions that you might put in your offer to purchase:

> ✔ Making the purchase subject to whether you can get finance to purchase the property
>
> ✔ Making the purchase subject to a satisfactory building inspection report
>
> ✔ Stipulating a longer or shorter settlement period

✔ Stipulating a lower deposit amount (5 per cent rather than 10 per cent, for instance)

✔ Stipulating items of furniture or fittings to be included in the negotiated price

Making your offer subject to conditions may give you a chance to pull out of the sale if you encounter problems, but the vendor isn't obliged to accept your conditions. If you're buying in a very heated market, and other buyers are as keen on the property as you are, the vendor may accept another offer with fewer conditions. Conditions are part of the negotiation process, just like price.

If you're very keen on a property and the vendor has particular needs — for a longer or shorter settlement, or even a larger deposit, for instance — you may be able to gain a more favourable position over another less flexible potential buyer if you can meet those needs.

Put in an *unconditional offer* (an offer with no conditions of your own attached) if you've thoroughly checked out the property, you're absolutely certain that you want it and you have the finance to pay for it. As soon as the vendor accepts the offer, you're legally obliged to go through with the sale (subject to a cooling-off period where applicable — see Chapter 13).

Understanding what happens after the vendor agrees to your offer

After some to-ing and fro-ing, the day may come when the agent calls you to tell you that the vendor agrees to your last offer price. Or the agent may come back with a price from the vendor that you're happy to agree to.

As soon as you agree on an offer, you should ask the agent to call the vendor to come in to sign and exchange a contract of sale with you (see Chapter 13). At this point in the process, you can also negotiate further conditions that you want to write into the contract (remember, though, the vendor may not agree to them). You're also required to hand over a cheque for a 10 per cent deposit or another amount that you've negotiated.

Avoiding being 'gazumped'

Even if the seller accepts your offer, the agreement isn't legally binding until you exchange signed contracts for that property with the vendor. Until this time, the vendor can accept a higher offer from another buyer. This process is called gazumping, and is a real problem in private treaty sales, especially in a heated market.

Getting on with the exchange — quickly!

Even though friends of mine carefully researched the auction processes, they didn't pay much attention to what happens when you buy a property by private treaty sale. When they found a house that was advertised at a price that was well within their budget, the first mistake they made was to offer a higher price than the property was advertised for. That offer immediately signalled their keen interest in the property. Unsurprisingly, the vendor happily accepted their offer. That was when they made their second mistake. Instead of insisting the vendor meet them immediately to sign and exchange the contracts of sale, they signed a contract and handed over their deposit to the agent to pass on to the vendor. Later that day, the agent called to tell them that another buyer had put in a higher offer. My friends were not told how much the other offer was, but were told they could send in a sealed bid (a document containing the amount they were prepared to pay, sealed in an envelope), and the person with the highest bid would be able to buy the property.

Without knowing what the other offer was, my friends panicked, thinking they could either lose the property with a bid of just a few hundred dollars less than the other party, or unnecessarily put in an overbid of thousands of dollars. Seeking advice from other friends, one recommended they seek the service of a buyers' agent (an agent with expertise in buying and negotiating for property who acts solely for you, the buyer, rather than the selling agent). He met them at the real estate agent's office, had some words with the agent and emerged to tell them a figure they ought to offer to secure the property. They made the offer and gratefully took possession of their new home 60 days later.

To this day, my friends are unsure if another genuine buyer existed. But the agent certainly took advantage of their ignorance. The lesson: When the vendor accepts your offer, request the agent immediately arrange for you and the vendor to meet and sign on the dotted line and exchange contracts before another 'buyer' appears.

Being gazumped can be very frustrating, and costly, if you've already incurred the expenses of carrying out a building inspection report and engaging a conveyance or solicitor, or if you're very fond of the property.

Avoid being gazumped by exchanging signed contracts with the vendor as soon as possible after you both agree to a price.

Looking at Other Selling Methods

The auction system (refer to Chapter 11) and sale by private treaty sale (see the section 'Checking Out a Private Treaty Sale' earlier in this chapter) are the most widely used ways of buying a property. In this section, I discuss two other ways in which properties can be put up for sale — sale by set date and sale by expression of interest. These methods have their own conventions, so if you're not confident about how to go about putting in your offer, ask the real estate agent for guidance.

Set sales

A *sale by set date* (also known as a *set sale*) is part auction, part tender. This selling method advertises a property for sale with a single price or price range, and a time and date by which a purchaser must make an offer. Unlike an auction, each buyer can put in just the one bid and doesn't know what other potential purchasers are bidding.

A sale by set date can benefit the vendor because this method concentrates the interest of buyers to a relatively short period — usually around four weeks — and ensures that buyers put in their highest possible bid in order not to miss out on the property. Critics of the system describe it as unfair to purchasers because they have just one chance to make an offer, and that a fear of missing out on the property can mean they pay more than they should.

During the set period, buyers give the agent a formal expression of interest in a sealed envelope. At the end of the sale period the agent gives all the offers to the vendor. The vendor can accept the highest offer or, if none meets his expectations, he can ask one of the prospective buyers to negotiate a higher price. He can also re-list the property for another set period, stage an auction (refer to Chapter 11) or list it for private treaty sale (refer to the earlier section 'Checking Out a Private Treaty Sale').

If you're a purchaser interested in a property for sale by set date, you can put in your best offer based on the advertised price and wait to see if you're successful. Don't go above your maximum limit: You may well end up with the property, though at a higher price than it is worth, and with a long time to regret your rashness.

Expressions of interest

A *sale by expression of interest* is often used by vendors who want to be discreet about the fact that they are selling their home, or who may want to get a sense of the market interest in their property without going through the auction experience. The vendor gives no fixed price. Instead, buyers are asked to name their price based on what the property is worth to them. The sale may occur within a set period, or the process may run until the vendor chooses to accept an offer or take the property off the market. After making your offer, as with a private sale, you may be invited to make a further 'best offer' or even to go into a 'boardroom auction' to compete with others who have made an offer.

Proponents of this selling method say it focuses a buyer's attention on the positive attributes of a property, which encourages the buyer to name a personal-value price, instead of focusing on the property's negative attributes in order to reduce the advertised price.

An expression of interest sale comes with few rules, and even though you may have the chance to make a higher offer, knowing how big to make your offer to secure the property can be difficult. In order to maximise your chance of buying well in this situation, it helps to have a very clear and well-researched idea of the likely value of the home.

Chapter 13

Sold to the Highest Bidder! Now What?

· ·

In This Chapter

▶ Signing the contract

▶ Finalising your loan approval

▶ Checking the home's true value

▶ Making the property yours

▶ Arranging insurance

· ·

*B*uying a property is a major legal transaction and is subject
to a series of regulations and requirements — and some
pretty impressive paperwork. After a vendor accepts your offer,
or yours is the winning bid at an auction, you need to carry
out a few final steps before you're ready to break open the
champagne.

In this chapter, I take you through signing and exchanging the
contract of sale (the document that covers the actual purchase)
and handing over the deposit. And, before you carve your
signature in stone on this document, you need to make sure
your chosen lender is actually happy to lend on the specific
property you finally choose. (Occasionally, a lender may not be
as convinced about the value of your choice as you are.)

I cover the processes pre and post settlement (the day the
property becomes yours), handing over the cheque to the
vendor, and getting the keys of your new home into your own
hands. I also look at why insuring perhaps the biggest asset you
may ever own from the day it becomes yours (settlement day) is
so important.

Signing on the Dotted Line

Whether you purchase your property at an auction (refer to Chapter 11) or through a private treaty sale (refer to Chapter 12), in order to finalise the sale, you need to sign and exchange a contract of sale.

A contract of sale is a legal document that sets out the terms and conditions of the sale. A contract of sale must include

- ✔ A copy of the title documents (which records information about the ownership of the property, its boundaries and any *caveat* on the property). A caveat is a 'tag' on the title of the property that indicates someone other than yourself and your lender has an ownership stake in the property, perhaps because of an unpaid debt.

- ✔ A *zoning certificate* (which explains the uses a property can be put to).

- ✔ Any council restrictions on the use of the property.

- ✔ Items such as floor coverings, curtains or other fittings that are either included or excluded in the contract.

- ✔ The deposit you're expected to pay.

- ✔ The purchase price.

- ✔ The *settlement period* (the nominated time between signing and exchanging your contract and getting those precious keys into your own eager hands).

Understanding the contract of sale document requires an attention to detail and knowledge of contract and property law that few people acquire outside of law school. Unless you're prepared to carry the responsibility — legally and financially — your best advice is to get your solicitor or conveyancer to look over the document to make sure every clause and condition is as it should be.

Knowing what to look for in a contract of sale

You can request a copy of the contract of sale for any property you're keen on from the selling agent. But when you're sure you've found the property you definitely want to purchase, the questions you need to ask (and that your solicitor or conveyancer checks) when assessing the information contained in the contract include the following:

- ✔ Is the property described in the contract the same as the one you're planning to buy?

- ✔ Are the property boundaries correct — is the building well inside the boundaries?

- ✔ Do any restrictions or caveats apply to the property that may prevent you making renovations or improvements in the future?

- ✔ Are any items not mentioned in the contract that you believe should be included in the purchase?

Don't presume that everything you see within and without the property is to be included in the transfer on settlement (for more information about the settlement process, see the section 'Settling on Your Property' later in this chapter). The general rule to be aware of is that any items attached and integral to the building, such as a hot-water system and fixed carpets, are automatically included. Other items such as curtains and blinds, light fittings, washing machines and even a dishwasher need to be specifically mentioned in the contract to ensure inclusion.

Making special conditions on the contract

You may have the opportunity to ask to put special conditions into a contract before you sign it. Your solicitor or conveyancer negotiates this process with the vendor's solicitor or conveyancer.

You can add special conditions to the contract for the following when buying by private treaty sale (refer to Chapter 12), but not at auction (refer to Chapter 11):

- ✔ **Building inspection report:** You can pull out of the sale if the inspection report uncovers major problems with the property.

- ✔ **Finance:** The sale can only go ahead if your lender approves your loan application.

✔ **Sale of your property:** You can pull out of the sale if you fail to sell your property.

✔ **Valuation:** You can pull out of the sale if a valuer or your lender decides the property is worth less than you're paying.

Other conditions you may want to write into your contract (when buying by either private sale or at an auction) are to do with

✔ A longer or shorter settlement period.

✔ A lower deposit amount — say, 5 per cent rather than 10 per cent.

✔ Repairs to be carried out, such as a dangerous power box to be replaced.

✔ Specific furniture or fittings to be included in the negotiated price.

The vendor is under no obligation to accept any special conditions you want written into the contract of sale. Your best approach is to request special conditions when negotiating the sale price or to help seal the deal.

Exchanging contracts and handing over the deposit

After you're happy with the wording of the contract, in some states you *exchange contracts* to finalise the transaction. Both you and the vendor sign two copies of the contract and then exchange them. You can exchange the copies of the contract by hand or by post. Your solicitor or conveyancer or real estate agent can arrange the exchange. (In Queensland, South Australia, Tasmania and Western Australia, no exchange of contracts occurs, because only the one contract document is required. The seller signifies her acceptance of a buyer's offer by counter-signing the contract.)

As purchaser, you hand over the deposit to the selling agent, not to the vendor. The selling agent puts the money into an account to be held in trust for the vendor. The money is handed over to the vendor along with the full purchase price a few weeks down the track when you finally settle on the property. Any interest earned on the deposit amount is split evenly between you and the vendor of the property. In some states, the interest earned on deposit amounts goes into an indemnity fund, which pays for services such as consumer advice lines. In Western Australia, the interest earned is used to fund First Home Buyer Accounts, which in turn provides money that first home buyers can use to help pay any transaction costs involved in buying their home.

If you buy through a private treaty sale (refer to Chapter 12), you may have up to seven days to pay the deposit, or may be able to arrange to pay it in instalments. If you buy at an auction, you have to pay the whole of the deposit immediately, so have your chequebook ready. If you're buying after having sold your previous home, you may be able to use funds from the deposit given to you by the buyer of your home. You need to negotiate previously with your buyers to be allowed to release their deposit to use for the deposit on your new home.

Argh! We made a mistake: Enter, the cooling-off period

In all states and territories, except Western Australia, you're entitled to a cooling-off period when you buy through a private treaty sale. During this specified period of time, you may withdraw your offer for whatever reason. If you do withdraw from the sale, you're refunded your deposit but, ordinarily, you have to pay a small forfeit amount for doing so. (See Table 13-1 for the cooling-off periods and forfeit amounts in each state and territory.)

Many buyers use this cooling-off period to carry out a building inspection. If the report reveals major problems with the property, you have the option to pull out of the sale. Alternatively, you can use that information to negotiate a lower price or some other condition with the vendor. The vendor may agree to repair the plumbing system, for instance.

Use the cooling-off period to contact the lender and get final approval for a loan. Given you only have a few days to withdraw from the sale, you need to encourage the lender to move fast on its decision.

Table 13-1	Cooling-Off Periods and Forfeit Amounts		
State/ Territory	*Cooling-Off Period*	*Forfeit Amount*	*Waiver Condition*
ACT	Five business days after the contracts have been exchanged	0.25% of the purchase price ($250 per $100,000)	You can waive the five-day cooling-off period by giving the vendor a copy of a certificate that has been signed by your solicitor.
NSW	Five business days starting on the day of exchange and ending at 5 pm on the fifth business day	0.25% of the purchase price	You can waive the cooling-off period if you give the seller a Section 66W Certificate prepared by an independent conveyancer or solicitor.
NT	Three business days starting the day the contract is signed and exchanged	Buyer can withdraw from the contract within this time without penalty and without any explanation	The cooling-off period may be waived, reduced or extended by negotiation and agreement.
Qld	Five business days	0.25% of the purchase price	You can waive the cooling-off period after seeing a solicitor and filling out a PAMD Form 32a Lawyers Certification.
SA	Two clear business days after the contract was made	No forfeit	You can waive the cooling-off period after seeing a solicitor, who explains the consequences of giving up your rights and provides you with a solicitor's certificate.
Tas	Two day cooling-off period, but only on the first property on which a buyer makes an offer	No forfeit	No waiver is possible.

State/ Territory	Cooling-Off Period	Forfeit Amount	Waiver Condition
Vic	Three clear business days (beginning at midnight of the day you sign the contract)	The vendor can withhold $100 or 0.2% of the purchase price, whichever is more	You can no longer elect to waive the cooling-off period in Victoria.
WA	No cooling-off period	–	–

Waiving your cooling-off period

In the Australian Capital Territory, New South Wales, Northern Territory, Queensland, and South Australia, buyers can choose to waive their right to a cooling-off period (refer to Table 13-1 for waiver conditions for each state and territory).

In a hot property market, choosing to waive your cooling-off rights can be a way to get an edge over another buyer who isn't prepared to waive those rights. Vendors prefer to deal with a buyer who's prepared to go into a contract with no threat of withdrawing within the cooling-off period.

Suggesting or encouraging buyers to waive their cooling-off rights is illegal for vendors.

As a buyer, if you wish to waive your cooling-off rights, you need to be very certain that nothing is standing in your way of buying the property. You must also get legal advice on the consequences of waiving the cooling-off period, before the contracts are signed and exchanged.

Securing Your Final Loan Approval

Before you start seriously looking for your new home, you need to have already talked to a lender to get pre-approval for the amount you want to borrow (refer to Chapter 10). This approval gives you a clear picture of how much you can afford to spend on a home.

Even if you have pre-approval to borrow a certain amount, the lender still needs to give their final approval to lend you money against the particular home you choose to buy. Ideally, you get this final approval before you sign the contract of sale (refer to the section 'Signing on the Dotted Line' earlier in this chapter). If for some reason the lender refuses to lend you the money you need against that particular property, you can be in danger of having to pull out of the purchase and of losing your deposit.

Getting a Valuation Done

You're ecstatic about the home you want to purchase and you're convinced about the great deal you're about to do on the property. But, stop, step back and take a breath because the lender is the final arbiter of whether the property is actually worth what you're offering to pay for it.

Ordinarily, the process of valuing a property is a formality. The lender may send out its valuer to see the property and assess whether it is indeed worth what you're proposing to pay for it. The valuer may take a 'drive-by', look at the property from the street and give a judgement based on the value of similar homes in the area. Now and then a valuer may give a valuation from the comfort of her office. The valuer may use this method if she has recently seen other homes in the area, and is confident that your purchase price is well within the valuation range.

Occasionally, though, the valuer decides that the property isn't worth what you're offering to pay for it. In this case, the lender may offer you a loan with a higher loan-to-value ratio (LVR). For instance, if you're counting on a loan for 80 per cent of the home's value, you may instead need to take a loan for 90 per cent of the home's value.

Upping the LVR above 80 per cent means you have to pay mortgage insurance (refer to Chapter 10), which can cost several thousand more dollars. If the lender offers to up the LVR, you may want to rethink whether the property is worth buying after all — that is, if you're in the position to be able to pull out of the sale.

You can't withdraw from the purchase made at an auction, even if you're not able to get final approval for a loan on a property purchase, without a significant penalty. You may be able to negotiate to just lose the 10 per cent deposit, instead of suffering a greater penalty such as being sued. Do your research and don't let the charged atmosphere of an auction force you to pay more than your upper limit or what a property is worth.

Settling on Your Property

Settlement is the day when all the legal and financial threads associated with your home purchase are tied up. By the end of the day, you can finally take possession of your new home.

The lead-up to settlement looks similar to the following:

✓ **The actual day on which you settle is nominated on the contract of sale** when you first exchange contracts with the vendor (refer to the section 'Signing on the Dotted Line' earlier in this chapter). By this day, all the legal work must be done on both sides. Also, by this date, you need to organise for the lender to hand over the full purchase price of the home to the vendor.

✓ **You visit the property before settlement day** and again after all the furniture has been removed to ensure no nasty surprises await you. If any windows are broken or the plumbing no longer works, for instance, you notify your solicitor or conveyancer, who then aims to negotiate and resolve the issue with the vendor before settlement.

✓ **Around two weeks before settlement day** your solicitor or conveyancer arranges for you to sign a document that confirms the transfer of the property into your name. Your solicitor or conveyancer hands this document to your lender at settlement, who registers it at the state or territory Land Titles Office on your behalf. Upon registration, the property is changed over to your name.

✓ **One week before settlement** your solicitor or conveyancer notifies you of the exact date and time of settlement and the amount of funds you're required to provide prior to settlement.

As important as settlement day is, you don't actually need to be there yourself. This meeting is a face-off between solicitors and lenders, and you and the vendor are entirely unnecessary to the process at this stage. The following parties attend:

✓ Your solicitor or conveyancer

✓ The vendor's solicitor or conveyancer

✔ A representative of your lender

✔ A representative of the vendor's lender, if they have a mortgage

Here's what happens on settlement day:

✔ Your lender authorises payment of the loan money to the vendor's lender.

✔ Your solicitor or conveyancer authorises the vendor to collect the deposit money from the estate agent where it has been held in trust.

✔ Your solicitor or conveyancer pays adjustments or receives reimbursements such as taxes, council and water rates that are listed as prepaid by the vendor.

✔ Your solicitor or conveyancer hands over the Transfer of Land document, as well as the certificate of title, to the lender, who holds it in trust until the home loan is completed.

✔ Your solicitor or conveyancer pays the stamp duty on the home loan.

✔ You have the keys and the house is yours.

✔ You take time to celebrate!

Using the devil in the detail to default legally

If either party fails to have all the legal and financial proceedings tied up on settlement day, the transaction can be cancelled by the other side — without a forfeit penalty. Settlement day happened just this way to a friend of mine — to his relief.

Soon after my friend exchanged contracts to a home, he discovered he had to move interstate for work purposes. While he'd resigned himself to the idea of becoming a landlord instead of a resident in his own home, he was delighted to hear from the vendor's solicitor that the settlement papers weren't ready on the nominated settlement day.

He had an option to give the vendor the benefit of an extension, but took advantage of this unexpected turn of events to exercise his rights to pull out of the purchase, leaving him free to buy his new home interstate instead.

Insuring Your Biggest Asset

Before you celebrate you must do one more thing before you can truly relax into home ownership. You must, absolutely must, organise home insurance. Taking out building insurance on your home is required for final approval for a home loan. The lender wants you to protect what is actually its asset until you pay the loan off in full. You should also consider insuring the contents of your new home. (See the sidebar 'Ensuring your property is really insured'.)

Protecting the biggest asset you may well ever own makes perfect sense. Too many home owners find out the hard way about the costs of skimping on insurance. The consequences of a number of high-profile disasters around the country in recent years, such as bushfires, cyclones and even hailstorms, have been a very vivid illustration of how people can be left thousands of dollars out of pocket, and in some cases homeless, because they ignore the possibility of the worst-case scenario of their home being damaged or destroyed.

Insuring the building

Insuring the actual building (*building insurance*) is cheaper than insuring its contents (*contents insurance*, see the section 'Insuring your possessions' later in this chapter) because the likelihood of your home being destroyed by fire or some other natural disaster is much lower than being burgled.

Ensuring your property is really insured

Officially, the responsibility for your new home goes to you on settlement day, so you should ensure that any insurance policy you take out begins the day you get the keys in your hands. However, the previous home owner may not have home insurance.

So, if you want to be absolutely sure that you're going to be compensated if by some quirk of fate your new home is burnt down, flooded or damaged in some other way before you move in, you may want to start your insurance as soon as you exchange contracts.

Part III: Borrowing For, Buying and Protecting Your Home

Insurers offer the following policies on building insurance:

- **Sum insured policy:** The most common type of building insurance policy in Australia is the sum insured policy. This policy insures your building for a particular amount. You nominate how much you want to insure your home for and the insurer agrees to pay costs up to this figure. The higher the sum you choose to insure for, the higher the premiums you pay.

  A sum insured policy puts the onus on you to make sure you have enough cover. It can be tempting to underestimate how much rebuilding your home really costs and so keep the costs of premiums down. But, if something happens to your home, you have to cover any costs above the maximum sum insured yourself. In the 2003 Canberra bushfires, at least half of those who lost their homes were found to be underinsured.

- **Total replacement policy:** This policy covers the total cost of rebuilding your home to its current standard and quality. There is no agreed maximum figure and the insurer charges you according to what it thinks rebuilding your home is going to cost. Premiums for this kind of policy are more expensive than for a 'sum insured policy' but you're guaranteed to have all your costs covered.

- **Indemnity policy:** This policy is often also called a market value policy. Instead of paying for new materials to rebuild your home, the insurer only pays an amount equivalent to the current state of your home. The older your home is, the lower the amount the insurer pays.

The financial services watchdog, ASIC (Australian Securities & Investments Commission) has a very helpful series of articles on home insurance on its consumer education website www.fido.gov.au ('fido', watchdog, get it?). It also has tips on how to shop around for a lower-cost policy without compromising your cover. To access the information, go to Products and click on Insurance.

Calculating the costs of rebuilding your home

One common way to work out how much it can cost to replace your home is to take a valuation of your home and subtract the value of the land (as set out on your rates notice). Theoretically, this method leaves you with the cost of the actual building. However, working out the value of your home this way is likely to leave you seriously underinsured because it ignores the real costs of materials as well as all the other costs involved in rebuilding, such as

- ✔ Demolishing and removing debris from the site.

- ✔ Living in alternative accommodation while your house is being rebuilt.

- ✔ Hiring architects or other professionals to draw up plans.

- ✔ Lodging plans with your local council.

- ✔ Replacing the garden and landscaping and/or retaining walls.

- ✔ Rebuilding on a difficult site.

Most home insurers provide *online calculators* (or *web calculators*) on their websites to help you make a more accurate estimate of actual rebuilding costs. But, a 2005 report by ASIC, 'Getting home insurance right — a report on homebuilding underinsurance', points out that the results that the websites come up with can vary enormously depending on what approach they use. (Find the report at www.fido.gov.au.)

The two main methods of calculating rebuilding costs are as follows:

- ✔ **The cost per square metre method:** This method uses a calculation based on the size of the house and the material it is built from. These calculators apply an average figure to each house and don't take into account the age of the house nor any other features that may make the house more expensive to rebuild.

- ✔ **The elemental estimating method:** This method assesses in detail the different elements of the building to price rebuilding costs 'from the ground up'. More detailed versions use local wage and material rates and other construction data.

The more questions a web calculator asks you about your home, the more accurate its estimate is likely to be. A good calculator asks how many bathrooms you have, whether your house is on a slope, its age and about the quality of the internal finishings. You may spend up to 15 minutes completing the questionnaire but you end up being confident that the estimate properly reflects the costs of rebuilding your home.

To get the best out of using web calculators, ASIC makes these suggestions:

- Check if the calculators ask for your postcode or merely which state you live in. If it only asks for your state, the calculator is likely to be using average figures for building costs that may not be right for your home.

- Test the calculators by using a friend's new-home details to see whether the figure it suggests is close to what it cost your friend to build. This way you get an idea about which calculators are more accurate.

- Use a number of calculators that ask different questions to see what figures they come up with. This method gives a much better idea of rebuilding costs than using just the one calculator.

Insuring your possessions

After you scrimp and save for the deposit on your new home and shell out for stamp duty, legal fees and building insurance, the last thing you may want to do is voluntarily pay out more to insure your belongings.

Depending on factors such as where you live, premiums on contents insurance can be as much as double the cost of building insurance (refer to the section 'Insuring the building' earlier in this chapter). But you need to balance that cost against the very real possibility of being burgled, or of your possessions being damaged or destroyed in a fire or flood or some other accident. After you add up the replacement cost of what you own, it may well be worth paying out a few extra hundred dollars a year in contents insurance to cover the considerable costs of replacing them.

The cost of your premium depends on how much you choose to insure your belongings for. Once again, it may be tempting to underinsure but, if your home is cleaned out in a burglary, you only get back the maximum you insure for. For example, if the amount stolen adds up to $35,000, and the maximum you insure for is $15,000, you're out of pocket $20,000 if you want to replace everything.

You can pay lower premiums. Here's how:

✔ **Bundle policies:** While you can buy building insurance and contents insurance separately, most insurers also offer combined home and contents insurance policies. You may want to shop around to see whether you can get a better deal with a bundled home and contents insurance policy.

✔ **Take on a higher excess:** The excess is the amount you pay towards the cost of a claim. For instance, accepting an excess of $1,000 on a claim can halve your annual premium.

✔ Tell the insurer

- If you have a security system.

- If the house is usually occupied during the day.

- If you haven't previously made a claim on an insurance policy.

Calculating the value of your possessions

Take the time to list your possessions in detail. Here's how:

✔ Get a notebook and do a stocktake of everything you own — room by room. Don't forget things like blinds, carpets and light fittings.

✔ Make an estimate of the replacement cost of each item.

✔ Use a digital camera to photograph each room, including particular items. This documenting helps as proof if you ever have to claim on your insurance. Keep a copy of the photos on a portable memory drive and lodge it somewhere outside the home for added safety, or upload them to one of the websites that let you store your photos online, such as Flickr (www.flickr.com) or Picasa Web Albums (picasaweb.google.com).

✔ Visit an insurer's website for a calculator that takes you through every room and offers suggested replacement prices for commonly owned items. (*Note:* You can also add 'special items' that aren't included in the list.) You can then use the total amount calculated to get a quote for the likely cost of premiums.

Some contents insurance policies don't include items such as computers, bicycles, mobile phones or computer gaming equipment in their standard cover. You may be able to get cover for these as 'special items' for an extra cost.

Part IV
The Part of Tens

Glenn Lumsden

*'Call me a hopeless romantic,
but I've always dreamt of buying
a quaint, rustic cottage in the country,
bulldozing it and building six units.'*

In this part ...

*E*very *For Dummies* book includes a Part of Tens. This part offers facts that are worth remembering and includes tips and more tips. The ten tips included here are essential for new home buyers. I've also provided a checklist of things to look for when inspecting a potential property, broken into the ten main areas you should focus on.

Chapter 14

Ten Things to Remember as a First Home Buyer

In This Chapter

▶ Making sure you're ready for the biggest financial commitment of your life

▶ Keeping your emotions in check when you buy

▶ Knowing that the mortgage eventually is going to reduce

*B*uying your first home is a huge leap. And it's one made more difficult by the fact that property prices are high, no matter where you look. Most first home buyers always have a tough time, though. They usually have to look in areas outside their preferred location or buy a property that's smaller or more rundown than they prefer. The important thing is to get your foot on the first rung of the property ladder — even if you have to lower your expectations a bit. But, not before you're ready — financially and psychologically. This chapter offers some tips to help you take heart.

Buy When You're Ready to Buy

When you're looking for a property, everyone you know is an expert about when is the best time to buy. They tell you the market is going up fast, so you need to buy now, not in six months' time; or that the market's going to crash, so you ought to wait another year to catch the bargains when interest rates go up.

Ignore them! Yes, all of them. The right time to buy a property is when you're ready to buy.

You know you're ready to buy when

- ✔ You find yourself dreaming about renovating your own home.

- ✔ You find yourself incessantly looking at the property section of the local newspaper or browsing the real estate listings on the internet.

- ✔ You start putting every last penny into the bank, rather than spending it on new clothes, going out or other treats.

Given the huge financial commitment involved in buying a property, you need to be psychologically ready for that step. Assuming you're going to hang on to the property for a while and you find a property that suits at a price you can afford, who cares what the wider market is doing?

Think Outside the Square

If you can't find anything you can afford in the suburb or area of your choice, you may need to think laterally or scale down your expectations just to get your foot on the first rung of the property ladder. Traditionally, first home buyers tend to look beyond their first choice to find a home they can afford.

To find somewhere more affordable, investigate suburbs just beyond those of your first preference. These nearby suburbs may have similar qualities to those you have your heart set on — they're just a bit further out than you may like. They can also offer other unexpected benefits, such as bigger properties and bigger yards and a neighbourhood more conducive to raising a family in the longer run.

Don't forget, you're not alone. The middle suburbs and many country towns are filling up with people just like you who are priced out of suburbs closer to the city and who eventually put their own stamp on the 'new' area.

Another alternative to your first choice is to buy a property still within your chosen area but that needs a lot of work — or one that originally may not have been a residence at all. First home buyers are a creative-thinking lot and are able to convert old warehouses, factories or shops into interesting new homes. (Chapter 7 covers all your renovating options.)

Look at Your First Purchase as a Springboard

As property owners, Australians tend not to buy just the one property and stay in it for the rest of their lives. If the first property you buy isn't the property you can imagine living in forever, think of it as just your first step onto the property ladder. In four or five years, you can sell it on to someone who is in the same position you're in today. Between when you buy and that time, your equity in the property builds up — from the repayments you make on the loan and hopefully from the increase in the value of the property itself — and you can use that financial gain to buy a property that better suits your needs.

Borrow No More Than You Can Afford

Temptation can come knocking, especially in a hot market when prices are rising quickly. Before you know it, you want to go beyond your budget to buy the home of your dreams. And lenders are only too happy to lend you as much as they think your income can bear, even if you don't have enough money, after making the required mortgage repayments each month, to step outside your new front door for the next few years. (Chapter 2 gives you all you need to know about the costs of buying a home.)

You need to cover more than the cost of the actual property. You have to foot the bill for a number of transaction costs and costs associated with getting a loan and getting legal advice. These costs can really send you over the financial edge if you don't budget for them.

Owning a home also involves expenses you may not have had to carry while you were renting. You're now the one who has to pay the council and water rates, for that new hot water system and to keep the house looking good over the years. Stretch the repayments too far over the limit, and owning a new home isn't going to be much fun at all.

Another Property Is Always around the Corner

When you miss out on a property that tugs at your heart, you may feel like you're never going to find a property you can both love and afford. Keep going. Fortunately, new properties keep coming on to the market each week, and eventually you're going to find the one that fits your criteria and your budget.

You may need to make a compromise on your criteria here or there, but don't settle for something you're not going to be happy living in for at least a couple of years. Chopping and changing properties more often than that is too expensive to contemplate.

Have faith that with consistent searching and effort the right property eventually comes along and is available at a price that you're able and willing to pay.

Don't Pay Too Much for a Property

Each property has a fair value. Don't be too desperate to find a home. You don't want to pay more for a property than it is really worth — in terms of its location and in terms of the property itself. First, paying too much can mean you have less to spend on improving your property. Second, you're going to have less equity in the property, and your loan-to-value ratio (refer to Chapter 13) may go over the 80 per cent level — meaning you have to pay mortgage insurance, which adds several thousand to your purchase price.

Do your research on how much properties in a particular area are worth, and make sure you get a building inspection report so you're aware of any problems with a property and how much it costs to repair them.

Keep Your Emotions in Check When Looking at a Home

Deciding you want to buy a home can be a bit like falling in love — sometimes your emotions can overwhelm your reason. You can fall for a property that looks gorgeous on the outside but may not be suitable to your needs. That cute white picket fence and those gorgeously painted ceiling roses may conceal a host of structural problems that could cost a fortune to fix up.

Retaining a business-like reserve when you're looking at one of the biggest purchases you're ever going to make pays you back handsomely. Take along a hard-headed friend you can trust to point out negatives when you look at properties. And if you really fall in love, get a thorough building inspection done before you make any serious offers. You should at least know about a property's faults before you commit to it.

Be Sceptical of Selling Agents

With rare exceptions, remember that the real estate agent isn't your friend — even if the agent pretends to be. It's not that agents are against you; the agent's just working for the sellers of the homes the agency represents. The agent's primary interest — and, in fact, a legal obligation exists — is to sell those properties for the highest prices possible. So when agents take you aside to tell you about the special prices they can get for you, be aware that they probably say that to everyone.

That's not to say that an agent can't help you find the home you're looking for. When you get to know the agents in the area, they're more than happy to inform you about properties that fit your bill. Agents can help you to forge a win-win situation that helps both their clients and you. Just don't expect any special favours just for you.

If you want an agent whose loyalty is totally dedicated to you, get yourself a buyers' agent. (Refer to Chapter 4.)

Renovating Can Wait

Most first home owners don't have much spare money to think about anything but the most basic renovations after they buy a home. But rushing into the renovations may not be the best approach. You need to give yourself some time to live in a property to see how you can improve it to better suit you and your family.

By living in the home for some time, you get a sense of how your family uses the property and you can identify

- ✔ How much time you need to save some money to put towards your renovation.
- ✔ How much you can afford to spend on your renovations.
- ✔ How the inside interacts with outdoors.
- ✔ How the sun moves through the home.
- ✔ What are the bad features you just have to remove.
- ✔ What are the good features you want to enhance.
- ✔ Which rooms work and which don't.

The Mortgage Does Go Down — Eventually

When you buy your first property, your mortgage can feel like a huge weight around your neck. You're committing to an enormous amount of money, it's true. And for the first couple of years, you may have to deny yourself many of the treats you're used to — eating out, buying CDs, travelling overseas — just to scrape together those monthly repayments.

After a few years of owning your own home, financially positive things begin to happen:

- ✔ You pay down the principal of the loan and the interest repayments start decreasing as well — almost infinitesimally at first but, after a few years, the interest amounts become noticeably smaller.

✔ As long as you stay employed, your wages are probably going to keep increasing. That means that the interest payments become smaller in another way — as a proportion of your income.

✔ If you buy well, the value of your home may also go up, so that the amount you owe to the lender also becomes smaller (as a proportion of your home's value). At the same time, your equity in your home becomes greater — without you doing anything much at all.

Of course, if you decide to borrow against the increased equity in your home, you're heading for a bigger loan and being back where you started — but at least you know you've got a growth asset on your hands that you can sell if your financial situation changes for the worst.

For more information on how a mortgage works and how to sift through the variety of options available, refer to Chapter 10.

Chapter 15

Ten Areas (Almost!) to Check at Open Homes

In This Chapter

▶ Detailing the important features of each area of the house — inside and out

▶ Working out what's necessary, and what's not

▶ Determining whether a room will suit your lifestyle

*I*n the excitement of finding your (potential) dream home, the job of checking for all the necessities, and some niceties, can easily be overlooked. In this chapter, I cover some basic items you should look for in just about every room or space in an average house or flat.

Checking for these key things will help avoid any last-minute panic when you're signing the contract to buy the home, desperately trying to remember whether you checked the water pressure or if the oven worked properly.

Kitchen

You spend a lot of time in the kitchen, so it's vital to ensure this area in your new home is going to meet your specific needs (even if you end up renovating later). Here's a list of some key kitchen features to look for as you hunt around an open house:

✔ **Benchtops and splashbacks:** Do you prefer granite benchtops and glass splashbacks, or laminate and tiles? Check the condition of the benchtops and of the grout and sealant around the tiles, sinks and splashbacks. Also check the amount of bench space and whether it provides you with enough preparation room.

✔ **Cooktop and oven:** How will you heat your food — gas? electricity? induction heating? thermonuclear power? (Keep in mind electricity is more expensive than gas.)

✔ **Extraction fan/range hood:** Check for an extraction fan — you'd be amazed how many homes don't have one and you often can't install one retrospectively. Also check the effectiveness of the fan — and the noise level!

✔ **Fridge space:** Have a look at the space for the fridge. Is it wide or high enough to fit the fridge you already own?

✔ **Floors:** What are the floors covered with? Are you happy to care for a wooden floor, or would you prefer to quickly mop tiles? Avoid carpet!

✔ **Hidden extras:** Does the kitchen come with a dishwasher already installed — or at least have a space (preferably next to the sink) to install one easily? What about some standing room? I don't know about you, but people at my dinner parties always end up hanging around while I finish preparing the food!

✔ **Power and phone points:** How many power points have been installed, and where are they placed? Are there enough points to accommodate a fridge, toaster, kettle, microwave and other less-frequently used appliances? Is there somewhere to plug in a phone or modem?

✔ **Storage solutions:** There's lots to store in a kitchen, so inspect the pantry and the number (and size) of the cupboards. Make sure you don't lose too much cupboard space to a hot-water service, dishwasher pipes or sink plumbing.

Bathroom

The bathroom in your new property might have last been renovated in the 1950s, meaning every item is a fetching shade of pink. But if your budget won't stretch to renovating the bathroom as soon as you move in, you'll be stuck with the current fittings for a little while. Examine this list of features to see whether the bathroom is functional for your needs:

- ✔ **Bath/shower:** Does the bathroom come with a bath, shower, both or a 'shub' (shower over a tub)? If there's only a shower, can you live without long baths after a hard day at work? Or are you more of a 'four-minute shower' person? (And congratulations if you are, given the droughts we tend to have in Australia!) If you have children, or are planning to, having a bath might be a must-have. If a short but sharp shower is important to you, remember to check the water pressure.

- ✔ **Bathroom vanity:** No, I'm not talking about spending too much time in front of the mirror! I'm referring to the sink and cupboard unit that's fairly standard in a bathroom. Does it come with a mirror? If the vanity doesn't have in-built drawers or cupboards, is there additional storage, or at least room to install a stand-alone set of drawers to house all your essential bits and pieces?

- ✔ **Power points:** Even if you're pretty low-maintenance, you probably use a few electric appliances in the bathroom, such as a hairdryer, electric toothbrush, shaver or hair straightener. Check the availability and placement of power points. Or, you might be into the bare essentials, and not need any of this at all!

- ✔ **Steam clearing:** You'll need something to remove the steam while you're bathing, to prevent mould from appearing on the bathroom walls. Is there an extraction fan? At the very least, you'll want a window that opens — but if the bathroom's on the ground floor, make sure the window has a lock to prevent unwanted visitors (human and otherwise) from creeping inside. Also check what the window looks out on.

✔ **Washing machine taps:** If there's no separate laundry in the house, or no communal laundry in the apartment block, then you'll probably find some washing machine taps in the bathroom. Check that there's enough space to fit your washing machine, and some room to sort your washing.

In modern properties or renovations, you might come across what's known as a *Euro laundry*, which usually means space for the washing machine (and perhaps dryer) is tucked away in a cupboard or in the kitchen. Check the space provided is sufficient.

Lounge

The lounge is the perfect place for entertaining guests and spending time with family. But what if you move in and find there's not enough room for your lounge suite? Here are some features to look for before you commit to buying a property:

✔ **Extra space:** Lots of lounges flow on to balconies or into the backyard. Does the property have doors or windows that allow you to bring the outside in?

✔ **Heating and cooling:** Do you swelter in summer without air-conditioning or do you really feel the cold in winter? Or do you prefer to keep your gas and electricity bills down? Numerous heating and cooling options are available: Reverse-cycle or split-system air-conditioners, ducted heating and cooling, open fire places, ceiling fans, hydronic heating, bar heaters and gas wall panels are all possible. Check out the heating and cooling options provided and whether they fit in with your requirements.

If the property doesn't come with any heating or cooling options, you can always buy a free-standing floor fan and heater.

✔ **Flooring:** Tiles, floor boards or carpet are the main flooring options in a living area; think about what works best for your location and lifestyle (and whether you can afford to change the current flooring, if it doesn't suit your needs).

✔ **TV and phone connections:** Some people prefer to keep
the TV out of the lounge, but if this isn't the case for you,
check for an aerial plug. Paid TV services may also be a
non-negotiable in your household; if so, you'll want to see
if the cabling has already been installed. (Don't forget to
check for aerials and satellite dishes outside!) Similarly,
you may want a phone in the lounge and, given the rise
of internet television, an internet connection in this room
could be very handy too if you want to avoid cables trailing
through the house or apartment.

Dining Room

Older properties usually have a separate, or formal, dining room.
If you do a lot of entertaining and have a large dining table, take
some measurements of your table and chairs *before* you head off
to the open home, to ensure it will fit into the dining area.

If formal dining isn't really your style, check whether another
use of the separate dining room is possible and practical.

More modern homes or renovations will often have open plan
dining areas, usually adjoined to the kitchen, lounge or both.
This means that the space is not (usually) as restricted as a
separate dining room. Check that the flow of the open plan
space fits in with your lifestyle.

Bedrooms

When looking at the main bedroom of the property, check the
following:

✔ **Clothes storage:** You're going to need to hang up your
clothes (unless you're a teenage boy — in which case,
plenty of floor space is probably your best bet). Some
wardrobes come with built-in shelving units, but if the
wardrobe installed only has hanging space, check you
can fit a chest of drawers in the room. If the room has no
storage (sometimes the case in older properties), you may
need to purchase a free-standing wardrobe.

✔ **Ensuite:** For some, not having an ensuite isn't a deal-breaker, but if you have children or often have guests staying, you may consider it to be. If this is the case, check whether the bedroom has an ensuite and that it meets your needs.

✔ **Flooring:** Carpet? Wooden floorboards? Remember that this will affect the temperature of the room throughout the year, so take the climate of your location into consideration.

✔ **Heating and cooling:** For maximum comfort in the summer months, and to stop you from freezing in winter, don't forget to look for heating and cooling systems, in whatever form you prefer (air-conditioning, ceiling fans, under-floor heating and so on).

✔ **Phone and TV connections:** If you like to watch the TV in bed or while you're getting dressed in the morning, ensure the bedroom has an aerial plug. You may also want a phone jack near the bed.

For properties with more than one bedroom, apply most of the preceding points to the second and subsequent bedrooms.

If you're planning to turn one of the bedrooms into a study, make sure to check for sufficient power points for all your computer equipment.

Laundry

Many older and/or larger homes have a separate laundry, and you may feel having this extra space is an added feature. If the property you're inspecting has a separate area for laundry, here's a list of what to look for:

✔ **Bench space:** If you've got a top-loading washing machine, then you may want to look for extra bench space for folding clothes, storing washing powders and hosting a central repository of unmatched socks (where *do* the other halves of the sock pairs go?!).

✔ **Dryer brackets and ducting:** Bringing your own dryer? Investigate whether there are brackets to attach the machine to the wall, and ducting to move the hot air outside.

✔ **Sink and cabinet:** A deep sink in the laundry is useful for soaking and rinsing — or bathing small children if the property doesn't have a bath! If you do have children, check whether the cabinet can be secured, so you can store nasty liquids and powders out of harm's way.

Garage

The number of cars/bikes/jet skis you own, or intend to own, will determine the suitability of the garage (if the property comes with one). When looking at parking options, keep the following in mind:

✔ **Parking that comes with apartment blocks:** In this situation, the parking is usually shared, and the options will be allocated parks, or first-in, first-serve. If you're lucky, there might also be a storage cage for all those odds and ends, like the fake Christmas tree and the bicycle that you really must start using more often ... Check the security and lighting in this shared space.

✔ **Parking that comes with houses or units:** In a stand-alone property, the parking options might include a covered garage or a driveway. If the property includes a covered garage, check how secure it is and whether it provides internal access. In some older properties, the covered garages are quite narrow, so check whether the car you have will fit, along with everything else you'd like to keep locked up and under cover. If the only parking option is the driveway, check how many cars it's possible to fit.

✔ **No parking at all:** If on-street parking is the only option, check the parking regulations in the area — you might need a permit to park outside your home, which is an additional annual cost.

Backyard or Balcony

Having a backyard is part of the Great Australian Dream, right? If the property you're considering has a backyard (or a balcony), work your way through this checklist of features:

- ✔ **Barbeque:** Another quintessential Australian feature — the barbie. If there isn't a plumbed-in gas pipe attached to the house, then you've got a bit of freedom to move your BBQ around the backyard. Check what options are available. If you're looking at cooking on a balcony, make sure that it is well ventilated.

- ✔ **Fences:** Whether you've got pets or children, it's essential to have the backyard fenced to stop runaways. Check the condition of the fence and find out how old it is. If the property has a balcony, ensure that railings are sufficient and secure.

- ✔ **Lighting and power points:** To enjoy long summer evenings out in the backyard, you'll need some lights outside the house, or an easily accessible power point to set up some temporary lighting. After all, how else are you going to string up fairy lights at Christmas?

- ✔ **Maintenance requirements:** Do you dream of creating a backyard escape and being surrounded by trees and plants, or do you prefer low-maintenance decking or pavers? Check whether enough space is available, and whether you're happy with the level of maintenance required.

- ✔ **Somewhere to sit:** Does the property come with a deck or paved area to put some outdoor furniture? Or, at least, a flat bit of grass?

- ✔ **Washing line:** Having a washing line will save you hundreds of dollars — sunlight is free, and dryers cost money to purchase and operate. If a washing line is already provided, check that it's not only unobtrusive but also positioned to catch good sunlight — north facing is ideal. If a washing line isn't already set up, check that there's somewhere you could install one.

Street Appeal

Everyone knows that you shouldn't judge a book by its cover, and the same goes for a house. But when you're making such a large purchase, it's natural to want to make sure everything is perfect, inside and out. Here are some ideas of what to look for when you're approaching (or leaving) the open home inspection:

- ✔ **Facade:** First impressions count, and in the case of a house or apartment block, it's the facade that creates this impression. Is the paint fresh or starting to peel? Is the colour scheme a bit dated? If the house has wooden cladding, check it's not showing signs of rot.

- ✔ **Landscaping:** Is the front yard a jungle of overgrown weeds? If you've got green thumbs, a challenging garden project may be exciting for you. But if you're a novice with plants and a lawnmower, and have little interest in learning how to do these chores, are you willing to pay someone to bring the front yard to a suitable standard, and to maintain it afterwards?

- ✔ **Privacy:** Do you like a front yard or apartment block that is quite open to the street, or do you prefer more privacy? The type of plants and fence used in the front yard or outside the apartment block can affect how much passers-by can look in, and how secure the property is. If you prefer more privacy and security, look for higher fences in good condition.

Index

• A •

advertising brochures, being wary of, 136–137
apartment living, 45. *See also* high-rise apartment living
apartments
  buying 'off the plan', 135–137
  checklist for buyers, 137–138
  purchase as investment, 53–54
  scarcity value of, 54
architects
  choosing, 146–148
  use for home design, 143–144
architectural periods and styles in housing, 94–102
Art Deco home style, 100
aspect of house
  effect on light, 47
  and position on block, 141
assessing properties, 79–81
auctions
  bidder registration required, 58
  bidding rules, 188–189
  deposit required, 27
  making offers after passed in, 192–193
  making pre-auction offers, 193–194
  problems with selling prices, 185–186
  procedure, 186–187
  pros and cons, 184
  tactics, 190–191
  and winning bidder, 192
Australian Capital Territory (ACT)
  auction bidding rules and regulations, 188
  cooling-off period, forfeit amount and waiver conditions, 212
  making an offer in, 200
  Office of Regulatory Services, 65
  owner–builder regulations, 113, 152
  stamp duty in, 29
  WorkCover authority in, 112
average annual percentage rate (AAPR) of interest on loans, 173–174

• B •

backyard or balcony, desirable features of, 240
banks as mortgage lenders, 171
basic variable interest-rate loans, 165–166
bathrooms
  desirable features of, 235–236
  number of, 45
  renovating, 105
bedrooms
  desirable features of, 237–238
  number of, 46
bidding at auctions, rules and regulations, 188–189
blocks of land
  assessment of, 141
  building on difficult sites, 142
  restrictions on building, 140
body corporate fees. *See* owners' corporation fees
borrowing money
  costs of, 27–30
  within means, 227
builders
  getting quotes from, 120
  project management by, 119–121
  signing contracts with, 120–121, 149
Builders All Risk Insurance for owner–builders, 151
building
  on difficult sites, 142
  sequence of events, 134–135
building by owners. *See* owner–builders

building designers
  choosing, 146–148
  deciding to use, 145
  hiring, 117–119
building inspections
  cost of, 31
  getting pre-purchase report,
    58, 85–86
building insurance policies, 217–218
building material, choice of, 45
building permits, 108, 153–154
building societies as mortgage
    lenders, 171
buyers' agents
  and auction bidding, 64
  claims made by, 60–61
  cost of using, 63
  finding a competent, 61–62
  limits on actions of, 64–65
  and *Trade Practices Act 1974*
    compliance, 64–65
buying
  checklist of preferred features, 48–49
  choosing time for, 19–20, 225–226
  costs of, 24–27
  dealing with real estate agents,
    55–57
  government charges on, 28–29
  lateral thinking in, 226
  legal fees, 30
  'off the plan', 135–138
  on your own, 38
  parents helping with, 39–41
  preparation for, 18–19
  readiness for, 10–11
  versus renting, 11–12
  with friends, 38–39

● **C** ●

Californian bungalow home styles,
    99–100
car parking options, 46, 138, 239
cash rate of interest, effect on home
    loan interest rates, 163
caveats on property, 208
certificates for specific works, 151
city fringes, moving to, 51
colonial home styles, 95

comparison rate of interest, 165
completion certificates, 117
concept plans, drawing up, 148
Construction Risk Insurance for
    owner–builders, 151
consumer agencies in states and
    territories, 65
contents insurance
  budgeting for, 31, 34–35
  calculating sum to be insured,
    221–222
  cost of premiums, 220–221
contracted stage payments, 117
contracts
  exchanging, 210–211
  signing after reading, 194
  signing with builders, 120–121, 149
contracts of sale, 208–210
conveyancing, cost of, 30
cooling-off period
  after private treaty sale, 193
  entitlement to, 211–212
  waiving, 212–213
cost per square metre method of
    calculating rebuilding costs, 219
costs in buying
  land in new developments, 140
  summary of, 24–26
costs of home-owning
  maintenance, 33–34
  monthly checklist, 32–33
  planning for future cost rises, 35
  rates, fees and insurance, 34–35
  regular living costs, 35
council rates, 34
council regulations in new
    developments or in country, 140
councils
  and owner–builders, 151, 153–154
  problems getting applications
    through, 109
country
  escaping to, 52–53
  out-of-season problems with living
    in, 54
credit files, 179–180
credit history, 159
credit unions, mortgage loans
    from, 171
credit-impaired loans, 177–179

• D •

deposit guarantees, 42
deposits
 paying, 210–211
 raising, 26–27
 saving for, 35–42
designers. *See* building designers
designing a home, 142–149
development approvals
 for owner–builders, 153–154
 for renovations, 109
dining room, desirable features
  of, 237
display homes. *See also*
   house-and-land packages;
   housing estates
 assessing, 131–134
 inclusions and exclusions in, 132
 optional extras in, 132
 resisting upgrading pressure, 133
do-it-yourself (DIY) renovations
 ability assessment, 110–112
 as owner–builder, 113–117
 safety standards required
   for, 112
do-it-yourself (DIY) websites for
   property, 73
Domestic Building Contracts
   when hiring tradespeople,
   116–117
draftspersons, use of, 145–146
drive-by inspections, 78
dummy bidding at auctions, 58, 184
Dutch Colonial home styles, 100

• E •

early modern home styles, 100–101
early Victorian home styles, 96–97
easements, 141
Edwardian home styles, 98–99
elemental estimating method of
   calculating rebuilding
   costs, 219
exit fees on leaving mortgage loan,
   174–175
expression of interest, sale by, 206

• F •

50 per cent rule for renovation
   expenditure, 106
*Fair and Square: A Guide to the Trade
   Practices Act for the Real Estate
   Industry*, 64–65
features of homes checklist, 48–49
Federation home styles, 98–99
fee structures for buyers' agents, 63
fees for architects and designers, 118
finance, cost of borrowing, 27–30
financial commitment, size of, 23–24
financial research companies, 169
First Home Owner Grant (FHOG), 17–18
First Home Savers Accounts, 36–37
fixed-rate loans, 162–164
floor plans
 assessing during inspection, 83
 choice of, 46
foreclosure, 159
forfeit amounts, 211–213
friends, buying with, 38–39
fringes of city, moving to, 51

• G •

garden, choice of, 46
gazumping, avoiding, 204–205
Georgian home styles, 95–96
gifts to use as deposit, 40
goods and services tax (GST), 151
government charges on buying, 28–29
growth asset, property as, 15

• H •

heritage restrictions, 90–91
high-rise apartment living, 53–54
holding deposits, 202
home building insurance, 31
home improvements, 21
home indemnity insurance
 for owner–builders, 151
 for renovation work, 111–112
home insurance
 after buying, 217–222
 budgeting for, 34
 for renovation work, 111–112

home ownership
  advantages of, 14
  as investment, 14–16
  as tax-friendly investment, 16
home replacement cost calculation,
      218–220
home warranty insurance
  for owner–builders, 115, 151
  for renovation work, 111–112
home-owning costs. *See* costs of
      home-owning
house-and-land packages, 51.
      See also display homes;
      housing estates
house-building
  by project builders, 135
  sequence of events, 134–135
housing, architectural periods and
      styles, 94–102
housing estates. *See also* display
      homes; house-and-land packages
  buying house-and-land package,
      130–131
  buying land first, 129–130
  developers of, 128–129
  investigating home in, 127–128
  pros and cons, 126
  resisting pressure to upgrade, 133

• *I* •

ideal home. *See also* searching,
      property
  designing, 142–149
  desirable features of, 44–49
improvements to homes, 21
indemnity building insurance policy,
      218
information about potential
      purchases, organising, 70–71
instalment contracts for vendor
      finance, 180
insurance
  of building, 217–218
  of contents, 31, 34–35, 220–221
  home building, 31
  online calculators, 219
  for owner–builders, 151
  for renovation work, 111–112

interest rates on loans
  comparison rate, 165
  fixed-rate versus variable-rate,
      162–164
  splitting the difference, 164–165
  vendor finance, 181
internet searching, property, 71–73
investments
  home ownership as, 14–16
  using to raise deposit, 41

• *J* •

joint-purchase arrangements, 39

• *K* •

kitchens
  desirable features of, 233–234
  renovating, 105

• *L* •

land
  assessment of blocks, 141–142
  building on vacant block, 140
land to value ratio, 53–54
landlords and renting, 13, 15
late Victorian home styles, 97–98
laundry, desirable features, 238–239
legal fees, 30
light
  affect of aspect on, 47
  assessing during inspection, 83
line of credit loans, 167
living at home while saving, 37
living costs, budgeting for, 35
loans. *See* mortgages
location
  and choosing property, 43–44,
      78–79
  trade-off against preferred home
      style, 49–54
lounge, desirable features of, 236–237
low-doc (low-document) loans,
      176–177
lump sums as gifts from parents, 40

• M •

managed funds, investing in to raise deposit, 41
margin loans, 169
Mediterranean home styles, 100
mid-Victorian home styles, 97
mod cons, choice of, 46
modernist home styles, 101–102
money, costs of borrowing, 27–30
mortgage broker, choosing, 171–174
Mortgage and Finance Association of Australia (MFAA), 173
mortgage managers (originators), 171
mortgage offset accounts, 165
mortgages
  basic variable interest-rate, 165–166
  borrowers outside standard criteria, 175–179
  changing lenders, 174–175
  connection to other facilities, 169–171
  documents required by lender, 161–162
  establishment fee, 27
  financing through developer, 133–134
  fixed rate versus variable, 162–164
  insurance of, 161
  interest rates on, 162–165
  lenders, 171–172
  lending criteria for, 159–161
  line of credit, 167
  obtaining from bank, 133
  obtaining pre-approval of loan amount, 170
  operation of, 158–159
  professional package, 167–168
  securing final approval, 213–214
  service fee on, 27
  stamp duty, 30
  stand-alone, 168–169
  standard variable interest-rate, 166

• N •

neighbours in apartments, 138
New South Wales (NSW)
  auction bidding rules and regulations, 188
  cooling-off period, forfeit amount and waiver conditions, 212
  making an offer in, 200
  Office of Fair Trading, 65
  owner–builder regulations, 113, 152
  stamp duty in, 29
  WorkCover authority in, 112
newspaper property guides, 73–74
no-doc (no-document) loans, 176–177
non-conforming loans, 177–179
Northern Territory (NT)
  auction bidding rules and regulations, 188
  cooling-off period, forfeit amount and waiver conditions, 212
  Department of Justice — Consumer Affairs, 65
  making an offer in, 201
  owner–builder regulations, 113, 152
  stamp duty in, 29
  WorkCover authority in, 112

• O •

occupancy certificates, 151
'off the plan' buying, pros and cons, 135–138
offers
  after property passed in at auction, 192–193
  contract signing and exchange, 203
  making in private treaty sale, 199–202
  making through real estate agent, 60
  putting conditions on, 202–203
'on the market', during auctions, 189
open for inspections
  making schedule for, 81–82
  what to look for during, 82–84, 233–241
outgoings, calculating monthly payments, 32–35
overcapitalising on renovation, 105–107
owner–builders
  calling in qualified tradespeople, 116–117
  considerations for, 149–150
  courses for, 153

owner–builders *(continued)*
  home warranty insurance
      requirements, 115
  obtaining council approvals, 153–154
  options for, 152–153
  project management by, 117
  regulations covering in states and
      territories, 113–115, 152
  relationships with tradespeople, 154
  responsibilities of, 150–152
owners' corporation fees, 30, 34, 138

● *P* ●

parents
  helping with buying, 39–41
  living with while saving, 37–38
parking. *See* car parking options
passed in
  making offers afterwards, 192–193
  property at auction, 190
payment defaults, 177
perfect home. *See* ideal home
period homes
  choice of, 47
  heritage restrictions, 90–91
  idiosyncrasies of, 89–90
  pros and cons of buying, 88–89
  renovating, 92, 102
  restoring original features, 93–94
permits for renovations, 107–109
planning permits
  for owner–builders, 153–154
  for renovations, 109
planning submissions, 153–154
plans, finalising, 148–149
pools and spas, 47
position. *See* location
possessions
  calculating value of, 221–222
  insuring, 220–221
pre-approval of loan amount, 170
pre-auction offers, 193–194
prices
  beating down, 198–199
  making an offer, 199–202
  negotiation in private treaty sale,
      196–198
private sale, 72–73, 200

private treaty sales
  negotiating a price, 196–198
  procedure, 195–196
problems, assessment during
      inspection, 84–85
professional home loan packages,
      167–168
progress payments, 117
project builders, 135
project management
  by architect or designer, 149
  for owner–builders, 117
project managers
  builders as, 119–121
  hiring, 117–119
property assessment after short-
      listing, 79–81
property inspections
  assessing potential problems, 84–85
  schedule for, 81–82
  what to look for, 82–84
property lift-out guides in
      newspapers, 73–74
public transport, checking location
      of, 79

● *Q* ●

qualified tradespeople, calling in,
      116–117
Queensland (Qld)
  auction bidding rules and
      regulations, 188
  cooling-off period, forfeit amount
      and waiver conditions, 212
  making an offer in, 201
  Office of Fair Trading, 65
  owner–builder regulations, 114, 152
  stamp duty in, 29
  WorkCover authority in, 112
Queenslander home styles, 99
quotes, obtaining from builders, 120

● *R* ●

real estate agents
  being sceptical of, 229
  dealing with, 55–57
  limits on actions of, 64–65

motivation of, 56–57
obtaining help from in finding
    property, 59, 74–75
and property values, 57–58
questioning about property, 58
and *Trade Practices Act 1974*
    compliance, 64–65
websites of, 73
real-estate speak, understanding, 77
rebuilding, calculating costs of,
    218–220
refinancing a mortgage, 174–175
removal costs, 31
renovation and restoration of period
    homes, 92–94
renovations
    challenge of, 48
    funding, 123–124
    living through, 121–123
    making livable, 104–105
    planning, 107–110
    structural improvements to, 105–107
renting
    advantages and disadvantages of, 12
    versus buying, 11–12
researching properties for sale, 71–75
Reserve Bank of Australia (RBA), cash
    rate of interest set by, 163
reserve prices, 186
rural properties, 52–53

• **S** •

safety on building sites, 151
safety standards required for
    renovation work, 112
sale by expressions of interest, 206
sale by set date, 205–206
saving for a deposit
    by deposit guarantee, 42
    by investing, 41
    by living with parents, 37–38
    First Home Savers Accounts, 36–37
    on your own, 38
    with friends, 38–39
    with parental help, 39–41
savings histories, 160
scarcity value of apartments, 54
sea-changing, 52–53

searching, property
    being persistent, 228
    and ideal home, 20–21
    narrowing down, 76–79
    strategy for, 70–75
second mortgages, 40
selling agents. *See* real estate agents
selling price estimates, problems
    with, 185–186
service fees on loans, 27
set sales, 205–206
settlement process, 208, 215–216
shares, investing in to raise
    deposit, 41
single people buying houses, 38
soil types, effect on block choice, 141
soundproofing in apartment
    blocks, 138
South Australia (SA)
    auction bidding rules and
        regulations, 188–189
    cooling-off period, forfeit amount
        and waiver conditions, 212
    First Home Bonus Grant, 17
    making an offer in, 201
    Office of Consumer and Business
        Affairs, 65
    owner–builder regulations, 114, 152
    stamp duty in, 29
    WorkCover authority in, 112
space, assessment during inspection,
    83–84
Spanish Mission home styles, 100
special conditions in contracts,
    209–210
special levy on apartment or unit
    owners, 34
stamp duty
    levels in states and territories,
        28–29
    on mortgages, 30
    savings by buying 'off the plan', 136
    as a state tax, 17
standard variable interest-rate loans,
    166
storage areas
    in apartments, 138
    assessment during inspection, 83–84
    importance of, 48
street appeal, 83, 241

sum insured building insurance policy, 218
sun, orientation with respect to, 47

• *T* •

Tasmania (Tas)
auction bidding rules and regulations, 189
Consumer Affairs and Fair Trading, 65
cooling-off period, forfeit amount and waiver conditions, 212
making an offer in, 201
owner–builder regulations, 114, 152
stamp duty in, 29
WorkCover authority in, 112
tax-friendly investment, home ownership as, 16
time to buy, choosing, 19–20, 225–226
total replacement building insurance policy, 218
Trade Practices Act 1974 and real estate industry compliance, 64–65
tradespeople and owner-builders, 116–117, 152, 154
travel expenses, property searching, 32
tree-changing, 52–53

• *U* •

unconditional offers, 203
units, buying 'off the plan', 135–138
up-and-coming suburbs, spotting, 50–51

• *V* •

valuation fee, 28
valuation of property, 214–215, 228
variable-rate loans, 162–164
vendor bids, 187

vendor finance, 180–181
vendors, dealing with real estate agents, 57
Victoria (Vic)
auction bidding rules and regulations, 189
Consumer Affairs Victoria, 65
cooling-off period, forfeit amount and waiver conditions, 213
First Home Buyer Bonus, 17
making an offer in, 201
owner–builder regulations, 114, 152
stamp duty in, 29
WorkCover authority in, 112
Victorian-era home styles, 96–98
viewline analysis, 91
views, importance of, 48

• *W* •

waiving cooling-off period in states and territories, 212–213
websites for real estate, 72–73
Western Australia (WA)
auction bidding rules and regulations, 189
cooling-off period, forfeit amount and waiver conditions, 213
Department of Commerce — Consumer Protection, 65
Home Buyers Assistance Account, 17
making an offer in, 202
owner–builder regulations, 114, 152
stamp duty in, 29
WorkCover authority in, 112
word of mouth in property searching, 75
WorkCover authorities in states and territories, 112

• *Z* •

zoning certificates, 208

Notes

Business & Investment

978-1-74216-971-2
$39.95

978-1-74216-853-1
$39.95

978-1-74216-852-4
$39.95

978-1-74216-939-2
$34.95

978-1-74246-874-7
$19.95

978-1-74216-962-0
$19.95

978-0-73140-827-6
$19.95

978-1-74216-941-5
$36.95

978-1-74216-942-2
$39.95

978-1-74246-848-8
$34.95

978-1-74031-146-5
$39.95

978-0-73140-940-2
$39.95

FOR DUMMIES®

Reference

978-1-74216-999-6
$39.95

978-1-74216-982-8
$39.95

978-1-74216-983-5
$45.00

978-0-73140-909-9
$39.95

978-1-74216-945-3
$39.95

978-0-73140-722-4
$29.95

978-0-73140-784-2
$34.95

978-0-73140-752-1
$34.95

Technology

978-0-47049-743-2
$32.95

978-1-74246-896-9
$39.95

978-1-74216-998-9
$45.00

978-1-74031-159-5
$39.95

Health & Fitness

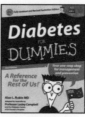

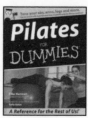

Living Gluten-Free	**Food & Nutrition**	**Diabetes**	**Pilates**
978-0-73140-760-6	978-0-73140-596-1	978-1-74031-094-9	978-1-74031-074-1
$34.95	$34.95	$39.95	$39.95

Fishing	**Golf**	**Cricket**	**Sailing**
978-1-74216-984-...			...73140-644-9
$39.95			$39.95

Being a Great Dad	**IVF & Beyond**	**Pregnancy**	**Baby's First Year**
978-1-74216-972-9	978-1-74216-946-0	978-1-74031-103-8	978-1-74031-042-0
$39.95	$39.95	$39.95	$39.95